CONTENTS

EDITOR'S WELCOME

Welcome to the first home plans book designed especially for urban and suburban living. With land costs on the rise, most city lots are becoming narrower and smaller. At the same time, most new home owners are looking for larger and more stylish homes. This outstanding collection proves that homes for narrower city lots can be as beautiful and comfortable as homes designed for wide country estates.

To create this book we examined over 4,000 home designs from 25 of America's leading residential design firms. We also carefully reviewed building and plan sale statistics over the past 5 years to select only the most popular home plans suited for city lots. Each home presented is less than 50 feet wide with most under 40 feet. Many are suited for "zero-lot lines" on "Z-line" configurations. The result is *Home Designs For Metropolitan Living* — the most comprehensive, innovative, and exciting anthology of home designs of its kind.

As you page through this book, you'll find well over 200 homes of every type and style — one-stories, two-stories, traditionals, contemporary designs, executive homes ranging from 1,000 to 3,800 square feet. You will also find a special category of exciting "new releases" — over 60 fresh, innovative designs.

Whether you live in the city, suburbs or a new development along the eastern, western or southern coastlines, in the spectacular mountains that make up the great Appalachians, Rockies, Cascades, and Sierra Nevadas, or among the hills, rivers, and valleys of the great mid-western plains — wherever you live, and whatever your lifestyle, you're bound to find your dream home in this book.

At HomeStyles "SOURCE 1" Designers' Network, we not only design home plans, we build dreams. For over 40 years (since 1946), we've supplied more than 175,000 home plans to professional builders, home owners, and do-it-yourselfers. Each have shared the common goal of building their dream home. The tremendous variety of designs represented in this book allows you to choose the home that best suits your lifestyle, budget, and building site.

Keep in mind that the most important part of a home design is the floor plan — the layout and flow of the rooms. If the floor plan excites you, minor changes are easily made by qualified professionals. Also, exterior styling can be easily modified — a traditional plan can be readily converted to a Spanish or Mediterranean style by changing the siding to stucco and using a tile roof rather than shingles or cedar shakes. The only limits to creative customizing are your own taste and ingenuity.

As you let your dreams run wild, you'll discover one of the most exciting aspects about this book is the tremendous savings that our home plans give to you. Custom designs cost thousands of dollars, usually 5% to 15% of the cost of construction. The design costs for a $100,000 home, for example, can range from $5,000 to $15,000. A "SOURCE 1" plan costs only $165 to $395 depending on the size of the home and the number of sets of blueprints that you order. When you order a "SOURCE 1" plan, you save the money you need to truly build your dream — to add a deck, swimming pool, beautiful kitchen, elegant master bedroom, luxurious bathroom, or other extras.

You can be assured of the quality of "SOURCE 1" plans. All of the blueprints are designed by members of the AIA (American Institute of Architects) and/or the AIBD (American Institute of Building Designers). Each plan is designed to meet nationally recognized codes — either the Uniform Building Code, the Standard Building Code, or the Basic Building Code — in effect, at the time that they were drawn. Please note that all "SOURCE 1" plans are designed to meet the specifications of seismic zones I or II. Because the United States has such temendous variety in geography and climate, each county and municipality will have its own codes, ordinances, zoning requirements, and building regulations. Therefore, depending on where you live, your plan may need to be modified to comply with your local building requirements — snow loads, energy codes, seismic zones, etc. If you need information or have questions regarding your specific requirements, call your local contractor, municipal building department, lumber yard, the AIBD(1-800-366-2423), or the NAHB (1-800-368-5242).

Building a home is truly the American dream. This book includes articles on how to select the right home design, money saving tips on cutting construction costs, and most importantly, over 200 new, up-to-date and best-selling home designs.

"SOURCE 1" doesn't just design homes, we build dreams! We hope that this book brings you one step closer to building yours.

CHOOSING THE DESIGN THAT'S RIGHT FOR YOU

For most of us, our home is the largest investment we will ever make. As a result, the style and type of home that we build is largely an economic decision. But of equal importance are issues of lifestyle, personal taste, and self-expression. Inevitably, our home is both our castle and our captor. We invest in it with the incomes that we earn from our weekday labor, and on the weekends, we invest in it with our saws, hammers, paintbrushes, and lawn tools. Our homes are truly an all-consuming labor of love.

Recognizing that love is in the eyes of the beholder, the following is a helpful guide to follow as you search for your dream home.

BUDGET

As a general rule, building a home costs between $60 and $100 per square foot of living space. However, as with most rules, the exceptions are greater than the rule. The greatest variables are land costs, labor and material costs, and individual tastes and style. The best bet is to contact your local builders association, lumberyard, or contractor.

Once you have an idea of what you can afford, determine any changes that you foresee in your income over the next five to ten years. For many, the future holds a greater income and therefore the possibility of a larger house. For others — young parents considering part-time work or empty-nesters soon to retire, the future may hold a reduction in income. Keep these considerations in mind as you evaluate your home plan needs.

LIFESTYLE

Just as your income may change, so too may your lifestyle. Select a plan that is flexible, versatile and adaptable. Young families may need a design that allows for expansion or flexibility in the floor plan. A 10' x 10' nursery may be adequate for a young child but will be terribly cramped for a teenager. On the other hand, a nursery today may become a den tomorrow.

For empty-nesters, there are other considerations. Children leave but they also return with friends, spouses, and grandchildren. The flexibility of the home design is a major consideration in dealing with these changes.

Your final lifestyle consideration is "aging." As we get older stairs become more difficult, doors are harder to open, and kitchens and bathrooms become more difficult to manage (especially in a wheelchair). If you plan on aging with your home, be sure to design your home so that it ages with you. Wider hallways, reinforced bathrooms for handgrips and railings, and gradual slopes in stairways are easy and less expensive to install at the time of construction. Renovating your home for wheelchair accessibility or handicapped living can be extremely costly down the line.

"Does the kitchen have a nook or breakfast bar?"

"Do we want a 'Great Room'?"

"How will it fit on our lot?"

"As we get older, will we want our home to be handicap accessible?"

"Is there enough storage space?"

"Can we add on later — a sunroom, deck or porch?"

"Do we want the master bedroom close to the kids or as far away as possible?"

"Can we afford it?"

"Is there expansion space — bonus room, unfinished basement or attic?"

"Where do I want the utility room — off the garage, near the kitchen or bedrooms, or in the basement?"

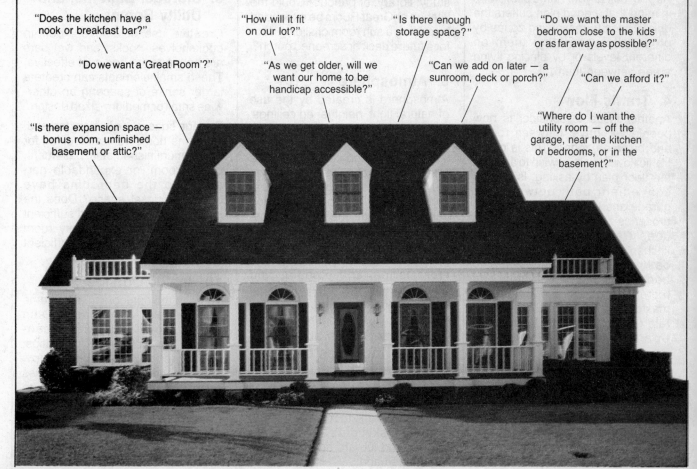

Plan E-3000

10 Most Popular Elements of a Good Home Design

1. Eye-Catching Exterior

Your house is a form of self-expression. Whether simple or subdued, stately or elegant, the exterior creates the first impression of your home. Does the exterior appearance of the home suit your tastes? If not, will changing the exterior materials or the color help?

2. Entryway Warmth

An inviting entryway sets the tone and atmosphere of your home. Does the entry have ample closet storage? Are the entrances covered or sheltered from rain or snow?

3. Zoning

There are three major zones in each home: working zones — kitchen, utility room, garage, bathrooms, and entryways; living zones — the living room, dining room, nook, family room, and/or Great Room; quiet zones — master bedroom, secondary bedrooms, library, den, and study.

As you look at your home plan, keep in mind that a good plan buffers the quiet zones from working zones by physically separating them on different levels or by placing living areas between them.

4. Traffic Flow

Another issue to consider is how people will travel between rooms and between zones. This is called traffic flow. You may wish to analyze the floor plan by asking: Is there a convenient path between the garage and the kitchen for carrying groceries and other supplies? How does traffic pass between the kitchen and other eating areas? Are bathrooms easily accessible to bedrooms and the family and recreation areas? Do I want the master bedroom close to or separate from the other bedrooms? Do I want the utility area in the basement, near the kitchen or near the bedrooms?

5. Openness, Flexibility, and Versatility

Look for a design that is open and airy and has rooms with multiple uses to change with your family's

Plan P-6563

needs. For example, the "Great Room" concept has become increasingly popular. In this idea, the kitchen, breakfast room, and family room work together as one large area yet function as separate spaces with their own identities. Also, ask yourself, can a nursery or spare bedroom be converted into a study, library, or parlour? Could the kitchen or Great Room be expanded by adding a sun room or sliding door for a future deck or screened porch?

6. Atmosphere

Atmosphere is created by the use of natural light, heightened ceilings, skylights, clerestory windows, and creative use of built-in artificial lights. Heightened ceilings create a greater sense of space and volume without increasing the actual dimensions of the room. A ceiling can also change the entire atmosphere of a room — vaulted and cathedral ceilings provide a contemporary "feel," trayed ceilings are more formal and elegant, and beamed ceilings create a casual and homey atmosphere.

7. Master Suites and Luxurious Master Bathrooms

A spacious, refreshing, and relaxing private bedroom retreat is highly popular. Walk-in closets, dual vanities, skylights, a separate shower and tub are added luxuries in high demand.

8. Kitchens

The kitchen has become a social center often incorporated with a breakfast nook and Great Room. A large, open kitchen with plenty of counter space, an island or peninsula counter, and a breakfast bar are highly desirable features.

9. Storage, Built-ins, and Utility Rooms

Creative use of alcoves, built-in bookshelves, nooks, and wet bars are both popular and cost effective. These small elements can create a larger sense of space in an otherwise small or medium-sized design.

Storage spaces are in high demand. Does the home you are looking for have an unfinished attic, basement, bonus room, or expandable garage? Do the bedrooms have adequate closet space? Does the kitchen have a pantry and sufficient cupboards? Does the utility room have extra storage and sufficient space?

10. Inside/Outside

To bring the outdoors in, new home designs are incorporating sun rooms, solariums, and greenhouses, as well as decks, patios, and porches. Creative window shapes and energy-efficient glass doors allow your home design to capture the beauty and freshness of the outdoors. If your home does not have a backyard deck or patio, could these be added without major expense?

4

COST-SAVING TIPS FOR BUILDING A HOME IN THE 90's

With construction costs and land values on the rise, record numbers of home builders are looking for money-saving ideas to build an affordable "dream home." Real estate, design costs, building materials, and contracting are the four areas that offer the greatest savings potential for new home buyers.

REAL ESTATE TIPS

The cost of land will vary depending on its location, whether or not it is developed or undeveloped, and whether the site poses any problems such as a difficult terrain, complicated configuration, or local zoning requirements.

1. When evaluating the land you wish to buy, keep in mind that undeveloped land is generally cheaper than developed land. It also has greater potential for appreciation as the surrounding area develops.

2. Despite potential problems, a difficult site can be a blessing in disguise. Although additional expenses may be required to excavate or provide access, the savings on the lot can be greater than the extra construction costs. Also, buying a problem site may enable you to live in a community you could not otherwise afford.

NOTE: Although unimproved and problem sites are cheaper, the costs of road access, electricity, water, and sewage must be carefully evaluated.

Plan P-7659

DESIGN TIPS

Once you have your lot, you must select a design that fits both your site and your lifestyle.

Identify your family's current and future needs and income. As a general rule, it is much safer to select a design that is within your budget and is flexible for future expansion. When selecting your "dream" design, keep in mind the following items:

1. Select a design that fits your site — one that will minimize excavation and grading.

2. There can be tremendous savings using predesigned blueprints from "SOURCE 1" or other reputable stock blueprint companies. Architects' fees for

custom drawn blueprints will range from 5% to 15% of the cost of building your home. Design costs for a $100,000 home, for example, can range from $5,000 to $15,000. However, complete construction blueprints are available from most stock design companies for $165-$395.

3. A rectangular design with simple roof lines is significantly less expensive than a home with numerous angles, nooks and crannies. Also, building up is significantly less expensive than building out. (A two-story home is less expensive than a one-story home with the same living space).

4. Look for a design that is open, flexible, and versatile allowing rooms to change as your family grows. Built-in furniture is a cost effective way of utilizing small spaces. It gives a sense of greater volume in a small home. Look for a home with unfinished space such as an unfinished basement or attic.

5. Decks, patios, screened in porches, greenhouses, and sun rooms add tremendously to the comfort and pleasure that you'll have in living in your home. They also translate to increased value for resale!

6. Design your home for energy efficiency. 2x6 construction of the walls may be more expensive

Plan R-1028

5

Plan H-930

in the short run, but these minimal costs will be paid back in energy savings.

Site your house correctly. A southern exposure in colder climates and a northern exposure in warmer climates will have a surprising effect on your fuel bills.

MATERIAL TIPS

The materials used to build your home are the most expensive costs of construction. Don't compromise on materials to save money! Savings can be made in using pre-manufactured materials and standard sizes.

1. Limit custom work! As attractive as elaborate detailing can be, the cost is often exorbitant. Look for mass produced detailing wherever possible.

2. Areas such as the kitchen and the bathroom are often very expensive to build due to the number of appliances, cabinets and features. Your builder and local supplier can design the kitchen and bathroom to take advantage of pre-designed cabinetry and counters.

CONTRACTING TIPS

Cutting construction costs (i.e. labor and materials) requires experience, time, and organizational skills.

As a home builder you have four options:

1. A construction company;
2. A general contractor (carpenter/builder);
3. Act as your own general contractor;
4. Build your own home.

In all of these cases, the contractor is responsible for coordinating the work of all "trades" — electricians, plumbers, painters, builders, etc., securing permits, handling finances and ensuring quality. There are advantages and disadvantages to each option:

1. A general construction company may offer some cost savings because your project will be consolidated with a number of other concurrent projects and there may be labor savings with sub-contractors. However, your house is one of many and you will not have much personal contact with your builder.

2. The general contractor can provide more personalized attention than a construction company. However, you will have to spend more time reviewing and comparing competitive bids and possibly specifying materials. A general contractor usually works on a "cost-plus" basis — the costs of materials and sub-contractors' charges plus the contract fee. This can either be a fixed cost or a percentage of the cost.

3. Acting as your own general contractor significantly reduces costs but also significantly increases the time and responsibility you must commit to the project. In this role, you have the responsibility of hiring, supervising, securing permits, and getting materials. This requires knowledge of local building codes and means working with construction specialists. Although the savings are significant, you must weigh the extensive commitment and time involved against having the work done by a professional.

4. The most cost efficient approach is to act as your own contractor and builder. In this case you eliminate all the costs except for materials. This option can be rewarding but requires a tremendous commitment of time — first in educating yourself, and then in doing it.

Plan E-2208

Angled Windows and Flowing Space

- This highly popular compact home proves that even smaller homes can be big on style and convenience.
- The bay windowed living room and dining room combine to create a large space for entertaining.
- A sunny nook adjoins the kitchen, which includes a pantry.
- The master suite includes a private bath, roomy wardrobe closet and a double-door entry.
- The sheltered entry invites guests and family alike, and a convenient utility area is situated in the garage entry area.
- Optional third bedroom can be used for a den or tv room, open to the nook if desired.

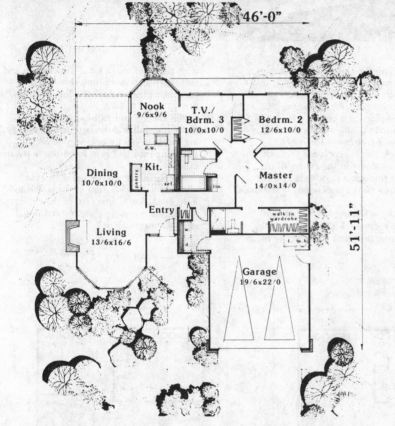

46'-0"

51'-11"

Nook
9/6x9/6

T.V./
Bedrm. 3
10/0x10/0

Bedrm. 2
12/6x10/0

Dining
10/0x10/0

Kit.

pantry

Master
14/0x14/0

ref.

lin.

Entry

walk in
wardrobe

Living
13/6x16/6

f. w.h.

Garage
19/6x22/0

Plan R-1028

Bedrooms: 2-3	**Baths:** 2

Total living area:	1,305 sq. ft.
Garage:	429 sq. ft.

Exterior Wall Framing:	2x4

Foundation options:
 Crawlspace only.
(Foundation & framing conversion diagram available — see order form.)

Blueprint Price Code:	A

Plan R-1028

To order blueprints, call
1-800-547-5570 or see order form
and pricing information on pages 220-224.

7

FRONT VIEW

An Owner-Builder Special

Perfect for a beach, lake or mountain site, this no-nonsense, energy-conscious house plan has everything you need for a leisure home or retirement retreat. It is also just the right size for a small, passed-over lot in town.

The basic rectangular design escapes being ordinary due to a wide wrap-around deck entirely covered by the projecting roof line and the cedar board siding in a vertical channel rustic pattern.

The entry door opens into the living-dining area which is warmed by a central fireplace and enhanced visually with a vaulted ceiling, made possible by using scissor trusses for the roof.

The deck also is accessible through sliding glass doors in the center of the room and through a door next to the kitchen area on the wall opposite the main entry.

Suited for a sloping lot, the daylight basement version (H-833-7) offers a garage, large bedroom and a utility room with plenty of space for a work bench and storage. For those not interested in a basement plan, and for flat lot situations, order Plan H-833-7A.

The kitchen and bathroom share a plumbing wall and the basement utilities are located directly below, minimizing plumbing runs and heat loss from hot water pipes.

Exterior walls are framed with 2x6s, allowing R-19 insulation in the walls, and R-30 insulation is specified in the ceiling. All glazing is double-pane for additional energy conservation.

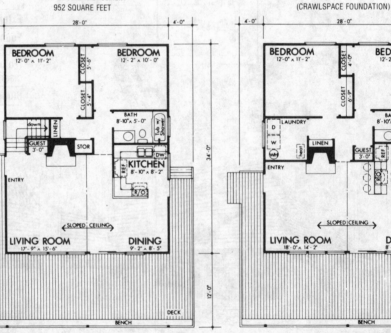

BASEMENT PLAN
952 SQUARE FEET

PLAN H-833-7
WITH DAYLIGHT BASEMENT
952 SQUARE FEET

PLAN H-833-7A
WITHOUT BASEMENT
952 SQUARE FEET
(CRAWLSPACE FOUNDATION)

Total living area: 952 sq. ft.
(Not counting basement or garage)

Blueprint Price Code A

Plans H-833-7 & H-833-7A

8

FRONT VIEW

Strong Design, Dramatic Interior

A strong exterior form and dramatic use of interior space combine to make this an interesting and attractive plan. Multi-level construction and open planning have resulted in a thrifty use of living area. The spacious feeling that enhances the living room opens from the elevated den and extends to the 20' high ridge beam and exposed rafters that cover both rooms.

A second bedroom and a complete bathroom with stall shower is conveniently located on the balcony level for this part of the home. Nearby, a stairway landing leads up to the third and uppermost level of the dwelling. The master bedroom has its own complete bathroom and a good-size closet.

The combined living area of the kitchen, dining, living room, bedrooms one and two and the complete bathroom are included in a total area of 936 sq. ft. The second floor plan that includes the master bedroom and bath contains 252 sq. ft.

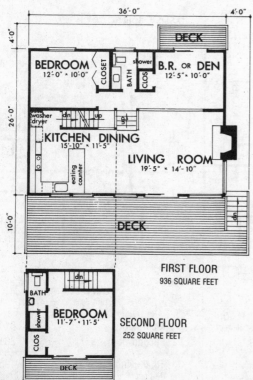

FIRST FLOOR
936 SQUARE FEET

SECOND FLOOR
252 SQUARE FEET

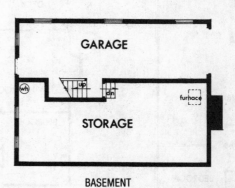

BASEMENT

PLAN H-863-2
WITH BASEMENT

First floor:	936 sq. ft.
Second floor:	252 sq. ft.
Total living area: (Not including basement or garage)	1,188 sq. ft.

Blueprint Price Code A

Plan H-863-2

To order blueprints, call
1-800-547-5570 or see order form
and pricing information on pages 220-224

Narrow Design Offers Two or Three Bedrooms

Designed for a sloping and narrow building lot, this 28' wide plan featuring a passive solar dining room can be varied for two or three bedrooms, and can also be built with or without a daylight basement.

The covered front entry to the 814 sq. ft. first floor also has a door leading in from the garage. An entry hall directs traffic to the main floor bedroom, full bathroom with washer and dryer, the stairway and to the living room/dining room/kitchen cluster.

The passive solar dining room has windows on three sides and a glass roof for collecting heat, plus a slate floor for heat storage. The kitchen is open to the dining area and is separated from the living room by a 7½' high wall.

A wood stove with exposed flue backed by ceiling-high exposed masonry adds radiant and stored heat to the living room.

Sliding glass doors from the living room and a French door from the passive sun room open onto a wood deck.

The second floor can be varied for two bedrooms with closets or as a master bedroom with full bath and large walk-in closet over the garage. Both variations have a balcony railing that looks over the vaulted-ceiling living room.

REAR VIEW

(EXTERIOR WALLS ARE 2x6 CONSTRUCTION)

PLAN H-946-2A
WITHOUT BASEMENT
(CRAWLSPACE FOUNDATION)

PLAN H-946-2B
WITH DAYLIGHT BASEMENT

PLAN H-946-1A
WITHOUT BASEMENT
(CRAWLSPACE FOUNDATION)

PLAN H-946-1B
WITH DAYLIGHT BASEMENT

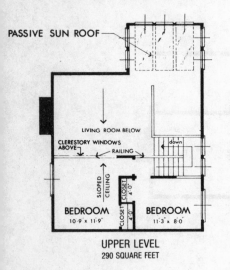

PLAN H-946-2A, 2B
(Three-Bedroom Version)

Main floor:	814 sq. ft.
Second floor:	290 sq. ft.
Total living area:	1,104 sq. ft.
(Not counting basement or garage)	

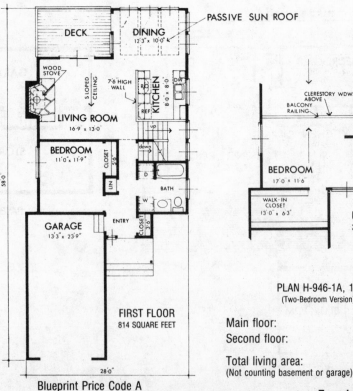

Blueprint Price Code A

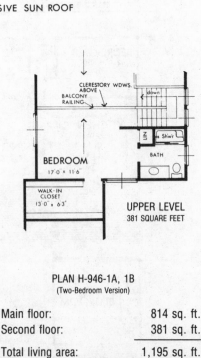

PLAN H-946-1A, 1B
(Two-Bedroom Version)

Main floor:	814 sq. ft.
Second floor:	381 sq. ft.
Total living area:	1,195 sq. ft.
(Not counting basement or garage)	

Plans H-946-1A, H-946-1B, H-946-2A & H-946-2B

To order blueprints, call 1-800-547-5570 or see order form and pricing information on pages 220-224.

Cozy Veranda Invites Visitors

Living:	1,266 sq. ft.
Garage & Storage:	550 sq. ft.
Porch	240 sq. ft.
Total :	2,056 sq. ft.

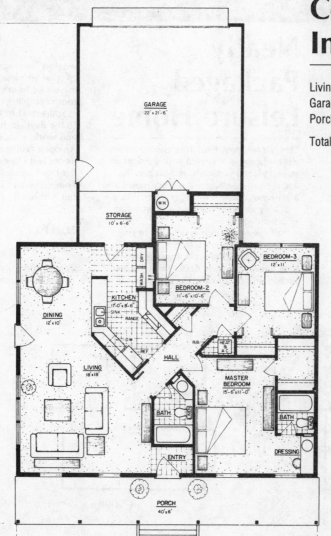

PLAN E-1217
WITHOUT BASEMENT

Exterior walls are 2x6 construction.
Specify crawlspace or slab foundation.

Blueprint Price Code A

Plan E-1217

Neatly Packaged Leisure Home

This pitched-roof two-story contemporary leisure home is accented with solid wood siding, placed vertically and diagonally, and it neatly packages three bedrooms and a generous amount of living space into a 1,271 sq. ft. plan that covers a minimum of ground space.

Half the main floor is devoted to the vaulted Great Room, which is warmed by a woodstove and opens out through sliding glass doors to a wide deck. The U-shaped kitchen adjacent to the Great Room has a window looking onto the deck and a circular window in the front wall. The master bedroom, a full bath and the utility room complete the 823 sq. ft. first floor.

Stairs next to the entry door lead down to the daylight basement, double garage and workroom, or up to the second floor. An open railing overlooking the Great Room and clerestory windows add natural light and enhance the open feeling of the home. The two bedrooms share another full bathroom.

Main floor:	823 sq. ft.
Upper floor:	448 sq. ft.
Total living area: (Not counting basement or garage)	1,271 sq. ft.

BASEMENT
PLAN P-520-D
WITH DAYLIGHT BASEMENT

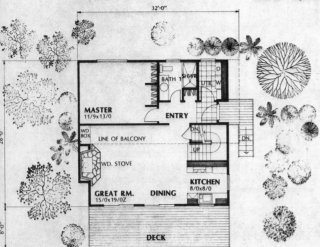

MAIN FLOOR

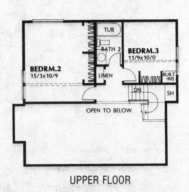

UPPER FLOOR

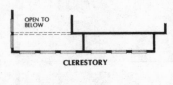

Blueprint Price Code A

Plan P-520-D

To order blueprints, call
1-800-547-5570 or see order form
and pricing information on pages 220-224.

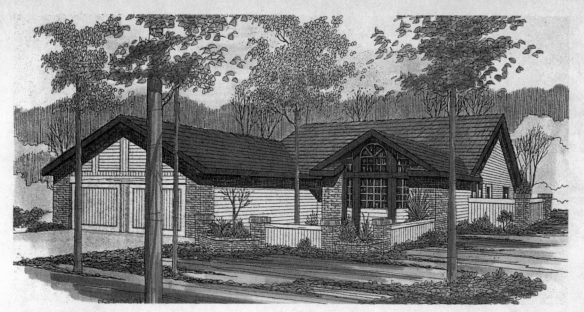

Economical and Stylish

A distinctive roof and window treatment on the kitchen extension lend a traditional look to this otherwise contemporary three-bedroom home of 1,362 sq. ft., which is only 40' wide to conserve lot space.

The brick and wood fence, with built-in planters, sets off the front courtyard and the walkway to the angled front door and entry hall. The vaulted, open-beam ceiling of the dining area and great room sweeps from the foyer to the large fireplace, flanked by windows, on the back wall.

The vaulted, U-shaped kitchen is washed with sunlight through the multi-paned arched window overlooking the front courtyard. A door from the dining area leads out to an optional courtyard and back to the large deck or patio set into the back corner of the house.

The large master bedroom suite has a sitting room, with a door leading to the patio, plus a dressing room, private bath and a spacious walk-in closet. The other two bedrooms share the hall bathroom.

In the daylight basement version of the plan, stairs replace the utility room just off the entry hall.

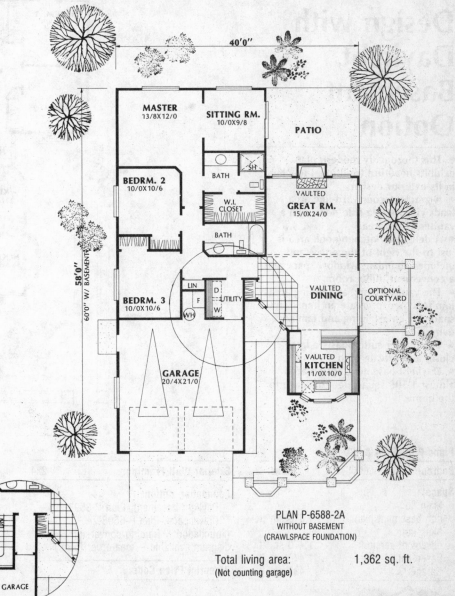

PLAN P-6588-2D
WITH DAYLIGHT BASEMENT

Main floor: 1,403 sq. ft.
Basement level: 1,303 sq. ft.

PLAN P-6588-2A
WITHOUT BASEMENT
(CRAWLSPACE FOUNDATION)

Total living area: 1,362 sq. ft.
(Not counting garage)

To order blueprints, call
1-800-547-5570 or see order form
and pricing information on pages 220-224

Blueprint Price Code A

Plans P-6588-2A & P-6588-2D

Narrow Lot Design with Daylight Basement Option

- This thoroughly modern plan exhibits beautiful traditional touches in its exterior design.
- A gracious courtyard-like area leads visitors to a side door with a vaulted entry area.
- A delightful kitchen/nook area is just to the right of the entry, and includes abundant window space and a convenient utility room.
- The vaulted living and dining areas join together to create an impressive space for entertaining and family living.
- The master suite boasts a large closet and private bath.
- Daylight basement option adds almost 1,500 square feet of space to the home.

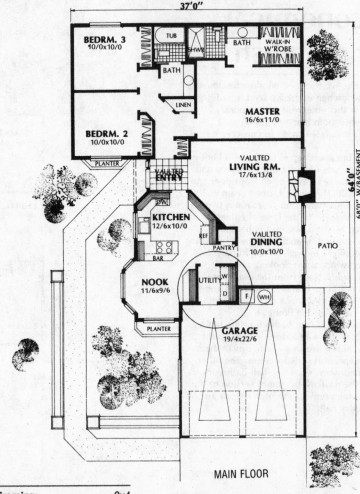

MAIN FLOOR

Plans P-6598-2A & -2D

Bedrooms: 3	Baths: 2

Space:

Main floor, non-basement plan:	1,375 sq. ft.
Main floor, basement version:	1,470 sq. ft.
Basement:	1,470 sq. ft.
Garage:	435 sq. ft.

Exterior Wall Framing: 2x4

Foundation options:
Daylight basement, Plan P-6598-2D.
Crawlspace, Plan P-6598-2A.
(Foundation & framing conversion diagram available — see order form.)

Blueprint Price Code: A

BASEMENT STAIR DETAIL

Plans P-6598-2A & -2D

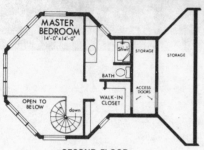

SECOND FLOOR
346 SQUARE FEET
134 SQUARE FEET — STORAGE

PLAN H-964-1B
WITH DAYLIGHT BASEMENT

PLAN H-964-1A
WITHOUT BASEMENT
(CRAWLSPACE FOUNDATION)

Octagonal Vacation Retreat

The octagonal shape of this plan is calculated to take 180-degree advantage of the view. All waking-hour activities are concentrated in a single Great Room, which combines living, dining and food preparation in one open area containing well over 500 sq. ft. When the huge, open deck is added to this, a total living area of more than 800 sq. ft. is to be enjoyed. Only the provocative spiral staircase provides any interruption of sight or movement.

The balance of the first floor is devoted to entry hall, well-appointed bathroom and spacious bedroom. Winding up the spiral staircase, one continues to enjoy a view of the Great Room while approaching the extraordinary master bedroom suite. Besides the large window-bound sleeping room, an exceptional private bath and dressing room occupy the 346 sq. ft. of the second floor.

If you choose the daylight basement version of this unusual home, a huge recreation room, a very spacious bedroom and a third complete bath are included. Laundry and storage space complete the lower floor plan. A beautiful covered patio under the deck is an optional possibility.

Finally, the oversized garage provides space for two automobiles, car and camper or boat, with plenty of space left over for equipment storage and work bench.

Exterior walls are framed in 2x6 studs.

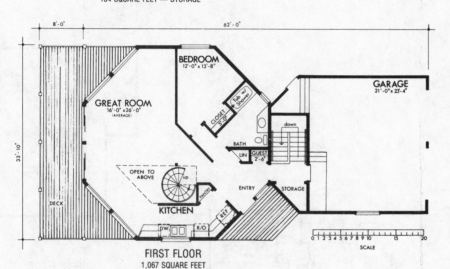

FIRST FLOOR
1,067 SQUARE FEET
512 SQUARE FEET — GARAGE

First floor:	1,067 sq. ft.
Second floor:	346 sq. ft.
Total living area: (Not counting basement or garage)	1,413 sq. ft.
Basement:	1,045 sq. ft.
Total with basement:	2,458 sq. ft.

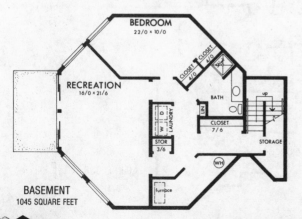

BASEMENT
1045 SQUARE FEET

Blueprint Price Code C With Basement
Blueprint Price Code A Without Basement

Plans H-964-1A & H-964-1B

To order blueprints, call
1-800-547-5570 or see order form
and pricing information on pages 220-224.

"Doll House" Design Big on Comfort

- Luxurious master suite includes deluxe bath.
- Both secondary bedrooms also have their own bathrooms.
- Vaulted living room ceiling creates feeling of more space.
- Living and dining areas combine to create space for entertaining.

Plan E-1312

Bedrooms: 3	Baths: 3

Space:

Upper floor:	313 sq. ft.
Main floor:	1,078 sq. ft.

Total living area:	1,391 sq. ft.

Exterior Wall Framing:	2x4

Foundation options:
  Crawlspace.
  Slab.
(Foundation & framing conversion diagram available — see order form.)

Blueprint Price Code:	A

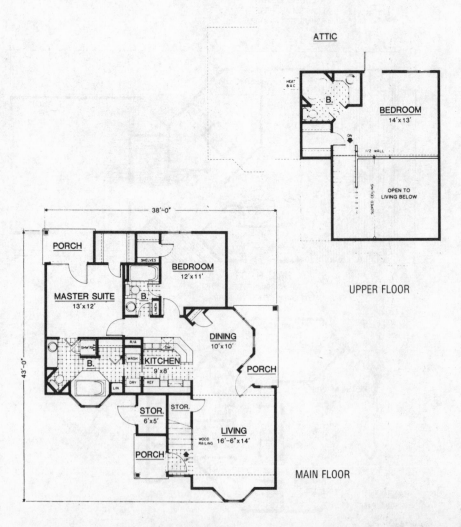

16

Plan E-1312

L-Shaped
Country-Style Home

PLAN E-1412
WITHOUT BASEMENT

Living	1400 sq. ft.
Utility & Storage	84 sq. ft.
Garage	440 sq. ft.
Porch	80 sq. ft.
Total	2004 sq. ft.

Exterior walls are 2x6 construction.
Specify crawlspace or slab foundation.

Floor plan labels:
PATIO
GARAGE
22'-0" x 20'-0"
DISAPPEARING STAIRS
BED ROOM 14'-0" x 10'-0"
KITCHEN 13'-0" x 12'-0"
DINING 14'-0" x 12'-0"
UTILITY & STORAGE 12'-0" x 7'-0"
SINK
RANGE
BAR
DISHWASHER
REFRIGERATOR
DRY.
WASH.
CLO.
HEAT & A/C
LINEN
HALL
BATH
PANTRY
BROOMS
W H
CLO.
BATH
BEAM
BOOKS DESK
BED ROOM 12'-0" x 11'-4"
CLO.
FLAT CEILING
SLOPE CEILING
LIVING 18'-0" x 16'-0"
BEAM
MASTER B. R. 15'-0" x 14'-0"
PORCH 20'-0" x 4'-0"
ENTRY
56'-0"
46'-0"

An Energy Efficient Home
Blueprint Price Code A

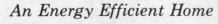
Plan E-1412

To order blueprints, call
1-800-547-5570 or see order form
and pricing information on pages 220-224.

Compact Design Works as a Single or a Duplex

- Compact design can be built as a single unit or a duplex; the latter, with zero clearance, may be done at a later date.
- Open layout of the first level promotes informal lifestyles; living and dining areas share a fireplace and sliding glass doors to a rear patio.

- U-shaped kitchen, a powder/laundry room and separate storage area complete the first level.
- Partially open stairway leads to three bedrooms and a full bath that make up the second level.

First floor:	448 sq. ft.
Second floor:	536 sq. ft.
Total living area: (Not counting garage)	984 sq. ft.

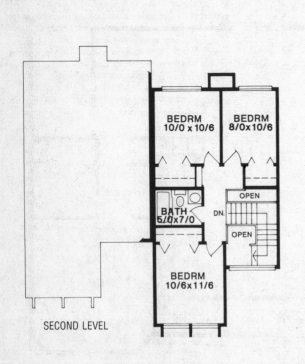

SECOND LEVEL

PLAN SD-8231
WITHOUT BASEMENT
(CRAWLSPACE FOUNDATION)

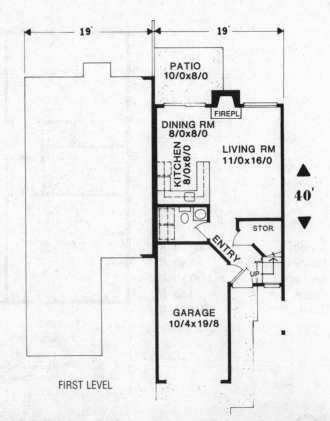

FIRST LEVEL

Blueprint Price Code A

Plan SD-8231

REAR VIEW

DECK

37'-3" 4'-0"

10'-0"

SLOPED CEILING

DINING
8'-4" x 11'-7"

KITCHEN
9'-0" x 9'-4"

DW

REF R/O

STOR

up down

LAUNDRY
W D

LIVING ROOM
17'-8" x 14'-11"

50'-0"

GUEST
3'-4"

BATH
6'-8" x 7'-5"

LIN

CLOSET
5'-0"

BEDROOM
10'-0" x 10'-0"

Shwr

BEDROOM
10'-0" x 10'-0"

ENTRY

STORAGE

CLOSET
5'-6"

GARAGE
11'-3" x 23'-8"

MAIN FLOOR
951 SQUARE FEET

PLAN H-925-1
WITH DAYLIGHT BASEMENT

DECK

SLOPED CEILING

WALK-IN CLOSET
7'-4" x 5'-0"

Tub w/ Shwr

BEDROOM
12'-0" x 13'-6"

BATH
9'-2" x 5'-0"

down

SECOND FLOOR
288 SQUARE FEET

STOR

WH heat

PLAN H-925-1A
WITHOUT BASEMENT
(CRAWLSPACE FOUNDATION)

Recipe for Easy Living

Take one 26' x 36' rectangular living space (951 sq. ft.), slice lengthwise, lower the rear portion three feet and place the whole on a slightly sloping lot. Add an attractive stairway, just five risers, to connect lower and upper sections. Divide the upper half of the rectangle into two bedrooms with a centralized bath; leave lower half as one large beautiful room sectioned off for living, dining and kitchen use. (A small laundry adjoining the kitchen space adds wonderfully to the utilization of this area; if you wish to have a basement, place the stairway in this laundry room.) Take a standard gable roof line and raise one end to form a master bedroom suite over the kitchen and dining area. Work in a full sized bath, walk-in wardrobe and 4' x 18' cantilevered deck. This will add 288 sq. ft.

Finally add a garage and covered walkway to the front and a 10' wide outdoor living deck at the rear. The results are sure to please.

First floor:	951 sq. ft.
Second floor:	288 sq. ft.
Total living area: (Not counting basement or garage)	1,239 sq. ft.

FRONT VIEW

Blueprint Price Code A

Plans H-925-1 & H-925-1A

To order blueprints, call 1-800-547-5570 or see order form and pricing information on pages 220-224.

Compact, Economical Three-Bedroom Home

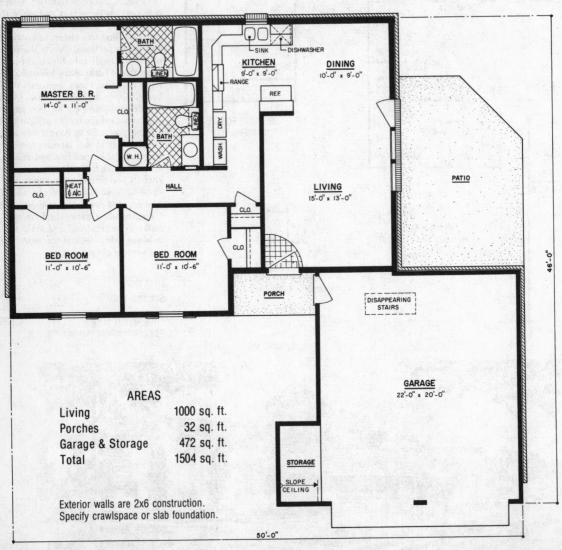

BATH

SINK   DISHWASHER

KITCHEN
9'-0" x 9'-0"

DINING
10'-0" x 9'-0"

RANGE

MASTER B. R.
14'-0" x 11'-0"

LINEN

REF.

CLO.

LINEN

BATH

WASH   DRY.

LIVING
15'-0" x 13'-0"

W. H.

PATIO

CLO.   HEAT & A/C

HALL

CLO.

CLO.

BED ROOM
11'-0" x 10'-6"

BED ROOM
11'-0" x 10'-6"

PORCH

DISAPPEARING STAIRS

46'-0"

GARAGE
22'-0" x 20'-0"

AREAS

Living	1000 sq. ft.
Porches	32 sq. ft.
Garage & Storage	472 sq. ft.
Total	1504 sq. ft.

Exterior walls are 2x6 construction.
Specify crawlspace or slab foundation.

STORAGE

SLOPE CEILING

50'-0"

An Energy Efficient Home

Blueprint Price Code A

Plan E-1001

Exterior walls are 2x6 construction.
Specify crawlspace or slab foundation.

Classic Saltbox with Open Interior Plan

Main floor:	1,088 sq. ft.
Storage:	32 sq. ft.
Porch:	40 sq. ft.
Expansion area:	580 sq. ft.

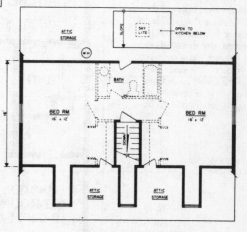

MAIN FLOOR

UNFINISHED UPPER LEVEL

Blueprint Price Code A

Plan E-1003

To order blueprints, call
1-800-547-5570 or see order form
and pricing information on pages 220-224.

Open Design in Compact Traditional

An instant feeling of spaciousness and openness is created in this hospitable residence with a vaulted Great Room and open-railed stairway. Additional appeal is lent by the wood-burning fireplace, which is visible from the kitchen and dining area, as well. The spacious kitchen has a pantry and a walk-in laundry room. The first floor master bedroom is isolated well away from living areas, yet conveniently accessible to the stairs for checking on small children in bedrooms above.

PLAN V-1098
WITHOUT BASEMENT
(CRAWLSPACE FOUNDATION)

First floor:	702 sq. ft.
Second floor:	396 sq. ft.
Total living area:	1,098 sq. ft.

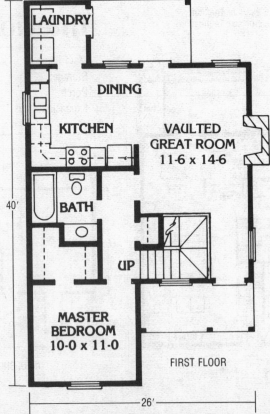

LAUNDRY

DINING

KITCHEN

VAULTED GREAT ROOM
11-6 x 14-6

BATH

UP

MASTER BEDROOM
10-0 x 11-0

FIRST FLOOR

40'

26'

8'-0" CEILINGS THROUGHOUT FIRST FLOOR

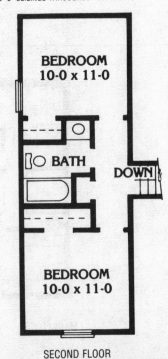

8'-0" CEILINGS THROUGHOUT SECOND FLOOR

BEDROOM
10-0 x 11-0

BATH

DOWN

BEDROOM
10-0 x 11-0

SECOND FLOOR

Blueprint Price Code A

Plan V-1098

To order blueprints, call
1-800-547-5570 or see order form
and pricing information on pages 220-224.

Eye-Catching Prow-Shaped Chalet

Steep pitched roof lines and wide cornices provide this handsome chalet with a distinct alpine appearance. The prow shape and large windows of the front wall along with the sturdy stone chimney are all calculated to enhance the character and stability of the dwelling. Heavy handsplit shakes add beauty to this attractive home.

The 10' deck provides an entry and at the same time an expansive outdoor living space. If the slope of your lot does not allow for a daylight basement, the plan is available without a basement.

A practical division of living and sleeping areas locates the living/dining room and kitchen at the front of the home, placing the two bedrooms at the rear. A hallway connects these two areas and midway a complete bathroom services the entire home. Laundry facilities flank one side of the central hallway.

An open staircase leads to a second floor where you will find another full bedroom, a complete bathroom and an open balcony.

First floor:	994 sq. ft.
Second floor:	486 sq. ft.
Total living area:	**1,480 sq. ft.**

(Not counting basement or garage)
(Exterior walls are framed in 2x6 studs)

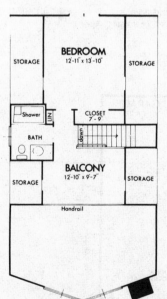

SECOND FLOOR
486 SQUARE FEET
WITHOUT STORAGE

PLAN H-886-3
WITH BASEMENT
PLAN H-886-3A
WITHOUT BASEMENT
(CRAWLSPACE FOUNDATION)

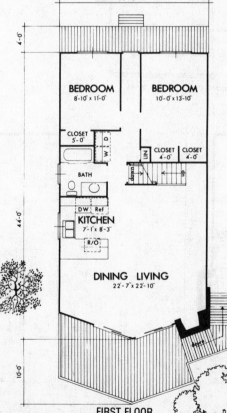

FIRST FLOOR
994 SQUARE FEET

Blueprint Price Code A

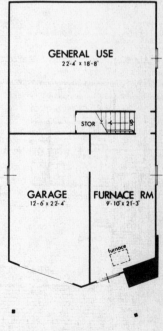

BASEMENT

Plans H-886-3 & H-886-3A

To order blueprints, call
1-800-547-5570 or see order form
and pricing information on pages 220-224.

FRONT VIEW

The Simple & Economical Housing Solution

Although primarily conceived as a second home, this compact plan could very well serve as a permanent residence for a small family. Only 26' x 28' in size, it provides a surprising amount of livability because every square foot is used with the utmost efficiency.

The great room which serves for living and dining is especially spacious, even more so when one considers the 6' x 26' deck that is so immediately accessible.

A small but efficient kitchen lies in a very central location to the left of the entry. Laundry facilities and storage closets are in the hallway leading to the bedroom and bath.

A large loft area overlooking the great room has infinite possibilities for extra sleeping quarters, a studio for artistic endeavors, a home office, recreation and many other uses depending on the inclination of the occupants. This upper space enjoys steady day-long natural lighting from the unique clerestory window arrangement overhead.

If your needs are simple and your pocketbook limited, this economical home may be the solution you seek.

Main floor:	728 sq. ft.
Loft:	432 sq. ft.
Total living area:	1,160 sq. ft.
(Not counting lower level garage)	

LOFT
LOFT
25'-3" x 16'-2"

SLOPED CEILING

down — RAILING

— CLERESTORY LINE

S.C.

S.C.

OPEN TO GREAT ROOM

SKYLIGHTS

LOFT
432 SQUARE FEET

CLERESTORY WINDOWS OVER LOFT AND STAIRS

MAIN FLOOR

4'-0" 26'-0"

BATH
14'-3" x 5'-0"

Tub w/ Shower

BEDROOM
10'-7" x 12'-6"

DW

W/D

KITCHEN
8'-6" x 8'-0"

GUEST STOR
3'-0"

REF

LIN   CLOSET   CLOSET
4'-0"   4'-0"

up

28'-0"

ENTRY

DINING

WOODSTOVE

down

GREAT ROOM
25'-3" x 13'-6"

DECK

6'-0"

MAIN FLOOR
728 SQUARE FEET

LOWER LEVEL

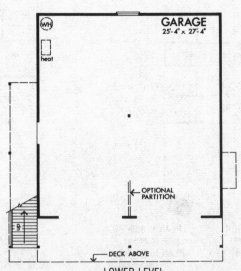

WH

heat

GARAGE
25'-4" x 27'-4"

OPTIONAL PARTITION

DECK ABOVE

LOWER LEVEL
728 SQUARE FEET
(SLAB-ON-GRADE FOUNDATION)

HomeStyles SOURCE 1
DESIGNERS NETWORK

Blueprint Price Code A

Plan H-963-2A

To order blueprints, call
1-800-547-5570 or see order form
and pricing information on pages 220-224.

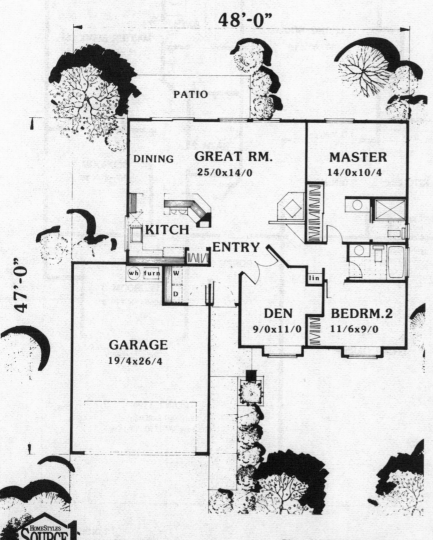

48'-0"

47'-0"

PATIO

DINING

GREAT RM.
25/0x14/0

MASTER
14/0x10/4

KITCH

ENTRY

wh furn W D

DEN
9/0x11/0

BEDRM.2
11/6x9/0

lin

GARAGE
19/4x26/4

For Singles or Starting Couples

The simple roof line and double-car garage effectively complement and enhance this 1,169 sq. ft., one-level home. The entry provides easy access to every room of the dwelling. The homemaker will love the kitchen built-ins and the separate laundry room.

This home also features the Great Room with a dining area. In addition, there is a nice den and two bedrooms. The master bedroom boasts a private bath and a large closet.

Perfect as a starter home, this floor plan arrangement will also be the ideal answer for the lifestyle of a the single working person.

Total living area: 1,169 sq. ft.
(Not counting garage)

PLAN R-1075
WITHOUT BASEMENT
(CRAWLSPACE FOUNDATION)

Blueprint Price Code A
Plan R-1075

Economy With A Touch of Class

Total living area: 1,198 sq. ft.
(Not counting garage)

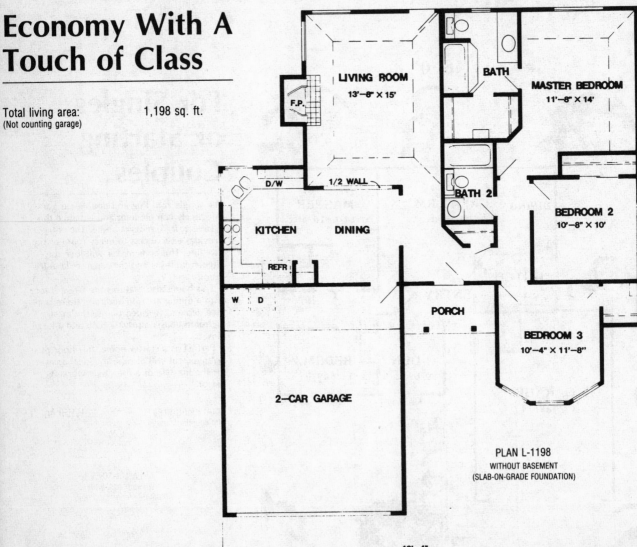

LIVING ROOM
13'-8" × 15'

F.P.

BATH

MASTER BEDROOM
11'-8" × 14'

D/W

1/2 WALL

BATH 2

KITCHEN   DINING

REFR

BEDROOM 2
10'-8" × 10'

W   D

PORCH

BEDROOM 3
10'-4" × 11'-8"

2—CAR GARAGE

PLAN L-1198
WITHOUT BASEMENT
(SLAB-ON-GRADE FOUNDATION)

43'—4"

Blueprint Price Code A
Plan L-1198

To order blueprints, call
1-800-547-5570 or see order form
and pricing information on pages 220-224.

Secluded Entryway in Compact Design

AREAS

Living	1200 sq. ft.
Porches	60 sq. ft.
Utility & Storage	100 sq. ft.
Total	1360 sq. ft.

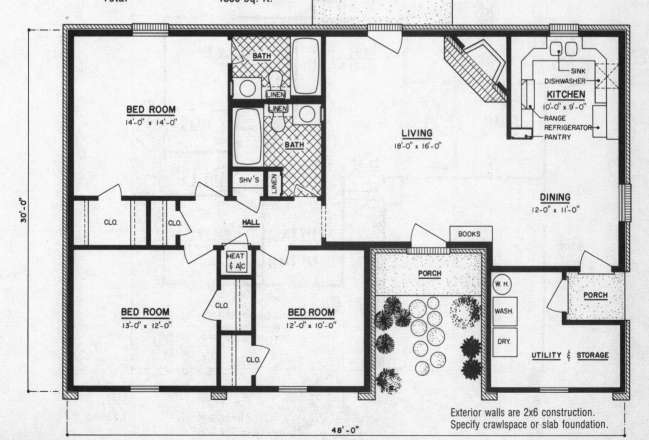

PATIO

BATH

LINEN

LINEN

BATH

SINK
DISHWASHER
KITCHEN
10'-0" x 9'-0"
RANGE
REFRIGERATOR
PANTRY

BED ROOM
14'-0" x 14'-0"

SHV'S

LINEN

LIVING
18'-0" x 16'-0"

DINING
12'-0" x 11'-0"

CLO.

CLO.

HALL

HEAT & A/C

BOOKS

PORCH

W. H.

WASH.

DRY.

PORCH

BED ROOM
13'-0" x 12'-0"

CLO.

BED ROOM
12'-0" x 10'-0"

CLO.

UTILITY & STORAGE

30'-0"

48'-0"

Exterior walls are 2x6 construction.
Specify crawlspace or slab foundation.

An Energy Efficient Home
Blueprint Price Code A

Plan E-1214

To order blueprints, call
1-800-547-5570 or see order form
and pricing information on pages 220-224.

Modest-Sized Home Offers
Large Dining/ Living Area

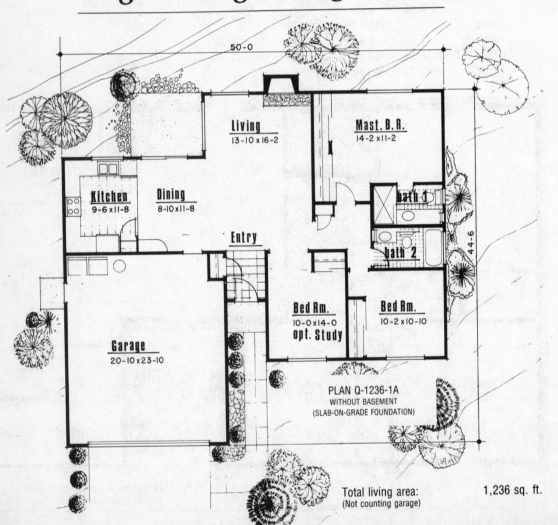

50-0

Living
13-10 x 16-2

Mast. B.R.
14-2 x 11-2

Kitchen
9-6 x 11-8

Dining
8-10 x 11-8

bath 1

bath 2

Entry

44-6

Garage
20-10 x 23-10

Bed Rm.
10-0 x 14-0
opt. Study

Bed Rm.
10-2 x 10-10

PLAN Q-1236-1A
WITHOUT BASEMENT
(SLAB-ON-GRADE FOUNDATION)

Total living area: 1,236 sq. ft.
(Not counting garage)

Blueprint Price Code A

Plan Q-1236-1A

CONTEMPORARY EXTERIOR

Two-Story with Alternate Exteriors

First floor:	846 sq. ft.
Second floor:	400 sq. ft.
Total living area:	1,246 sq. ft.

(Not counting basement or garage)

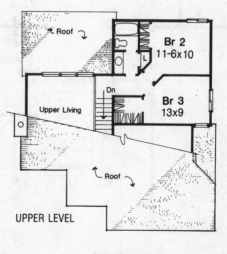

TRADITIONAL EXTERIOR

LOWER LEVEL

36'-8"

Deck

Dining 9x9-6

K 12x9

Mbr 14x12-8

Clerestory Above

Dn

Living 12-4x17
Vaulted Ceiling

Up

Plant Shelf

Garage 20x20

38'-8"

UPPER LEVEL

Roof

Br 2 11-6x10

Dn

Upper Living

Br 3 13x9

Roof

PLAN B-8323
WITH BASEMENT

(Both contemporary and traditional exteriors included in blueprints.)

Blueprint Price Code A

Plan B-8323

To order blueprints, call
1-800-547-5570 or see order form
and pricing information on pages 220-224

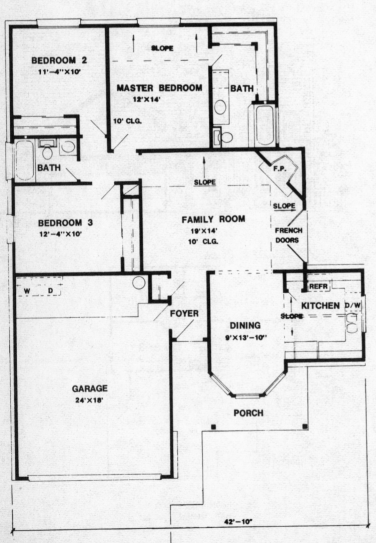

BEDROOM 2
11'-4"×10'

MASTER BEDROOM
12'×14'
10' CLG.

BATH

SLOPE

BATH

SLOPE

F.P.

BEDROOM 3
12'-4"×10'

FAMILY ROOM
19'×14'
10' CLG.

SLOPE

FRENCH DOORS

W   D

FOYER

REFR

KITCHEN D/W

SLOPE

DINING
9'×13'-10'

GARAGE
24'×18'

PORCH

42'-10"

Compact, Easy To Build

Total living area: 1,270 sq. ft.
(Not counting garage)

PLAN L-1270
WITHOUT BASEMENT
(SLAB-ON-GRADE FOUNDATION)

HomeStyles
SOURCE 1
DESIGNERS NETWORK

Blueprint Price Code A

Plan L-1270

To order blueprints, call
1-800-547-5570 or see order form
and pricing information on pages 220-224.

Compact Story-and-a-Half Home

AREAS

Main floor:	1,282 sq. ft.
Bonus (second floor):	644 sq. ft.
Storage:	54 sq. ft.
Porch:	48 sq. ft.

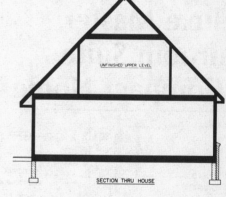

SECTION THRU HOUSE

Exterior walls are 2x6 construction.
Specify basement, crawlspace or slab foundation.

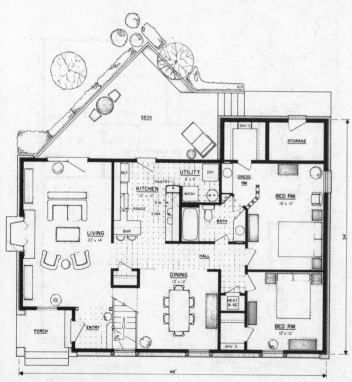

MAIN FLOOR

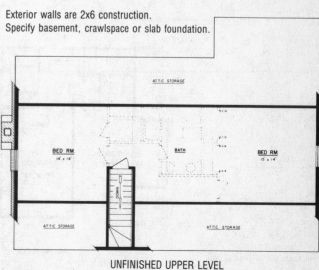

UNFINISHED UPPER LEVEL

An Energy Efficient Home
Blueprint Price Code A

Plan E-1215

HomeStyles SOURCE 1 DESIGNERS' NETWORK

Deluxe Master Bedroom Suite in Compact Home

First floor:	838 sq. ft.
Second floor:	453 sq. ft.
Total living area:	**1,291 sq. ft.**
(Not counting garage)	

OPTIONAL BEDROOM 4
164 SQ. FT.

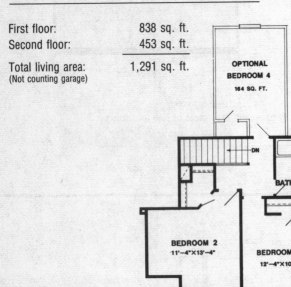

DN

BATH 2

BEDROOM 2
11'-4"X13'-4"

BEDROOM 3
12'-4"X10'

SECOND FLOOR

PLAN L-257-A
WITHOUT BASEMENT
(SLAB-ON-GRADE FOUNDATION)

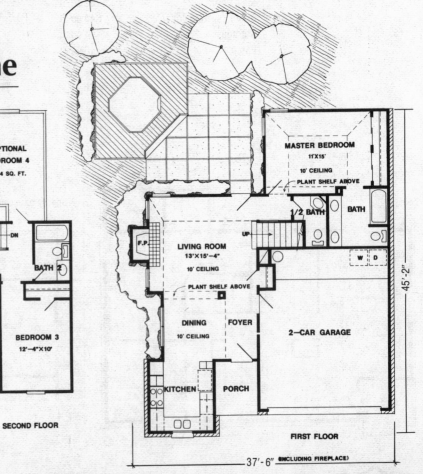

MASTER BEDROOM
11'X15'
10' CEILING
PLANT SHELF ABOVE

1/2 BATH   BATH

F.P.

LIVING ROOM
13'X15'-4"
10' CEILING

PLANT SHELF ABOVE

UP

W   D

DINING
10' CEILING

FOYER

2-CAR GARAGE

KITCHEN   PORCH

FIRST FLOOR

45'-2"

37'-6"
(INCLUDING FIREPLACE)

Blueprint Price Code A

Plan L-257-A

More for Less

Big in function but small in footage, this two-story passive solar design puts every inch of space to valuable and efficient use. The house can be constructed either as a free-standing unit or as part of a condo development.

The plan flows visually from its entry, through its high-ceilinged great room, to a brilliant south-facing sun room where solar heat is collected and stored in the ceramic-tiled floor.

Thick insulation in exterior walls and ceilings minimizes heat loss during the cold season. In summer, air flow is created by convection while eave overhangs protect against over-exposure.

The first floor, excluding sun room, provides 915 sq. ft. of living area, while the second floor adds 397 sq. ft., for a total of 1,312 sq. ft. Garage is 427 sq. ft.; optional basement is 915 sq. ft.

First floor:	915 sq. ft.
Second floor:	397 sq. ft.
Total living area:	1,312 sq. ft.
Garage:	427 sq. ft.
Basement (Optional):	915 sq. ft.

(Slab-on-grade option included.)

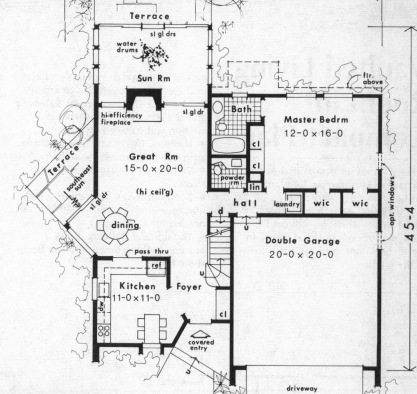

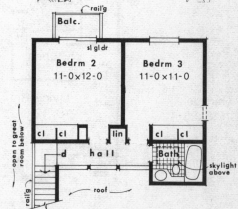

Blueprint Price Code A

Plan K-507-S

Vaulted Living Room in Compact Plan

● Here's another design that proves that a compact narrow lot plan need not be plain or unattractive.
● A sheltered entry leads into a raised foyer, which introduces the vaulted living room, the stairway to the second floor, and a short hallway to the kitchen.

● A cozy breakfast nook is included in the efficient, open-design kitchen.
● Also note the convenient half-bath and storage closet between the kitchen and garage entry.
● Upstairs, the master suite includes a private bath and large walk-in closet.
● Bedroom 2 also includes a large closet.
● Bedroom 3 can be used as a loft, library, exercise room or study if not needed for sleeping.
● The upstairs hallway offers a balcony looking down into the living room below.

Plan B-224-8512

Bedrooms: 2-3	Baths: 2½

Space:

Upper floor:	691 sq. ft.
Main floor:	668 sq. ft.
Total living area:	1,359 sq. ft.
Basement:	+/− 668 sq. ft.
Garage:	458 sq. ft.

Exterior Wall Framing: 2x4

Foundation options:
Standard basement only.
(Foundation & framing conversion diagram available — see order form.)

Blueprint Price Code: A

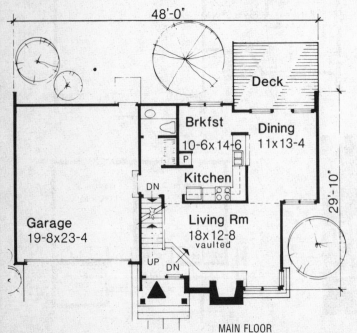

MAIN FLOOR

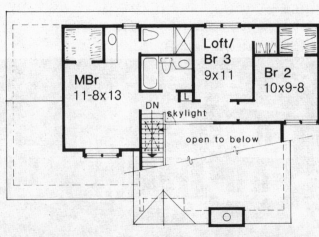

UPPER FLOOR

Plan B-224-8512

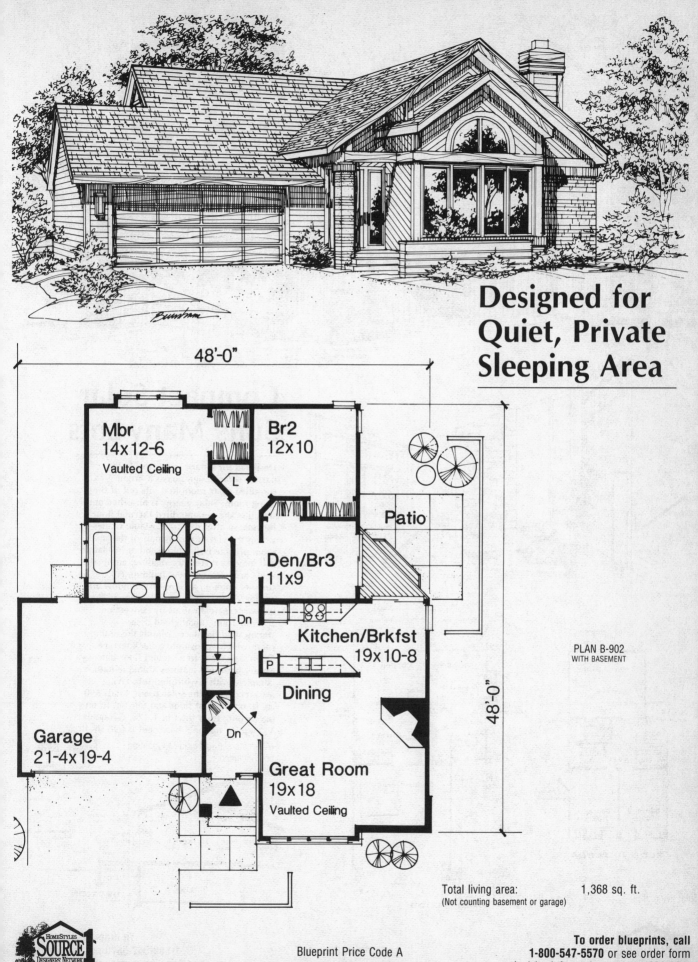

Designed for Quiet, Private Sleeping Area

48'-0"

48'-0"

Mbr
14x12-6
Vaulted Ceiling

Br2
12x10

Patio

Den/Br3
11x9

Dn

Kitchen/Brkfst
19x10-8

Dining

P

Dn

Garage
21-4x19-4

Great Room
19x18
Vaulted Ceiling

PLAN B-902
WITH BASEMENT

Total living area: 1,368 sq. ft.
(Not counting basement or garage)

Blueprint Price Code A

Plan B-902

To order blueprints, call
1-800-547-5570 or see order form
and pricing information on pages 220-224.

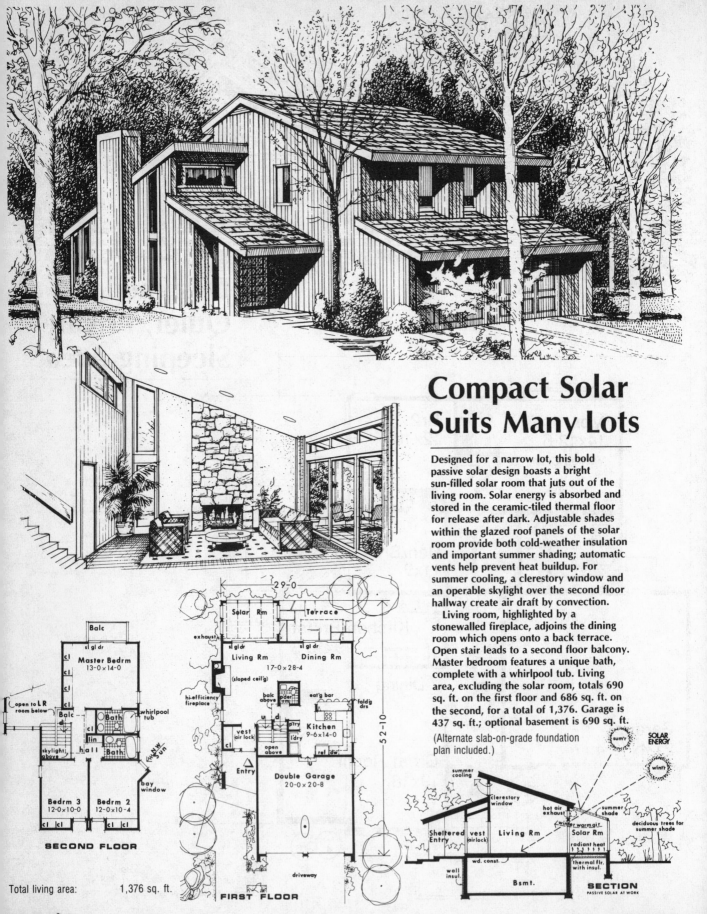

Compact Solar Suits Many Lots

Designed for a narrow lot, this bold passive solar design boasts a bright sun-filled solar room that juts out of the living room. Solar energy is absorbed and stored in the ceramic-tiled thermal floor for release after dark. Adjustable shades within the glazed roof panels of the solar room provide both cold-weather insulation and important summer shading; automatic vents help prevent heat buildup. For summer cooling, a clerestory window and an operable skylight over the second floor hallway create air draft by convection.

Living room, highlighted by a stonewalled fireplace, adjoins the dining room which opens onto a back terrace. Open stair leads to a second floor balcony. Master bedroom features a unique bath, complete with a whirlpool tub. Living area, excluding the solar room, totals 690 sq. ft. on the first floor and 686 sq. ft. on the second, for a total of 1,376. Garage is 437 sq. ft.; optional basement is 690 sq. ft.

(Alternate slab-on-grade foundation plan included.)

Total living area: 1,376 sq. ft.

Blueprint Price Code A

Plan K-521-C

To order blueprints, call
1-800-547-5570 or see order form
and pricing information on pages 220-224

Stately Veranda on Compact Home

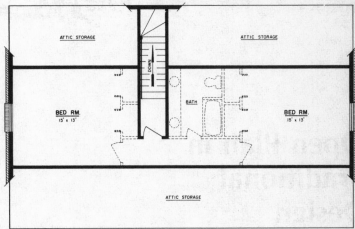

UNFINISHED UPPER LEVEL

LOWER LEVEL

Main floor:	1,384 sq. ft.
Storage:	56 sq. ft.
Porch:	313 sq. ft.
Upper level:	656 sq. ft.
Total area:	2,409 sq. ft.

Exterior walls are 2x6 construction.
Specify basement, crawlspace or slab foundation.

Blueprint Price Code A

Plan E-1317

Open Plan in Traditional Design

This design is popular for its simple yet stylish exterior, making it suitable for country or urban settings. The covered front porch and gabled roof extension accent the exterior while providing a sheltered area for outdoor relaxation.

A rear entrance leads from the carport to the utility room, which features a walk-in pantry. A storage area accessible from the carport hides lawn mowers and garden tools.

Inside, the kitchen features an island bar facing the bay-windowed dining room. This area combines with the living room, which has a fireplace and cathedral ceiling, to create one large gathering spot.

The master bedroom, tucked at the rear of the home and looking out to the backyard, has a walk-in closet and a private bath. A second full bath serves the remaining two bedrooms.

Total living area: 1,385 sq. ft.
(Not counting carport)

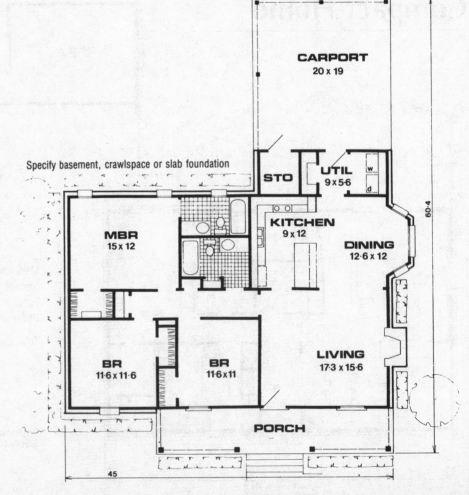

Specify basement, crawlspace or slab foundation

CARPORT
20 x 19

STO

UTIL
9 x 5·6

KITCHEN
9 x 12

DINING
12·6 x 12

MBR
15 x 12

LIVING
17·3 x 15·6

BR
11·6 x 11·6

BR
11·6 x 11

PORCH

60·4

45

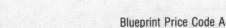
Blueprint Price Code A
Plan J-86155

To order blueprints, call
1-800-547-5570 or see order form
and pricing information on pages 220-224.

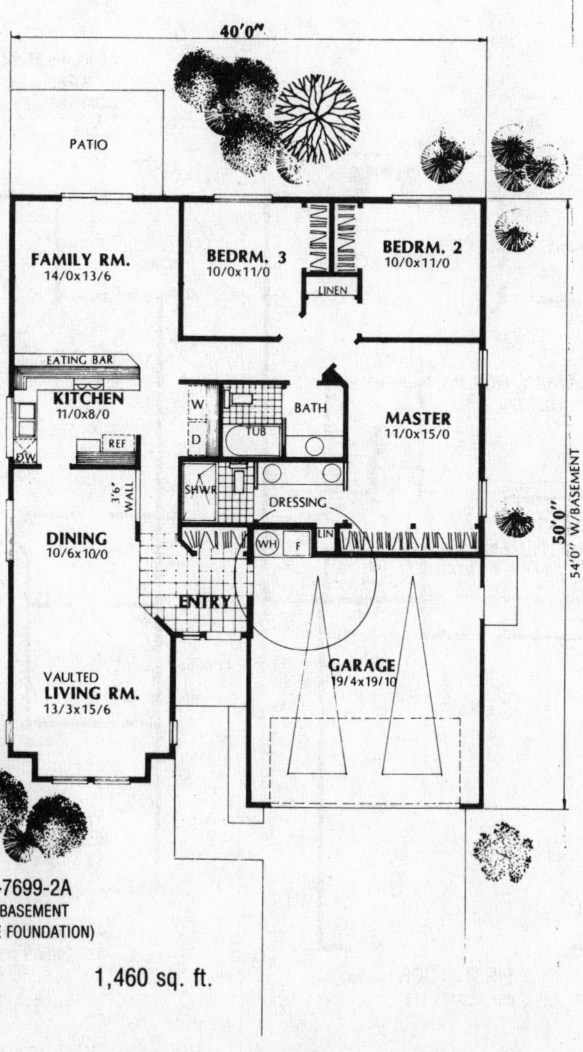

Compact Plan for Small Lot

PLAN P-7699-2D
WITH DAYLIGHT BASEMENT

Main floor:	1,509 sq. ft.
Basement level:	1,530 sq. ft.

PLAN P-7699-2A
WITHOUT BASEMENT
(CRAWLSPACE FOUNDATION)

Total living area: 1,460 sq. ft.
(Not counting garage)

Floor plan labels:
- PATIO
- FAMILY RM. 14/0x13/6
- BEDRM. 3 10/0x11/0
- BEDRM. 2 10/0x11/0
- LINEN
- EATING BAR
- KITCHEN 11/0x8/0
- BATH
- TUB
- MASTER 11/0x15/0
- W / D
- REF
- DW
- 3/6 WALL
- SHWR
- DRESSING
- DINING 10/6x10/0
- WH / F / LIN
- ENTRY
- VAULTED LIVING RM. 13/3x15/6
- GARAGE 19/4x19/10
- 40'0"
- 54'0" / 50'0" W/BASEMENT

Basement detail labels:
- STOR
- LINEN
- DN
- GARAGE

To order blueprints, call
1-800-547-5570 or see order form
and pricing information on pages 220-224.

Blueprint Price Code A

Plans P-7699-2A & P-7699-2D

Townhouse Living for Narrow Lots

Because of its 24' width this home can be constructed on a 40' lot (even less in some jurisdictions). This is about half the requirement of a one-story dwelling with similar features and floor space. Further, the home needs only half the foundation and roof required by a one-floor residence. Heating costs are reduced by the fact that the upper rooms are partially warmed by radiation from the lower floor that would otherwise be simply wasted in unused attic spaces. Through years of ownership, the burden of taxes would also be lightened greatly because of the smaller building site. Many other economies such as lower water heating bills due to the concentrated plumbing arrangement will also be enjoyed.

By its very shape and arrangement, this home lends itself beautifully to use as a duplex. When placed side by side along the garage, kitchen and family room wall, two units measuring 48' in width can be combined on a 60' x 100' lot for a double saving in land and construction costs. (Duplex version is Plan H-592-1A2.)

First floor:	655 sq. ft.
Second floor:	755 sq. ft.
Total living area: (Not counting garage)	1,410 sq. ft.

PLAN H-1427-1A
WITHOUT BASEMENT
(CRAWLSPACE FOUNDATION)

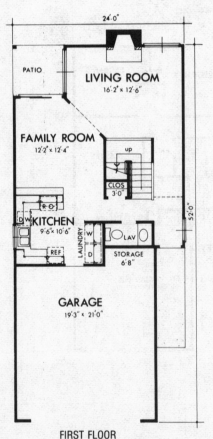

FIRST FLOOR
655 SQUARE FEET

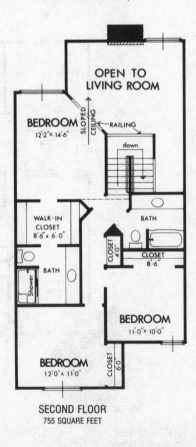

SECOND FLOOR
755 SQUARE FEET

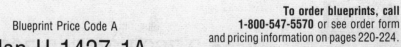

Blueprint Price Code A

Plan H-1427-1A

To order blueprints, call
1-800-547-5570 or see order form
and pricing information on pages 220-224

Compact Contemporary

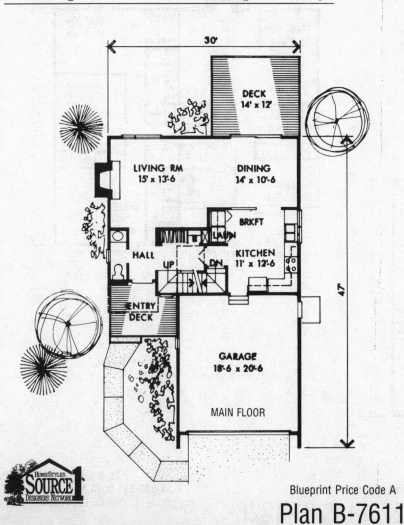

DECK
14' x 12'

LIVING RM
15' x 13'-6

DINING
14' x 10'-6

BRKFT

LAUN

HALL

UP

DN

KITCHEN
11' x 12'-6

ENTRY
DECK

30'

47'

GARAGE
18'-6 x 20'-6

MAIN FLOOR

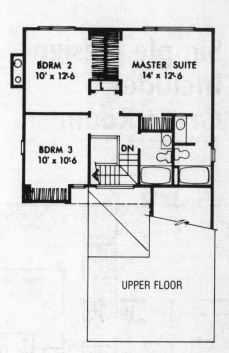

BDRM 2
10' x 12'-6

MASTER SUITE
14' x 12'-6

BDRM 3
10' x 10'-6

DN

UPPER FLOOR

PLAN B-7611
WITH BASEMENT

Main floor:	705 sq. ft.
Upper floor:	738 sq. ft.
Total living area:	1,443 sq. ft.
(Not counting basement or garage)	

HomeStyles
SOURCE 1
DESIGNERS' NETWORK

Blueprint Price Code A

Plan B-7611

To order blueprints, call
1-800-547-5570 or see order form
and pricing information on pages 220-224.

Simple Design Includes Great Room

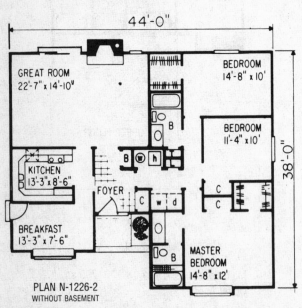

44'-0"

GREAT ROOM
22'-7" x 14'-10"

BEDROOM
14'-8" x 10'

BEDROOM
11'-4" x 10'

B

KITCHEN
13'-3" x 8'-6"

FOYER

C
w d

38'-0"

C
C

BREAKFAST
13'-3" x 7'-6"

B

MASTER
BEDROOM
14'-8" x 12'

PLAN N-1226-2
WITHOUT BASEMENT

(Specify crawlspace or slab foundation)

44'-0"

GREAT ROOM
22'-7" x 14'-10"

BEDROOM
14'-8" x 10'

BEDROOM
11'-4" x 10'

B

dn

KITCHEN
13'-3" x 8'-6"

FOYER

C
w d

38'-0"

C
C

BREAKFAST
13'-3" x 7'-6"

MASTER
BEDROOM
14'-8" x 12'

B

PLAN N-1226-1
WITH BASEMENT

Total living area: 1,480 sq. ft.
(Not counting basement or garage)

Blueprint Price Code A

Plans N-1226-1 & N-1226-2

To order blueprints, call
1-800-547-5570 or see order form
and pricing information on pages 220-224.

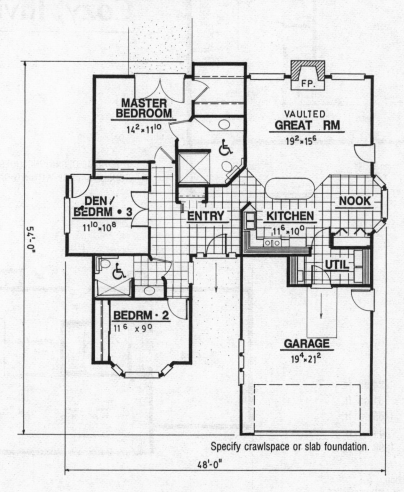

MASTER BEDROOM
$14^2 \times 11^{10}$

VAULTED
GREAT RM
$19^2 \times 15^6$

FP.

DEN/
BEDRM • 3
$11^{10} \times 10^8$

ENTRY

KITCHEN
$11^6 \times 10^0$

NOOK

UTIL

BEDRM • 2
$11^6 \times 9^0$

GARAGE
$19^4 \times 21^2$

Specify crawlspace or slab foundation.

48'-0"

54'-0"

Total living area: 1,484 sq. ft.
(Not counting garage)

PLAN I-1484-H
WITHOUT BASEMENT

Blueprint Price Code A

Plan I-1484-H

To order blueprints, call
1-800-547-5570 or see order form
and pricing information on pages 220-224.

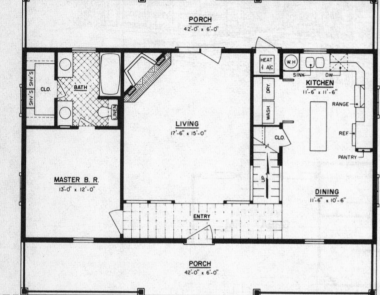

PORCH
42'-0" x 6'-0"

HEAT & A/C

KITCHEN
11'-6" x 11'-6"

SINK **DW**

W.H.

DRY

WASH

CLO.

RANGE

REF.

PANTRY

BATH

CLO.

SHV'S

LINEN

LIVING
17'-6" x 15'-0"

MASTER B. R.
13'-0" x 12'-0"

UP

DINING
11'-6" x 10'-6"

ENTRY

PORCH
42'-0" x 6'-0"

42'-0"

34'-0"

LOWER LEVEL

Compact, Cozy, Inviting

THIS HOME DESIGN INCLUDES A SEPARATE DOUBLE GARAGE WITH STORAGE.

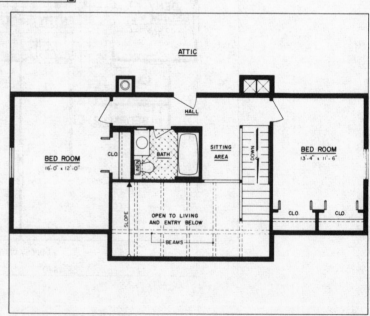

ATTIC

HALL

BED ROOM
16'-0" x 12'-0"

CLO.

LINEN

BATH

SITTING AREA

DOWN

BED ROOM
13'-4" x 11'-6"

CLO.

CLO.

SLOPE

OPEN TO LIVING AND ENTRY BELOW

BEAMS

UPPER LEVEL

AREAS

Living - Lower Level   924 sq. ft.
Living - Upper Level   561 sq. ft.
Living - Total   1485 sq. ft.
Porches   504 sq. ft.
Total   1989 sq. ft.

Exterior walls are 2x6 construction.
Specify basement, crawlspace or slab foundation.

An Energy Efficient Home

HomeStyles
SOURCE 1
DESIGNERS NETWORK

Blueprint Price Code A

Plan E-1421

To order blueprints, call
1-800-547-5570 or see order form
and pricing information on pages 220-224.

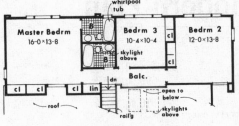

SECOND FLOOR

Master Bedrm 16-0×13-8 · Bedrm 3 10-4×10-4 · Bedrm 2 12-0×13-8 · whirlpool tub · skylight above · Balc. · open to below · skylights above · roof · rail'g

Compact Design Offers Affordable Luxury

This rustic two-story, three-bedroom contemporary home is clad in horizontal wood siding and topped with asphalt shingles. A massive stone chimney dominates the facade. An inviting entryway leads to an open, well-zoned plan. The living room is highlighted by a wood-burning fireplace and a sloping ceiling that sweeps up to the second story balcony. Operable skylights overhead brighten the interiors.

The formal dining room, adjacent to the living room, opens onto a backyard terrace. An efficient U-shaped kitchen boasts a glazed half-circular dinette for casual family meals.

On the upper level, three bedrooms and two full baths are connected by the open balcony that overlooks the living room below. The master bedroom features ample closets and a private bathroom, complete with a whirlpool tub.

First floor:	766 sq. ft.
Second floor:	739 sq. ft.
Total living area: (Not counting basement or garage)	1,505 sq. ft.
Garage:	440 sq. ft.
Optional basement:	766 sq. ft.

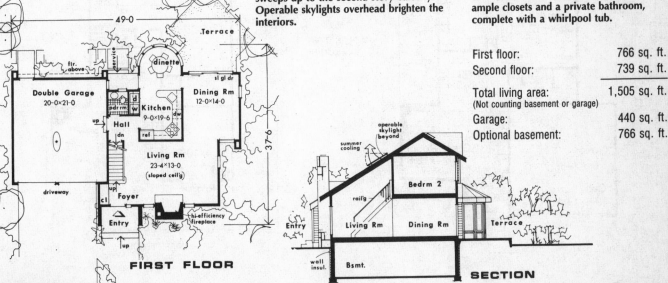

FIRST FLOOR

49-0 · 37-6 · Terrace · flr. above · service · dinette · sl gl dr · Double Garage 20-0×21-0 · Dining Rm 12-0×14-0 · pdr rm · Kitchen 9-0×19-6 · Hall · up · dn · ref · Living Rm 23-4×13-0 (sloped ceil'g) · driveway · up · cl · Foyer · Entry · up · hi-efficiency fireplace

SECTION

operable skylight beyond · summer cooling · Bedrm 2 · rail'g · Entry · Living Rm · Dining Rm · Terrace · wall insul. · Bsmt.

Blueprint Price Code B

Plan K-539-L

To order blueprints, call 1-800-547-5570 or see order form and pricing information on pages 220-224.

Traditional Flavor for Modern Plan

First floor: 817 sq. ft.
Second floor: 699 sq. ft.

Total living area: 1,516 sq. ft.
(Not counting basement or garage)

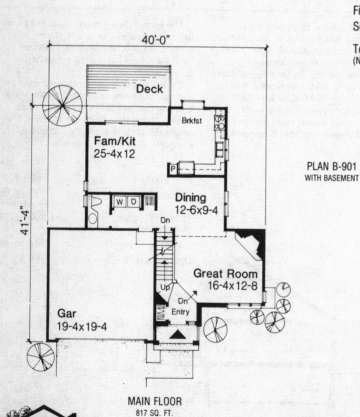

PLAN B-901
WITH BASEMENT

40'-0"

Deck

Brkfst

Fam/Kit
25-4x12

P

Dining
12-6x9-4

W D

Dn

Up

Great Room
16-4x12-8

Dn
Entry

Gar
19-4x19-4

41'-4"

MAIN FLOOR
817 SQ. FT.

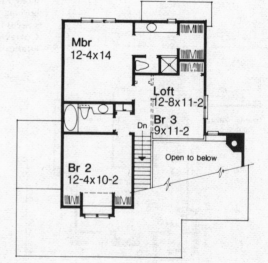

Mbr
12-4x14

Loft
12-8x11-2

Br 3
9x11-2

Dn

Open to below

Br 2
12-4x10-2

UPPER FLOOR
699 SQ. FT.

46

Blueprint Price Code B

Plan B-901

To order blueprints, call
1-800-547-5570 or see order form
and pricing information on pages 220-224

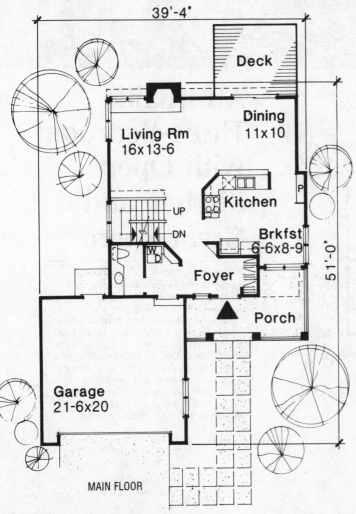

Compact Two-Story Offers Spacious Living/Dining Area

MAIN FLOOR

39'-4"

51'-0"

Deck

Living Rm
16x13-6

Dining
11x10

Kitchen

P

UP

DN

Brkfst
6-6x8-9

W D

Foyer

Porch

Garage
21-6x20

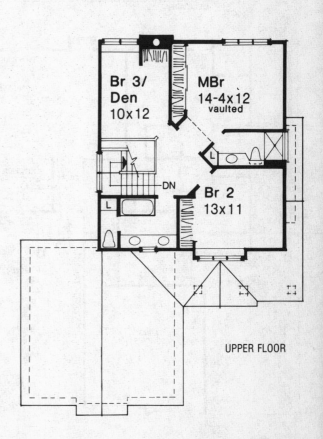

Br 3/
Den
10x12

MBr
14-4x12
vaulted

L

DN

L

Br 2
13x11

UPPER FLOOR

Main floor: 765 sq. ft.
Upper floor: 760 sq. ft.

Total living area: 1,525 sq. ft.
(Not counting basement or garage)

Blueprint Price Code B

Plan B-148-86

To order blueprints, call
1-800-547-5570 or see order form
and pricing information on pages 220-224.

Affordable Three-Bedroom with Open Kitchen and Great Room

Multiple gabled roofs with dramatic overhangs add to the exterior charm of this three-bedroom contemporary home. The interior is cozy, with plenty of features for folks who love outdoor living indoors. There's a garden area located just off the master bedroom's sitting area with privacy fence. Vaulted ceilings add a sense of the great outdoors to the large activity area, corner kitchen, and entry. The activity room also enjoys its own fireplace and snack bar and shares access to a rear wood deck with the master bedroom.

PLAN N-1276-1
WITH BASEMENT

PLAN N-1276-2
WITHOUT BASEMENT

Total living area: 1,533 sq. ft.

47'-0"

DECK AREA

EXPOSED RAFTERS ABOVE

MASTER BEDROOM
15'-0" x 12'-6"

ACTIVITY AREA
24'-6" x 18'-0"

VAULTED CEILING

SITTING AREA
6'-8" x 8'-0"

GREAT ROOM

SNACK COUNTER

ENTRY
VAULTED CEILING

KITCHEN
11'-6" x 12'-6"

63'-6"

BEDROOM 3
10'-0" x 10'-0"

D.   UTIL.
W.
L.T.

BEDROOM 2
10'-0" x 12'-0"

GARAGE
20'-6" x 21'-0"

Blueprint Price Code B

Plans N-1276-1 & N-1276-2

Open Kitchen/Family Room Combination

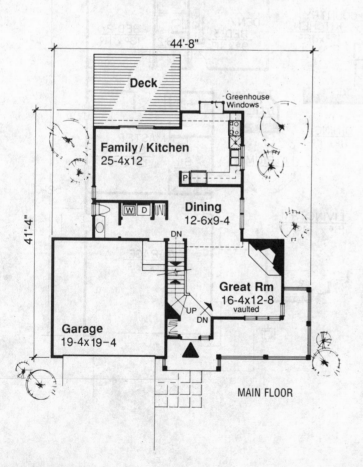

44'-8"

Deck

Greenhouse Windows

Family / Kitchen
25-4x12

W D

Dining
12-6x9-4

DN

Great Rm
16-4x12-8
vaulted

UP   DN

Garage
19-4x19-4

41'-4"

MAIN FLOOR

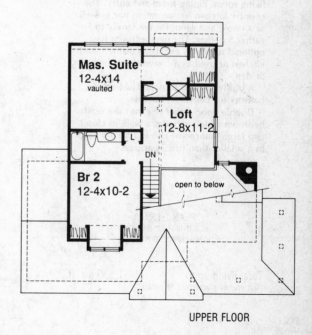

PLAN B-88006
WITH BASEMENT

Main floor: 818 sq. ft.
Upper floor: 732 sq. ft.

Total living area: 1,550 sq. ft.
(Not counting basement or garage)

Mas. Suite
12-4x14
vaulted

Loft
12-8x11-2

Br 2
12-4x10-2

DN

open to below

UPPER FLOOR

Blueprint Price Code B

Plan B-88006

To order blueprints, call
1-800-547-5570 or see order form
and pricing information on pages 220-224

Exciting Inside and Out

This beautiful contemporary plan is as exciting inside as it is on the outside. Dramatic stone columns flank the entry and provide support for the massive covered entry roof. The accent windows in front are reduced in size as they gradually step back from the entry wall, creating the illusion of spaciousness.

Upon entering the home, you are greeted by an atrium which faces the living room, dining room and entry. The country kitchen has an eating bar as well as a nook, and room for the family to gather together. The den/bedroom has optional use as an extension of the country kitchen or used as a conventional bedroom or den.

A utility room is provided just off the hallway for convenient access.

Double doors usher one into the master bedroom which includes a walk-in closet and large bathroom. This is a luxury home in a smaller-than-usual package.

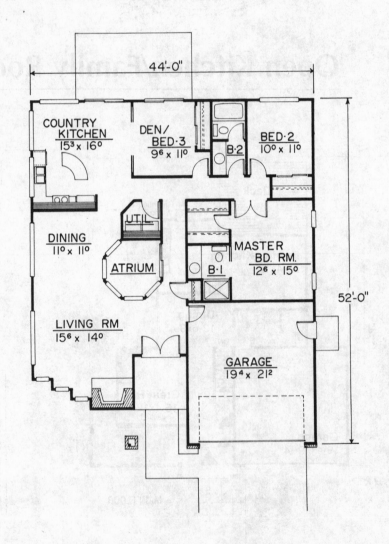

PLAN I-1550-A
WITHOUT BASEMENT
(CRAWLSPACE FOUNDATION)

Total living area: 1,550 sq. ft.
(Not counting basement or garage)

Blueprint Price Code B
Plan I-1550-A

Spacious Country Kitchen

Main floor:	834 sq. ft.
Upper floor:	722 sq. ft.
Total living area:	1,556 sq. ft.
(Not counting basement or garage)	

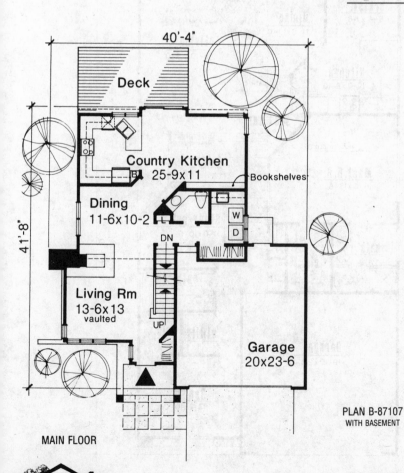

40'-4"

41'-8"

Deck

Country Kitchen
25-9x11

BF

Bookshelves

Dining
11-6x10-2

W
D

DN

Living Rm
13-6x13
vaulted

UP

Garage
20x23-6

MAIN FLOOR

PLAN B-87107
WITH BASEMENT

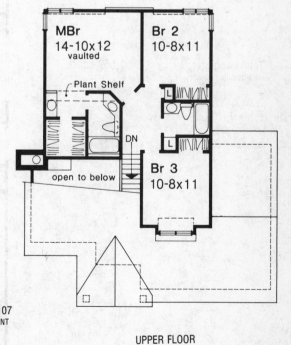

MBr
14-10x12
vaulted

Br 2
10-8x11

Plant Shelf

L

DN

L

open to below

Br 3
10-8x11

UPPER FLOOR

Blueprint Price Code B

Plan B-87107

To order blueprints, call
1-800-547-5570 or see order form
and pricing information on pages 220-224.

Economy Home for Small Lot

PLAN Q-1557-1A
WITHOUT BASEMENT
(SLAB-ON-GRADE FOUNDATION)

Total living area: 1,557 sq. ft.
(Not counting garage)

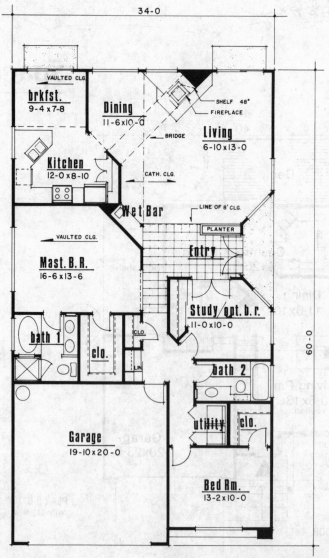

34-0

60-0

VAULTED CLG.

brkfst.
9-4 x 7-8

Dining
11-6 x 10-0

SHELF 48"
FIREPLACE

BRIDGE

Living
6-10 x 13-0

Kitchen
12-0 x 8-10

CATH. CLG.

Wet Bar

LINE OF 8' CLG.

PLANTER

Entry

VAULTED CLG.

Mast. B.R.
16-6 x 13-6

Study/opt. b.r.
11-0 x 10-0

bath 1

clo.

CLO.

LIN

bath 2

utility

clo.

Garage
19-10 x 20-0

Bed Rm.
13-2 x 10-0

Blueprint Price Code B

Plan Q-1557-1A

To order blueprints, call
1-800-547-5570 or see order form
and pricing information on pages 220-224.

Contemporary Mediterranean Perfect for Narrow Lots

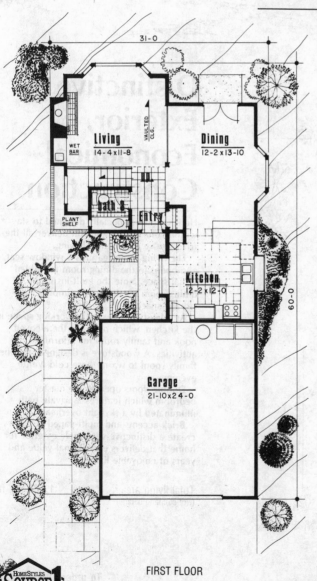

FIRST FLOOR

- Living 14-4 x 11-8
- Dining 12-2 x 13-10
- Kitchen 12-2 x 12-0
- Garage 21-10 x 24-0
- WET BAR
- Bath
- Entry
- PLANT SHELF
- VAULTED CLG.
- 31-0
- 60-0

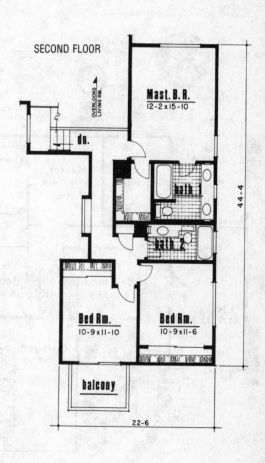

SECOND FLOOR

- Mast. B.R. 12-2 x 15-10
- Bath 1
- Bath 2
- Bed Rm. 10-9 x 11-10
- Bed Rm. 10-9 x 11-6
- balcony
- dn.
- OVERLOOKS LIVING RM.
- 44-4
- 22-6

First floor:	800 sq. ft.
Second floor:	765 sq. ft.
Total living area:	1,565 sq. ft.

Blueprint Price Code B

Plan Q-1565-1A

To order blueprints, call
1-800-547-5570 or see order form
and pricing information on pages 220-224

53

Distinctive Exterior, Economical Construction

Here's a house specially designed to stay within your budget and still deliver all the frills you've dreamed of having.

The living room features a window seat, and opens to the dining room for added visual space. Note the built-ins in the dining room for display or simply extra storage space.

An island provides extra working space in the kitchen, which opens to the alcoved nook and family room for informal activities. A woodstove is designed into the family room to warm those cold winter evenings.

Double doors open to the master bedroom which features a private bath illuminated by a skylight overhead.

Brick accents and multi-paned windows create a distinctive yet simple exterior for a home that delivers exceptional value and years of enjoyable living.

Total living area: 1,585 sq. ft.
(Not counting garage)

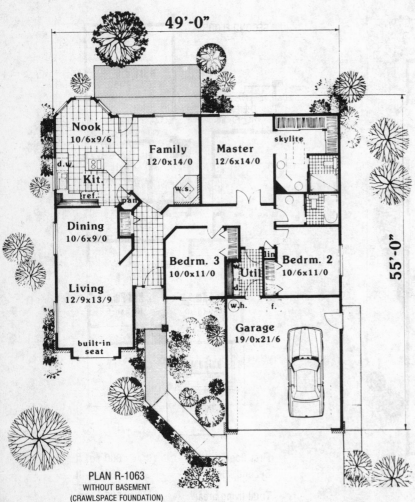

49'-0"

55'-0"

Nook
10/6x9/6

Family
12/0x14/0

Master
12/6x14/0

skylite

d.w

Kit.

ref.

pan

w.s.

Dining
10/6x9/0

Living
12/9x13/9

Bedrm. 3
10/0x11/0

Util.

Bedrm. 2
10/6x11/0

w.h.   f.

built-in seat

Garage
19/0x21/6

PLAN R-1063
WITHOUT BASEMENT
(CRAWLSPACE FOUNDATION)

Blueprint Price Code B
Plan R-1063

To order blueprints, call
1-800-547-5570 or see order form
and pricing information on pages 220-224.

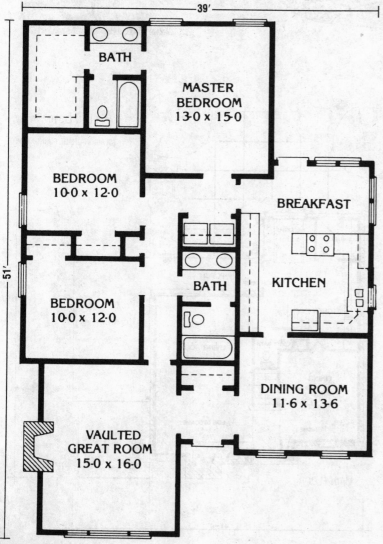

BATH

MASTER BEDROOM
13-0 x 15-0

BEDROOM
10-0 x 12-0

BREAKFAST

BATH

KITCHEN

BEDROOM
10-0 x 12-0

DINING ROOM
11-6 x 13-6

VAULTED GREAT ROOM
15-0 x 16-0

39'

51'

Appealing French Details

Authentic French details adorn the facade of this appealing one-story design. The slightly recessed doorway, arched windows, and curved shutters all add interest to this beautifully proportioned residence.

The vaulted ceiling of the Great Room makes this room appear much larger than its dimensions state. An oversized Palladian window creates a dramatic focal point and floods the room with natural light. The kitchen contains an unusual amount of cabinets and counter space.

Abundant closet space is provided for the inhabitants of the master bedroom. Also, note the convenient location of the laundry center, handy to both kitchen and bedroom areas.

PLAN V-1586
WITHOUT BASEMENT
(CRAWLSPACE FOUNDATION)

Total living area: 1,586 sq. ft.

9'-0" CEILINGS THROUGHOUT

Blueprint Price Code B
Plan V-1586

Classic Home for Small Lot

First floor:	839 sq. ft.
Second floor:	769 sq. ft.
Total living area:	1,608 sq. ft.

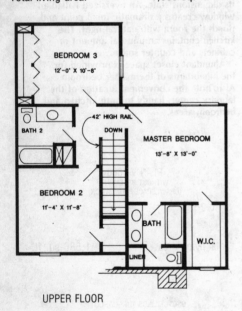

UPPER FLOOR

BEDROOM 3
12'-0" X 10'-8"

BATH 2

42" HIGH RAIL

DOWN

MASTER BEDROOM
13'-8" X 13'-0"

BEDROOM 2
11'-4" X 11'-8"

BATH

W.I.C.

LINEN

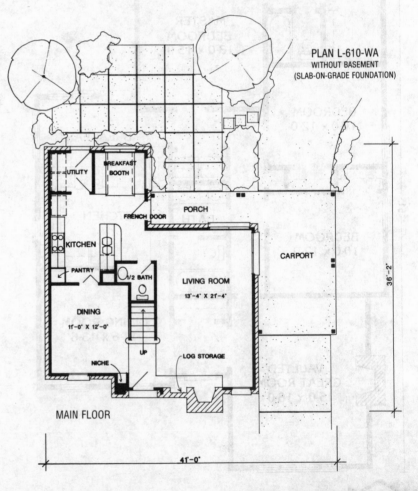

PLAN L-610-WA
WITHOUT BASEMENT
(SLAB-ON-GRADE FOUNDATION)

UTILITY

BREAKFAST BOOTH

FRENCH DOOR

PORCH

KITCHEN

PANTRY

1/2 BATH

CARPORT

LIVING ROOM
13'-4" X 21'-4"

DINING
11'-0" X 12'-0"

UP

NICHE

LOG STORAGE

MAIN FLOOR

36'-2"

41'-0"

Blueprint Price Code B

Plan L-610-WA

To order blueprints, call
1-800-547-5570 or see order form
and pricing information on pages 220-224

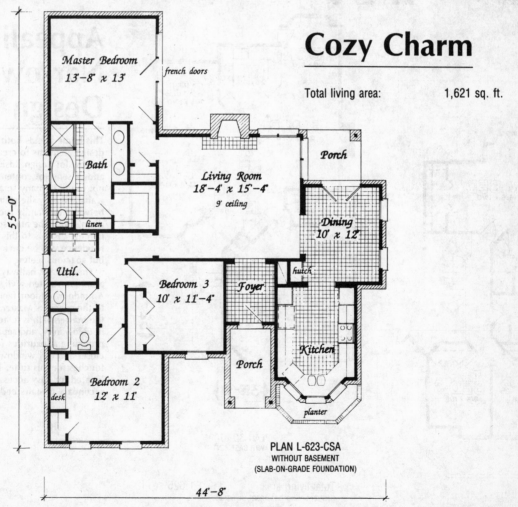

Cozy Charm

Total living area: 1,621 sq. ft.

Master Bedroom
13'-8" x 13'

french doors

Bath

linen

Living Room
18'-4" x 15'-4"
9' ceiling

Porch

Dining
10' x 12'

hutch

Util.

Bedroom 3
10' x 11'-4"

Foyer

Kitchen

desk

Bedroom 2
12' x 11'

Porch

planter

55'-0"

44'-8"

PLAN L-623-CSA
WITHOUT BASEMENT
(SLAB-ON-GRADE FOUNDATION)

Blueprint Price Code B

Plan L-623-CSA

To order blueprints, call
1-800-547-5570 or see order form
and pricing information on pages 220-224.

Appealing Narrow-Lot Design

This home blends both French and English design elements to create an appealing narrow lot design. Inside, an open plan adds a sense of contemporary grandeur not found in many small homes. With few walls and only the stair for division between the family room, living room, and dining area, the atmosphere is warm and homey. Visitors to this very appealing residence will be envious of the compact but spacious feeling.

The upstairs hallway is lined above with a unique vaulted skylight planting ledge. An indoor/outdoor feeling follows the hall to the spacious Master Suite. Featured in the master bath is a step-up tile tub, double vanity, and separate shower, all providing a luxurious feeling. A walk-in closet and bay window are added fine touches for this suite. The hall bath is located for easy access to the two secondary upstairs bedrooms.

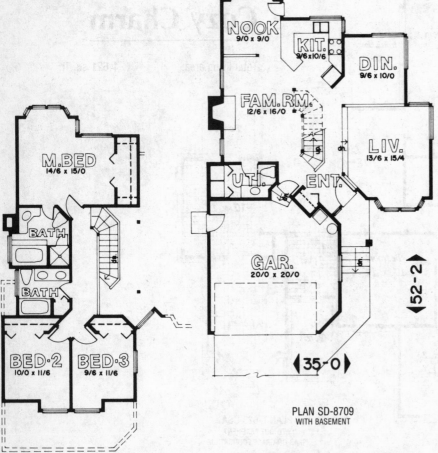

PLAN SD-8709
WITH BASEMENT

Total living area: 1,625 sq. ft.
(Not counting basement or garage)

Blueprint Price Code B
Plan SD-8709

To order blueprints, call
1-800-547-5570 or see order form and pricing information on pages 220-224.

Covered Entry Adds Distinctive Touch

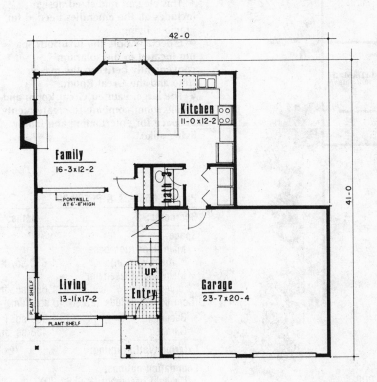

Kitchen
11-0 x 12-2

Family
16-3 x 12-2

PONYWALL
AT 6'-8" HIGH

bath

Living
13-11 x 17-2

UP
Entry

Garage
23-7 x 20-4

PLANT SHELF

PLANT SHELF

42-0

41-0

FIRST FLOOR

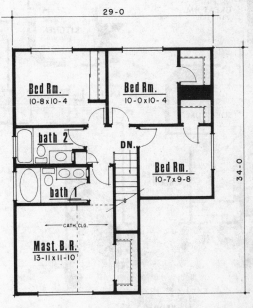

Bed Rm.
10-8 x 10-4

Bed Rm.
10-0 x 10-4

bath 2

DN.

Bed Rm.
10-7 x 9-8

bath

CATH. CLG.

Mast. B. R.
13-11 x 11-10

29-0

34-0

SECOND FLOOR

PLAN Q-1630-1A
WITHOUT BASEMENT
(SLAB FOUNDATION)

First floor: 876 sq. ft.
Second floor: 754 sq. ft.

Total living area: 1,630 sq. ft.
(Not counting garage)

HomeStyles
SOURCE
DESIGNERS NETWORK

Blueprint Price Code B

Plan Q-1630-1A

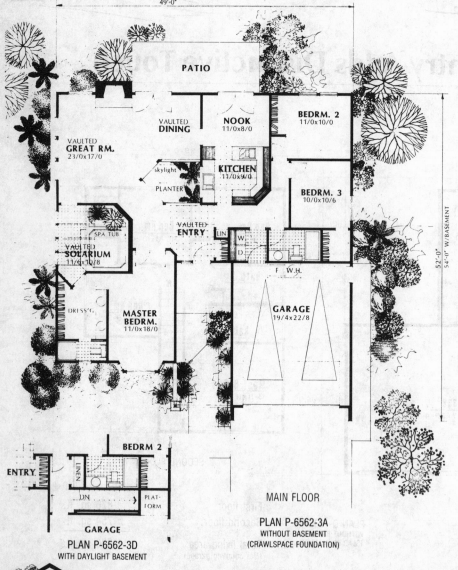

PATIO

VAULTED **DINING**

NOOK
11/0x8/0

BEDRM. 2
11/0x10/0

VAULTED
GREAT RM.
23/0x17/0

skylight

KITCHEN
11/0x9/0

PLANTER

BEDRM. 3
10/0x10/6

SPA TUB

VAULTED
ENTRY

LIN

VAULTED
SOLARIUM
11/6x10/8

W
D

F W.H.

DRESS'G

**MASTER
BEDRM.**
11/0x18/0

GARAGE
19/4x22/8

49'-0"

52'-0" W/BASEMENT
54'-0" W/BASEMENT

MAIN FLOOR

PLAN P-6562-3A
WITHOUT BASEMENT
(CRAWLSPACE FOUNDATION)

BEDRM 2

LINEN

DN

PLAT-
FORM

ENTRY

GARAGE

PLAN P-6562-3D
WITH DAYLIGHT BASEMENT

Master Suite Adjoins Spa Solarium

- This elegant mid-sized design includes all the amenities needed for gracious living.
- Especially note the luxurious spa tub located in the solarium conveniently between the master suite and the Great Room.
- The large, vaulted Great Room and dining room combine to create plenty of space for entertaining and family living alike.

Plans P-6562-3A & P6562-3D

Bedrooms: 3	Baths: 2

Space:

Main floor (non-basement version):	1,639 sq. ft.
Main floor (basement version):	1,699 sq. ft.
(Both figures include 123 sq. ft. solarium.)	
Basement:	1,699 sq. ft.
Garage:	438 sq. ft.

Exterior Wall Framing:	2x4

Foundation options:
Daylight basement (P-6562-3D).
Crawlspace (P-6562-3A).
(Foundation & framing conversion diagram available — see order form.)

Blueprint Price Code:	B

Plans P-6562-3A & P-6562-3D

Livability, Economy, Convenience

This home rates high marks not only for great livability but economy as well. To utilize the available square footage, the living and dining rooms are joined to create shared visual areas which enhance the feeling of spaciousness. This is further emphasized by the vaulted ceiling that highlights both rooms.

A convenient eating bar separates the kitchen and family room for informal dining. If you look closely, you'll find a pantry closet tucked inside the kitchen for additional storage space.

Note the side windows which frame the sliding glass door in the family room. The added window area provides extra light to cheerfully brighten the interior.

The master bedroom is generously sized and features a private bath.

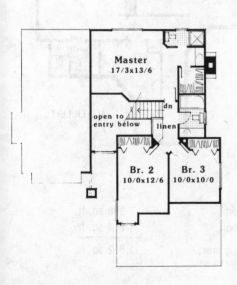

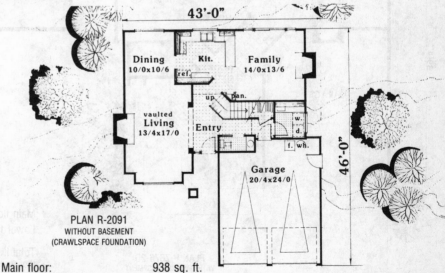

PLAN R-2091
WITHOUT BASEMENT
(CRAWLSPACE FOUNDATION)

Main floor:	938 sq. ft.
Upper floor:	703 sq. ft.
Total living area: (Not counting garage)	1,641 sq. ft.

Blueprint Price Code B

Plan R-2091

Bedrooms on Walkout Level

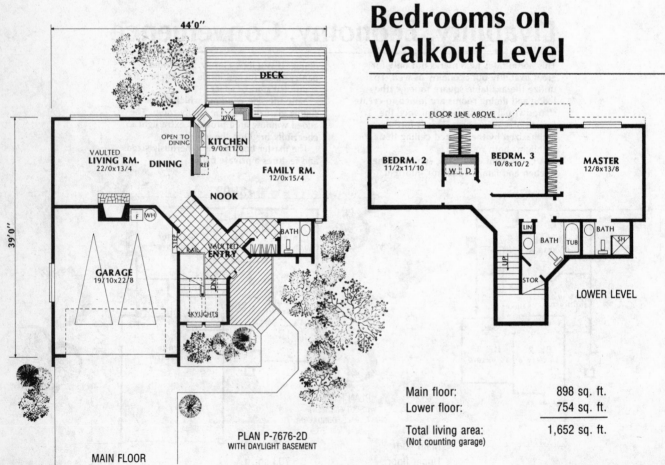

MAIN FLOOR

44'0"

39'0"

DECK

VAULTED LIVING RM. 22/0x13/4

DINING

OPEN TO DINING

KITCHEN 9/0x11/0

DW

REF.

FAMILY RM. 12/0x15/4

NOOK

F WH

BATH

VAULTED ENTRY

STEP

RAIL

GARAGE 19/10x22/8

DN

SKYLIGHTS

PLAN P-7676-2D
WITH DAYLIGHT BASEMENT

LOWER LEVEL

FLOOR LINE ABOVE

BEDRM. 2 11/2x11/10

W D

BEDRM. 3 10/8x10/2

MASTER 12/8x13/8

LIN

BATH

TUB

BATH

SH

UP

STOR

Main floor:	898 sq. ft.
Lower floor:	754 sq. ft.
Total living area: (Not counting garage)	1,652 sq. ft.

HomeStyles SOURCE 1
DESIGNERS' NETWORK

Blueprint Price Code B

Plan P-7676-2D

To order blueprints, call
1-800-547-5570 or see order form
and pricing information on pages 220-224.

Elegant Master Suite

This charming traditional home offers a multitude of fine features. The covered entry and vaulted foyer create an inviting atmosphere. The vaulted Great Room features a fireplace, covered patio, bar and lots of windows.

The gourmet kitchen with adjacent nook is ideal for the active family or a retired couple.

The elegant master suite features a spacious bath, walk-in closet and a reading alcove, and also opens to a private covered patio. A jacuzzi tub, separate toilet compartment and double vanity add a measure of convenience to the luxurious master bath.

This home totals 1,665 sq. ft. The residence has a depth of 65' and a width of only 44'

PLAN S-4789-B
WITH BASEMENT

Total living area: 1,665 sq. ft.
(Not counting basement or garage)

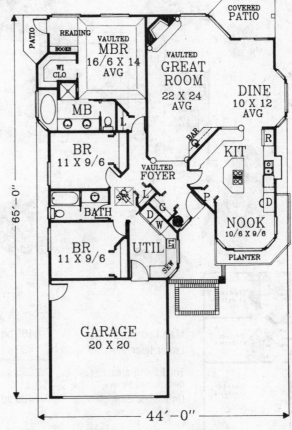

PLAN S-4789-A
WITHOUT BASEMENT
(CRAWLSPACE FOUNDATION)

Exterior walls are 2x6 construction.

To order blueprints, call
1-800-547-5570 or see order form
and pricing information on pages 220-224.

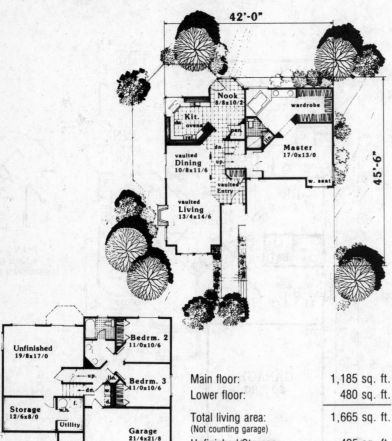

42'-0"

45'-6"

Nook
8/8x10/2

wardrobe

Kit.
oven

Master
17/0x13/0

vaulted
Dining
10/8x11/6

dn.

pan.

up.

w. seat

vaulted
Entry

vaulted
Living
13/4x14/6

Unfinished
19/8x17/0

Bedrm. 2
11/0x10/6

up.

Bedrm. 3
11/0x10/6

dn.

Storage
12/6x8/0

Utility

Garage
21/4x21/8

Main floor:	1,185 sq. ft.
Lower floor:	480 sq. ft.
Total living area: (Not counting garage)	1,665 sq. ft.
Unfinished/Storage:	495 sq. ft.

Exciting Design for Sloping Lot

This design adapts especially well to a side slope and offers an exciting floor plan.

The vaulted foyer opens to the living room which is highlighted by a cheerful fireplace and is also vaulted. A half-wall with overhead arch separates the foyer and hallway from the dining room without interrupting the flow of space.

The kitchen is designed for the serious cook and offers plenty of counter and cabinet space. The adjoining nook is vaulted with a walk-in pantry located in the corner. With eight-foot walls, the pantry's ceiling is low enough in the vaulted nook to provide an excellent shelf for displaying plants. A large overhead skylight not only provides a natural growing light but also illuminates the interior stairwell. A French door opens off the nook to a spacious deck — perfect for outdoor entertaining.

Separated from the rest of the household, the master bedroom located upstairs offers extra privacy and is a true haven from the day's worries. It boasts a relaxing whirlpool tub, dual vanities, and spacious walk-in closet.

Seven steps down from the main level you'll find two more bedrooms. Down another seven steps you'll discover a large unfinished recreation room — great for parties or, if desired, an informal family room. Don't overlook the large storage room located just off to the side.

Blueprint Price Code B

Plan R-4033

To order blueprints, call
1-800-547-5570 or see order form
and pricing information on pages 220-224.

Skylighted Passive-Solar Home

Fully glazed for expansive views, this comfortable contemporary home has a vaulted sun room for collecting and storing passive solar energy. Especially suited for a sloping site with a view, the house fits equally well on an urban lot or in a country setting. The main floor and daylight basement each have 863 sq. ft. of living space, and the upper floor adds 642 sq. ft.

Main floor:	863 sq. ft.
Upper floor:	642 sq. ft.
Total living area: (Not counting garage)	1,505 sq. ft.
Daylight basement:	863 sq. ft.
Total with basement:	2,368 sq. ft.

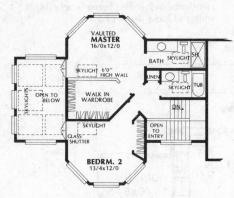

PLAN P-536-2A
WITHOUT BASEMENT
(CRAWLSPACE FOUNDATION)

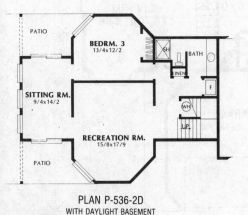

PLAN P-536-2D
WITH DAYLIGHT BASEMENT

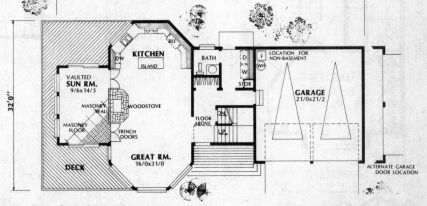

Blueprint Price Code C With Basement
Blueprint Price Code B Without Basement

Plans P-536-2A & P-536-2D

Quality Narrow-Lot Design

This 2,207 sq. ft. home will fit on a narrow lot. While only 34' wide, it includes the amenities often found only in larger custom homes.

As you enter the angled foyer you will see the family room featuring a fireplace. The powder room is easily accessible just off the family room. One of the central features of the residence is the open staircase which separates the formal and informal living areas. The open floor plan is ideal for entertaining with guests circulating easily between rooms.

The bar in the roomy kitchen is perfect for serving to the family room.

The upstairs master suite has a private bath with a double vanity, and both a shower and tub. The other two bedrooms are near a secondary bath which also has some special luxurious touches, such as a double vanity.

Having trouble finding that special plan for a difficult lot? Try this one!! As mentioned before this home is only 34' wide and has a depth of 52'.

Main floor:	831 sq. ft.
Upper floor:	688 sq. ft.
Total living area: (Not counting basement or garage)	1,519 sq. ft.

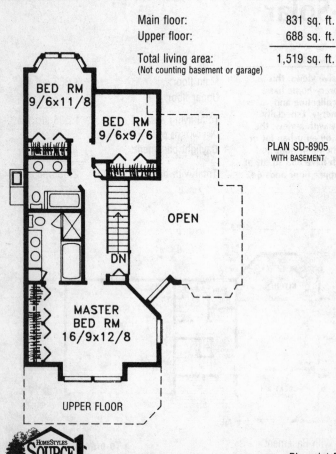

PLAN SD-8905
WITH BASEMENT

UPPER FLOOR

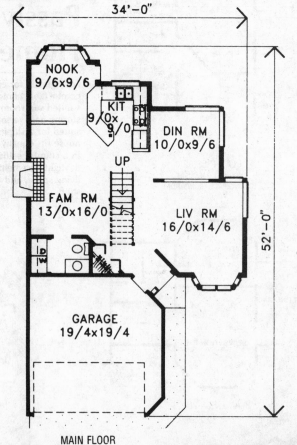

MAIN FLOOR

Blueprint Price Code B

Plan SD-8905

To order blueprints, call
1-800-547-5570 or see order form
and pricing information on pages 220-224.

Rustic Styling, Comfortable Interior

- Front-to-back split level with large decks lends itself to steep sloping site, particularly in a scenic area.
- Compact, space-efficient design makes for economical construction.
- Great Room design concept utilizes the entire 36' width of home for the kitchen/dining/living area.
- Two bedrooms and a bath are up three steps, on the entry level.
- Upper level bedroom includes a compact bath and a private deck.

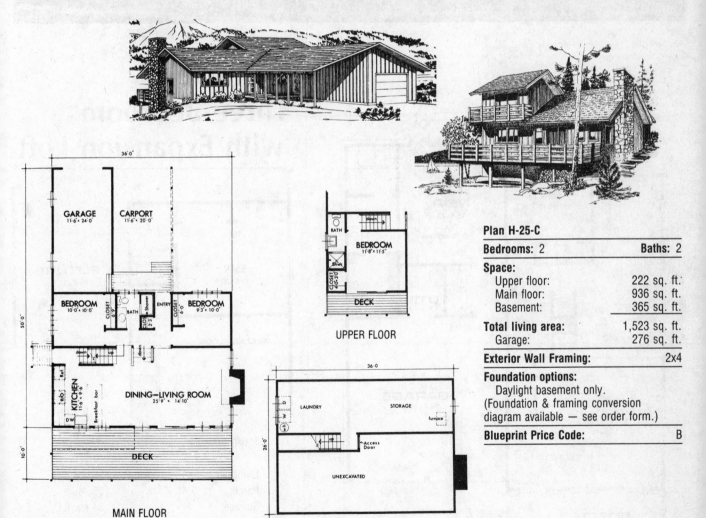

MAIN FLOOR

UPPER FLOOR

BASEMENT

Plan H-25-C

Bedrooms: 2	Baths: 2
Space:	
Upper floor:	222 sq. ft.
Main floor:	936 sq. ft.
Basement:	365 sq. ft.
Total living area:	1,523 sq. ft.
Garage:	276 sq. ft.
Exterior Wall Framing:	2x4

Foundation options:
Daylight basement only.
(Foundation & framing conversion diagram available — see order form.)

Blueprint Price Code: B

HomeStyles SOURCE 1 DESIGNERS NETWORK

Plan H-25-C

To order blueprints, call
1-800-547-5570 or see order form and pricing information on pages 220-224.

67

Compact Three-Bedroom with Expansion Loft

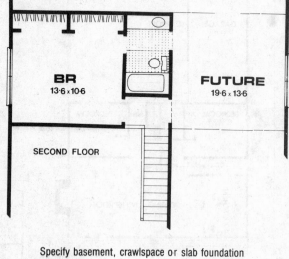

PORCH

BR
11·6 x 10·3

MBR
16·6 x 13
RAISED CEILING

KIT
10 x 8

BKFST
13 x 11

w
d

UTIL

LIVING
15·6 x 15

GARAGE
19·3 x 19·3

PORCH
20 x 6

FIRST FLOOR

50·4

40

BR
13·6 x 10·6

FUTURE
19·6 x 13·6

SECOND FLOOR

Specify basement, crawlspace or slab foundation

Living area:	1,523 sq. ft.
Porch:	155 sq. ft.
Storage:	34 sq. ft.
Garage:	390 sq. ft.
Total:	2,102 sq. ft.

Blueprint Price Code B
Plan J-8636

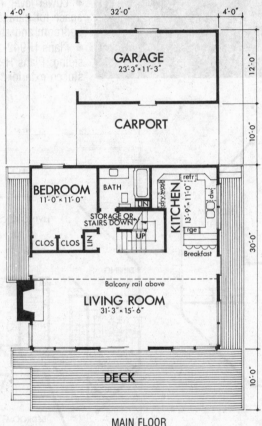

PLAN H-876-1
WITH BASEMENT
PLAN H-876-1A
WITHOUT BASEMENT
(CRAWLSPACE FOUNDATION)

FURNACE AND WATER HEATER
IN PLAN WITHOUT BASEMENT
ARE LOCATED IN CRAWLSPACE.

GARAGE
23'-3" × 11'-3"

CARPORT

BEDROOM
11'-0" × 11'-0"

BATH

LIN

KITCHEN
13'-9" × 11'-0"

refr
dry wash
dw
rge

**STORAGE OR
STAIRS DOWN**

UP

CLOS CLOS LIN

Breakfast

Balcony rail above

LIVING ROOM
31'-3" × 15'-6"

DECK

MAIN FLOOR

BEDROOM
11'-0" × 11'-0"

BATH

Shower

BEDR'M
8'-6" × 13'-5"

DOWN

CLOS CLOS LIN

BALCONY

UPPER PART OF LIVING ROOM

SECOND FLOOR

First floor:	960 sq. ft.
Second floor:	592 sq. ft.
Total living area:	1,552 sq. ft.
(Not counting basement or garage)	

Surprising Spaces via Beamed Ceilings

Here is a home that explodes into surprising spaces. That result is achieved primarily by the way the beamed living room area ceiling extends from the first floor plate level of the front window wall and rises a soaring two stories to a point midway over the depth of the home.

The angle at which the ceiling extends over the space below gives an attractive detail to the windows at each end of the room and the masonry of the log-sized fireplace. Due to the way the open stairways and balconies are used in conjunction with the window walls, the living areas manage somehow to be both cozy and expansive at the same time. The design certainly complements its environment, for it is possible to enjoy both a very well-lighted interior as well as see in every direction from two different floor levels.

The first floor, with no major doors to inhibit relaxed movement from area to area, is open and spacious, yet all the while each separate zone retains its own identity and privacy when desired.

Because of the vaulted ceiling, a balcony adjoining the two upstairs bedrooms and bath provides a good view of the spacious living area below.

Plans H-876-1 & H-876-1A

Unique Octagon Design

- Innovative roof design allows simpler, more economical construction than most other octagons.
- Spacious main floor includes all the features needed for year-round or recreation-site living.
- Living and dining rooms flow together to form a room more than 38' wide with a great panoramic view.
- Lower level includes plenty of space for garage, shop, den, another bedroom and storage.
- Plans H-942-1 & -1A are wood siding; Plans H-942-2 & -2A are stucco exterior.

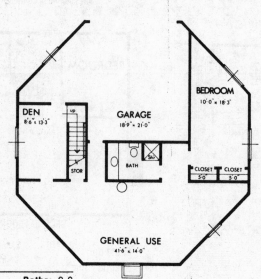

BASEMENT

1/16" = 1'

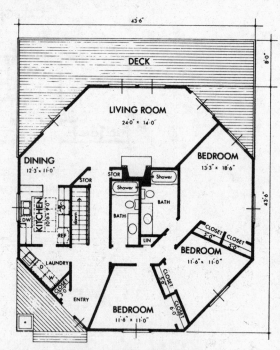

MAIN FLOOR

Plans H-942-1,-1A,-2,-2A

Bedrooms: 3-4	Baths: 2-3

Space:

Main floor:	1,564 sq. ft.
Basement:	1,170 sq. ft.
Garage:	394 sq. ft.

Exterior Wall Framing:	2x6

Foundation options:
Daylight basement, H-930-1, -2.
Crawlspace, Plans H-930-1A, -2A.
(Foundation & framing conversion diagram available — see order form.)

Blueprint Price Code:

Without basement:	B
With basement:	D

Plans H-942-1, -1A, -2 & -2A

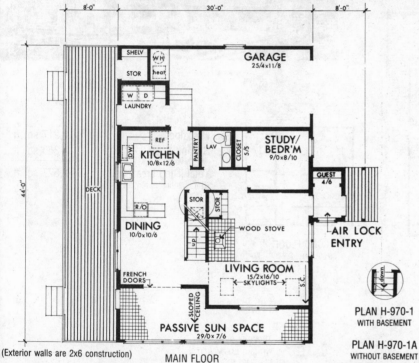

Main floor labels: GARAGE 25/4 x 11/8, SHELV, STOR, WH, heat, W, D, LAUNDRY, DW, REF, KITCHEN 10/8 x 12/6, PANTRY, LAV, CLOSET 5/5, STUDY/BEDR'M 9/0 x 8/10, GUEST 4/6, DECK, R/O, DINING 10/0 x 10/6, STOR, STOR, WOOD STOVE, AIR LOCK ENTRY, down, UP, FRENCH DOORS, SLOPED CEILING, LIVING ROOM 15/2 x 16/10, SKYLIGHTS, S.C., PASSIVE SUN SPACE 29/0 x 7/6

8'-0" 30'-0" 8'-0" 44'-0"

(Exterior walls are 2x6 construction) MAIN FLOOR

PLAN H-970-1
WITH BASEMENT

PLAN H-970-1A
WITHOUT BASEMENT
(CRAWLSPACE FOUNDATION)

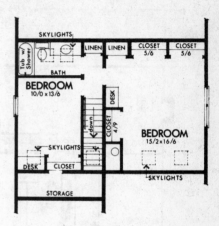

Second floor labels: SKYLIGHTS, Tub w/ Shower, LINEN, LINEN, CLOSET 5/6, CLOSET 5/6, BATH, BEDROOM 10/0 x 13/6, DESK, down, CLOSET 4/9, BEDROOM 15/2 x 16/6, DESK, SKYLIGHTS, CLOSET, STORAGE, SKYLIGHTS

SECOND FLOOR

First floor:	817 sq. ft.
Sunspace:	192 sq. ft.
Second floor:	563 sq. ft.
Total living area: (Not counting basement or garage)	1,572 sq. ft.
Airlock entry:	40 sq. ft.
Garage:	288 sq. ft.

The Simple Life at Its Best in a Passive Solar Design

This home's rustic exterior is suggestive of Carpenter Gothic Style homes or early barn designs. The wood shake roof and "board-and-batten" style siding help to carry out this theme. An air-lock entry provides a protected place to remove outer garments as well as serving as an energy-conserving heat loss barrier. As you pass from the entry into the cozy living room, there is an immediate perception of warmth and light. This room features a centrally located woodstove and two skylights.

Between the living room and the sun space are two double-hung windows to provide heat circulation as well as admit natural light. Further inspection of the ground floor reveals a delightful flow of space. From the dining room it is possible to view the kitchen, the wider portion of the sun space and part of the living room. An open staircase connects this room with the second floor.

The kitchen boasts modern appliances, large pantry and storage closets and a convenient peninsula open to the dining room. The remainder of the first floor includes a handy laundry room, an easily accessible half-bath and a bonus room with an unlimited number of possibilities. One such use may be as a home computer/study area. Upstairs, two bedrooms with an abundance of closet space share the fully appointed, skylighted bathroom.

A word about the passive sun room: It seems that solar design has come full circle, returning us to the concept that less is more. This sun room uses masonry floor pavers as heat storage and natural convection as the primary means of heat circulation. This serves to reduce both the potential for system failures and the heavy operating workload often found in more elaborate solar designs, not to mention the high cost of such systems.

Blueprint Price Code B

Plans H-970-1 & H-970-1A

To order blueprints, call
1-800-547-5570 or see order form
and pricing information on pages 220-224

DINING
11'-0" x 12'-0"

KITCHEN
9'-4" x 10'-6"

LIVING ROOM
19'-8" x 15'-4"

LAUNDRY

GUEST
4'-1"

BATH
10'-3" x 8'-9"

LINEN

CLOSET
8'-4"

BEDROOM
11'-6" x 13'-7"

BEDROOM
11'-6" x 13'-7"

ENTRY

STORAGE

CLOSET
6'-6"

GARAGE
12'-10" x 23'-8"

DECK

SLOPED CEILING

MAIN FLOOR
1217 SQUARE FEET

PLAN H-925-2
WITH DAYLIGHT BASEMENT

DECK

WALK-IN CLOSET
7'-5" x 5'-0"

BEDROOM
14'-0" x 14'-0"

BATH
9'-6" x 5'-0"

Shwr

SLOPED CEILING

SECOND FLOOR
360 SQUARE FEET

First floor:	1,217 sq. ft.
Second floor:	360 sq. ft.
Total living area:	1,577 sq. ft.
(Not counting basement or garage)	

PLAN H-925-2A
WITHOUT BASEMENT
(CRAWLSPACE FOUNDATION)

STOR   W&D   heat

Economical and Convenient

In an effort to merge the financial possibilities and the space requirements of the greatest number of families, the designers of this home restricted themselves to just over 1,200 sq. ft. of ground cover (exclusive of garage), and still managed to develop a

superior three-bedroom design.

From a covered walkway, one approaches a centralized entry hall which effectively distributes traffic throughout the home without causing interruptions. Two main floor bedrooms and bath as well as the stairway to the second floor master suite are immediately accessible to the entry. Directly forward and four steps down finds one in the main living area, consisting of a large living room with vaulted ceiling and a dining-kitchen combination with conventional ceiling height. All these rooms have direct access to an outdoor living deck of over 400 sq. ft. Thus, though modest and unassuming from the street side, this home evolves into

eye-popping expansion and luxury toward the rear.

To ease homemaking chores, whether this is to be a permanent or vacation home, the working equipment, including laundry space, is all on the main floor. Yet the homemaker remains part of the family scene because there is only a breakfast counter separating the work space from the living area.

Tucked away upstairs, in complete privacy, one finds a master bedroom suite equipped with separate bath, walk-in wardrobe and a romantic private deck.

The plan is available with or without a basement and is best suited to a lot that slopes gently down from the road.

HomeStyles **SOURCE 1** DESIGNERS NETWORK

Blueprint Price Code B

Plans H-925-2 & H-925-2A

To order blueprints, call
1-800-547-5570 or see order form
and pricing information on pages 220-224.

Covered Wrap-Around Deck Featured

A house-spanning deck is covered at the front of the home and wraps around to connect with the main entry and kitchen door.

An oversized fireplace is the focal point of the interior wall of the living room, which connects with an expandable dining area. Open planning is the theme of the interior, creating a feeling of spaciousness. The kitchen is tucked into one corner, but has open counter space, providing visual contact with the living room.

The two main floor bedrooms are good-sized and have sufficient wardrobe space. Other well planned hall closets provide more storage and linen shelves. A fully equipped bathroom is placed on a common plumbing wall next to the kitchen.

The living area of the main floor level comprises 952 sq. ft., and the basement level adds another 673 sq. ft., not counting the garage. Exterior walls are designed with 2x6 studs for R-19 insulation.

Main floor:	952 sq. ft.
Basement:	673 sq. ft.
Total living area: (Not counting garage)	1,625 sq. ft.

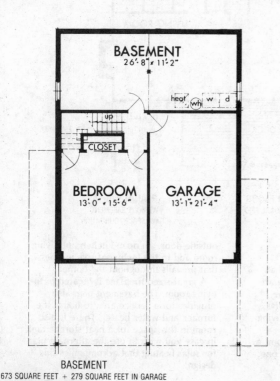

BASEMENT
26'-8" x 11'-2"

heat wh w d

up

CLOSET

BEDROOM
13'-0" x 15'-6"

GARAGE
13'-1" x 21'-4"

BASEMENT
673 SQUARE FEET + 279 SQUARE FEET IN GARAGE

4'-0" 28'-0" 4'-0"

34'-0"

12'-0"

BEDROOM
12'-0" x 11'-3"

CLOSET

CLOSET

BEDROOM
12'-2" x 10'-0"

down

LIN

BATH

ENTRY

CLOS

STOR

KITCHEN
8'-10" x 8'-7"

LIVING ROOM
17'-9" x 15'-7"

DINING
9'-2" x 8'-6"

DECK

MAIN FLOOR
952 SQUARE FEET

Blueprint Price Code B

Plan H-806-2

To order blueprints, call
1-800-547-5570 or see order form
and pricing information on pages 220-224

FRONT VIEW

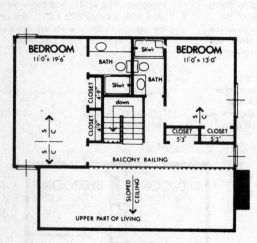

SECOND FLOOR
685 SQUARE FEET

First floor:	960 sq. ft.
Second floor:	685 sq. ft.
Total living area:	1,645 sq. ft.

(Not counting garage or basement)

(Exterior walls are 2x6 construction)

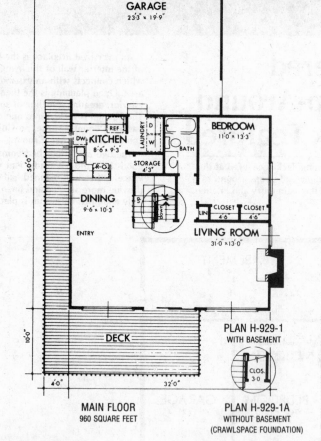

MAIN FLOOR
960 SQUARE FEET

PLAN H-929-1
WITH BASEMENT

PLAN H-929-1A
WITHOUT BASEMENT
(CRAWLSPACE FOUNDATION)

Contemporary Retreat

This home is a result of studies made of popular plans over the past years with the various features that seem to be uppermost in people's minds today in the selection of a recreational home. The plan illustrated

here is one of the most popular new versions of this type of housing. An excellent floor plan articulates around an open centrally located staircase. There are two bedrooms on the second floor, one with a private bath. A full bath is off the central hallway, which overlooks the living room below.

Besides one bedroom on the first floor, a laundry and complete bathroom flank one side of the hallway leading to the rear

outside door. An open kitchen and living room add to the feeling of spaciousness that prevails throughout the home.

A great-sized fireplace is located in the living room. The basement plan also provides for a service area to house the furnace and water heater. There is also room in this space for a heat storage tank in case you wish to use the alternate plan for solar heating that accompanies this design.

Blueprint Price Code B

Plans H-929-1 & H-929-1A

Sun Roof Focuses on Family Living

The intersecting pitched-roof lines of this striking contemporary home add eye appeal indoors and out. The living room sun roof gathers passive solar heat to be stored in the tile floor and the two-story high masonry backdrop to the wood stove.

Whether for a flat lot without a basement or for a sloping site with daylight basement, this home showers the residents with solar warmth. Exterior walls are framed in 2x6 studs for R-19 insulation.

FRONT VIEW

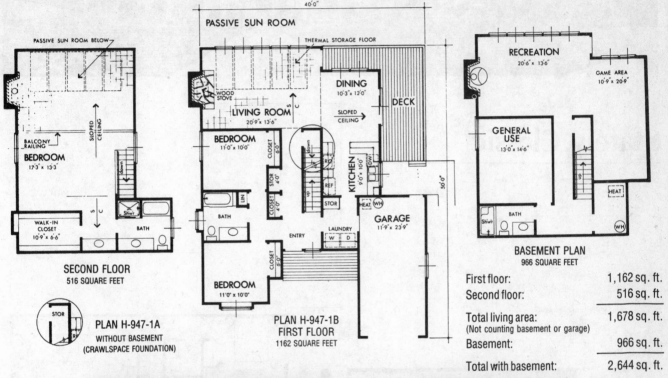

SECOND FLOOR
516 SQUARE FEET

PASSIVE SUN ROOM BELOW
SLOPED CEILING
BALCONY RAILING
BEDROOM 17'3" x 13'3"
down
WALK-IN CLOSET 10'9" x 6'6"
BATH
Shwr

STOR

PLAN H-947-1A
WITHOUT BASEMENT
(CRAWLSPACE FOUNDATION)

40'-0"

PASSIVE SUN ROOM

THERMAL STORAGE FLOOR

WOOD STOVE
LIVING ROOM 20'9" x 13'6"
DINING 10'3" x 12'0"
SLOPED CEILING
DECK
BEDROOM 11'0" x 10'0"
CLOSET 6'0"
STOR 4'0"
CLOSET 4'0"
down
up
REF
KITCHEN 9'0" x 10'0"
DW
STOR
HEAT WH
GARAGE 11'9" x 23'9"
BATH
LIN
ENTRY
LAUNDRY W D
CLOSET 5'0"
BEDROOM 11'0" x 10'0"
50'-0"

PLAN H-947-1B
FIRST FLOOR
1162 SQUARE FEET

RECREATION 20'-6" x 13'-6"
GAME AREA 10'-9" x 20'-9"
GENERAL USE 13'-0" x 14'-6"
HEAT
Shwr
BATH
WH

BASEMENT PLAN
966 SQUARE FEET

First floor:	1,162 sq. ft.
Second floor:	516 sq. ft.
Total living area: (Not counting basement or garage)	1,678 sq. ft.
Basement:	966 sq. ft.
Total with basement:	2,644 sq. ft.

Blueprint Price Code D With Basement
Blueprint Price Code B Without Basement

Plans H-947-1A & H-947-1B

To order blueprints, call
1-800-547-5570 or see order form
and pricing information on pages 220-224.

Stately Classic

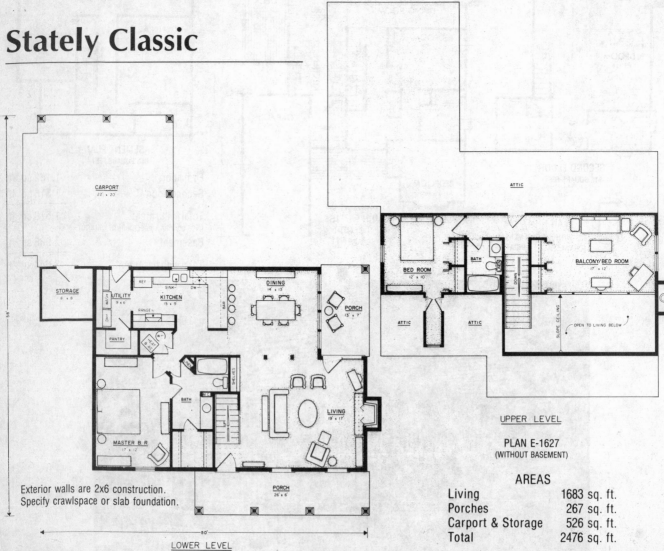

Exterior walls are 2x6 construction.
Specify crawlspace or slab foundation.

LOWER LEVEL

UPPER LEVEL

PLAN E-1627
(WITHOUT BASEMENT)

AREAS

Living	1683 sq. ft.
Porches	267 sq. ft.
Carport & Storage	526 sq. ft.
Total	2476 sq. ft.

An Energy Efficient Home

Blueprint Price Code B

Plan E-1627

To order blueprints, call
1-800-547-5570 or see order form
and pricing information on pages 220-224

Ideal Home for a Narrow Lot

Because this design is only 28' wide, it could be built on a 40' lot, local codes permitting.

An entry hall provides the introduction to the wide-open arrangement of the first floor. One is immediately drawn to the balconied staircase and bay window near the entrance.

On the first level, the Great Room, dining area and kitchen combine in such a way that no one need be excluded from activities or conversation. Still, each area has its separate identity: the Great Room with its fireplace, the dining area with its large outdoor deck visible through sliding glass doors, and the U-shaped kitchen separated from the other areas by the breakfast bar.

Upstairs, you will find three bedrooms and two baths. The master bedroom suite includes a large walk-through closet in addition to a private bath.

CLERESTORY WINDOWS OVER STAIRWAY

down

28'-0"

DECK

STONE HEARTH

WOODSTOVE

SKYLIGHT

FLAT CEILING LINE

GREAT ROOM
25'-2" x 19'-3"

up

STOR

RANGE

KITCHEN
12'-6" x 8'-0"

DW

OVEN

REF

LAUNDRY
W D

LAV

GUEST
5'-0"

ENTRY

54'-0"

heat

GARAGE
19'-4" x 21'-2"

MAIN FLOOR

PLAN H-1427-3A
WITHOUT BASEMENT
(CRAWLSPACE FOUNDATION)

PLAN H-1427-3B
WITH DAYLIGHT BASEMENT

First floor:	810 sq. ft.
Second floor:	880 sq. ft.
Total living area:	1,690 sq. ft.
Garage:	443 sq. ft.
Basement:	810 sq. ft.

OPEN TO LIVING ROOM

SLOPED CEILING

MASTER BEDR'M
14'-2" x 14'-6"
S.C.

RAILING

down

HIGH WINDOW

CLOSET 6'-0"

SKYLIGHT

CLOSET 6'-0"

STORAGE

BATH

Tub w/ Shower

WH

CLOSET 4'-0"

CLOSET 4'-0"

LINEN/STOR

Shw'r

BATH

BEDROOM
12'-2" x 11'-0"

S.C.

CLOSET 5'-8"

BEDROOM
10'-10" x 10'-0"

SECOND FLOOR

GENERAL USE

up

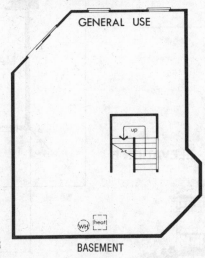

WH

heat

BASEMENT

Blueprint Price Code B

To order blueprints, call
1-800-547-5570 or see order form
and pricing information on pages 220-224.

Plans H-1427-3A & H-1427-3B

77

Victorian Ideal For Narrow Lot

This compact Victorian design incorporates four bedrooms and three full baths into a 30' wide home totaling only 1,737 sq. ft. of heated living area. The upstairs master suite features two closets, an oversized tub and a sitting room with vaulted ceiling and bay window. Two additional bedrooms and a second full bath are included in the 783 sq. ft. upper level.

A fourth bedroom and third full bath on the main floor can serve as an in-law or guest suite. Between the dining and breakfast rooms is a galley kitchen. The dining room has a bay window and the breakfast room a utility nook. A large parlor with a raised-hearth fireplace completes the 954 sq. ft. main floor.

Specify Elevation A or B when ordering. An attached two-car garage off the kitchen is also available upon request.

First floor:	954 sq. ft.
Second floor:	783 sq. ft.
Total living area:	1,737 sq. ft.

PLAN C-8347
WITHOUT BASEMENT

Specify crawlspace or slab foundation

First floor plan:

STUDY OR BEDROOM
11'-6"X12'-0"

BATH

WASH DRY

BREAKFAST
9'-0"X11'-8"

PANT.

CLOSET

FURN

COATS

REFG

STOOP

RAIL

PARLOR
18'-0"X13'-0"

RAIL

RANGE

KITCHEN
8'-0"X12'-0"

D.W.

SINK

UP

PORCH
18'-0"X6'-0"

RAIL

DINING ROOM
11'-4"X12'-8"

28'-6"

30'-0"

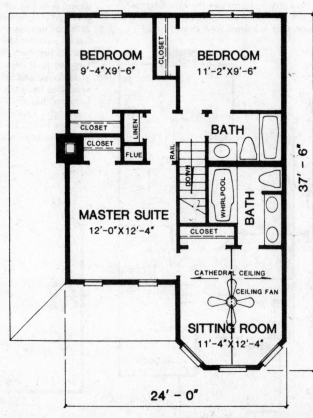

Second floor plan:

BEDROOM
9'-4"X9'-6"

CLOSET

BEDROOM
11'-2"X9'-6"

CLOSET

LINEN

CLOSET

BATH

FLUE

RAIL

DOWN

WHIRLPOOL

BATH

MASTER SUITE
12'-0"X12'-4"

CLOSET

CATHEDRAL CEILING

CEILING FAN

SITTING ROOM
11'-4"X12'-4"

37'-6"

24'-0"

ELEVATION B

Blueprint Price Code B

Plan C-8347

To order blueprints, call
1-800-547-5570 or see order form and pricing information on pages 220-224.

FRONT VIEW

Two-Level Home Features Dramatic Loft

- Clean, uncluttered lines give this basically traditional plan a modern look.
- Inside, the living room soars to a vaulted ceiling two stories above.
- The efficient U-shaped kitchen opens to a sunny nook in the front of the home.
- A formal dining room also features large front windows.
- Upstairs, two bedrooms share a connecting bath and open onto a balcony above the living room below.
- Also note the storage area over the garage.
- The plan version with a basement includes a lower level recreation room with a fireplace.

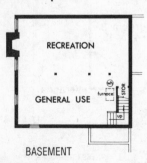

BASEMENT

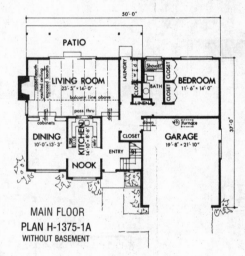

MAIN FLOOR
PLAN H-1375-1A
WITHOUT BASEMENT

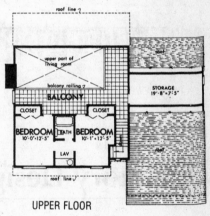

UPPER FLOOR

MAIN FLOOR
PLAN H-1375-1
WITH BASEMENT

Plans H-1375-1 & 1A

Bedrooms: 3	Baths: 2

Space:

Upper floor:	598 sq. ft.
Main floor:	1,153 sq. ft.

Total living area:	**1,751 sq. ft.**
Basement:	840 sq. ft.
Garage:	429 sq. ft.
Storage:	145 sq. ft.

Exterior Wall Framing:	2x4

Foundation options:
Standard basement, Plan H-1375-1
Crawlspace, Plan H-1375-1A
(Foundation & framing conversion diagram available — see order form.)

Blueprint Price Code:

Without basement:	B
With basement:	C

To order blueprints, call
1-800-547-5570 or see order form
and pricing information on pages 220-224.

HomeStyles SOURCE 1 DESIGNERS NETWORK

Plans H-1375-1 & H-1375-1A

FRONT VIEW

REAR VIEW

Graceful One-Story Design

Total living area: 1,753 sq. ft.

80

PLAN L-755-VA
WITHOUT BASEMENT
(SLAB-ON-GRADE FOUNDATION)

(Plans for a detached two-car garage included with blueprints.)

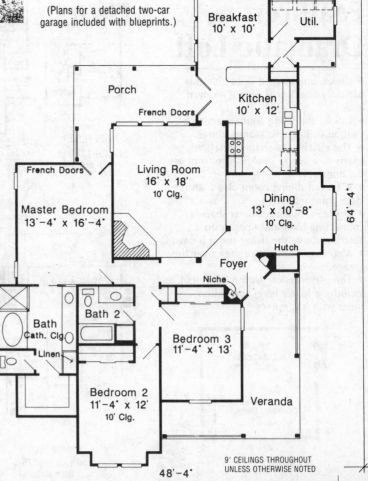

Breakfast 10' x 10'

Util.

Porch

French Doors

Kitchen 10' x 12'

Living Room 16' x 18' 10' Clg.

Dining 13' x 10'-8" 10' Clg.

French Doors

Master Bedroom 13'-4" x 16'-4"

Hutch

Foyer

Niche

64'-4"

Bath Cath. Clg.

Bath 2

Bedroom 3 11'-4" x 13'

Linen

Bedroom 2 11'-4" x 12' 10' Clg.

Veranda

9' CEILINGS THROUGHOUT UNLESS OTHERWISE NOTED

48'-4"

Blueprint Price Code B

Plan L-755-VA

To order blueprints, call
1-800-547-5570 or see order form
and pricing information on pages 220-224.

Luxury and Privacy on a Narrow Lot

This one-and-a-half-story home is less than 39' wide and 63' deep, and requires a lot of 50' x 100'. The large rear courtyard unites the house and yard, and creates a private backyard oasis.

The interior of the house is designed to focus attention on the courtyard and bring the outdoors in. Each room has a view of the courtyard, yet privacy is maintained by eliminating windows on the opposite side of the house.

Special features throughout the house draw in light and show off greenery. Plant shelves run along the railing above the foyer, and a box window/plant ledge rests above the kitchen sink. A window seat in the bedroom and corner windows in the living and dining rooms overlook the courtyard.

The open entry leading into the living room and dining room offers an unobstructed view of the landscape and the fireplace. Vaulted ceilings in the master bedroom, living room, and dining area reinforce the spacious, airy feeling.

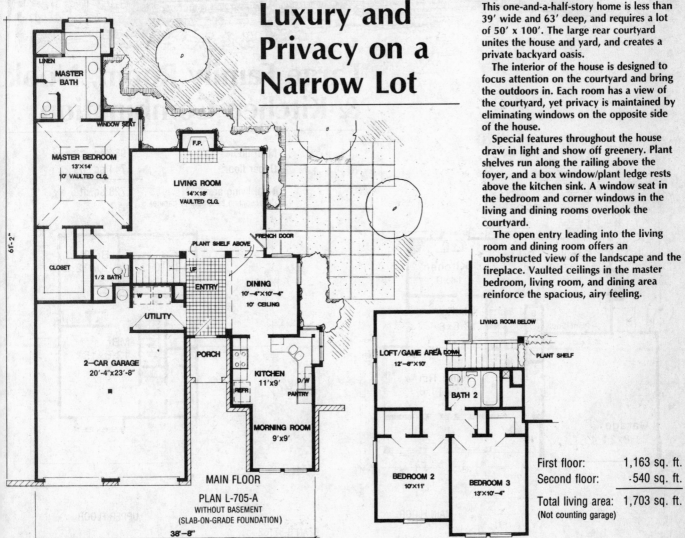

MAIN FLOOR

PLAN L-705-A
WITHOUT BASEMENT
(SLAB-ON-GRADE FOUNDATION)

First floor:	1,163 sq. ft.
Second floor:	.540 sq. ft.
Total living area:	1,703 sq. ft.

(Not counting garage)

To order blueprints, call
1-800-547-5570 or see order form and pricing information on pages 220-224.

Blueprint Price Code B

Plan L-705-A

Large Family Room, Nook & Kitchen Combination

Main floor:	984 sq. ft.
Upper floor:	744 sq. ft.
Total living area:	1,728 sq. ft.
(Not counting basement or garage)	

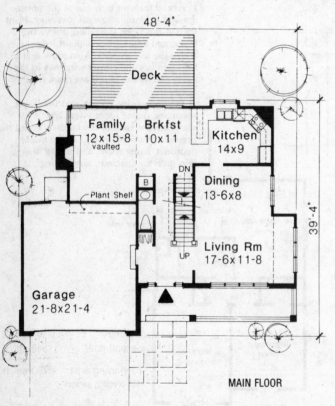

48'-4"

Deck

Family 12 x 15-8 vaulted

Brkfst 10 x 11

Kitchen 14 x 9

Plant Shelf

B

DN

Dining 13-6 x 8

UP

Living Rm 17-6 x 11-8

Garage 21-8 x 21-4

39'-4"

MAIN FLOOR

Br 3 13 x 10

Br 2 10 x 12-6

DN

MBr 13-6 x 15

UPPER FLOOR

PLAN B-87132
WITH BASEMENT

Blueprint Price Code B

Plan B-87132

Vaulted Ceiling in Master Bedroom

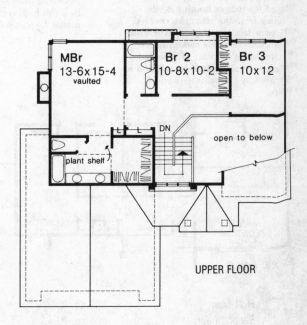

47'-0"

46'-4"

Deck

Brkfst
7-6x9-6

Kit

Dining
11-2x12

Family Rm
14x15-9

P

Bar

DN UP

Living Rm
16-6x14
vaulted

Garage
22x26-4

MAIN FLOOR

PLAN B-87102
WITH BASEMENT

MBr
13-6x15-4
vaulted

Br 2
10-8x10-2

Br 3
10x12

DN

open to below

plant shelf

UPPER FLOOR

Main floor:	926 sq. ft.
Upper floor:	806 sq. ft.
Total living area: (Not counting basement or garage)	1,732 sq. ft.

HomeStyles
Source 1
DESIGNERS NETWORK

Blueprint Price Code B

Plan B-87102

To order blueprints, call
1-800-547-5570 or see order form
and pricing information on pages 220-224.

Compact Design with Energy-Saving Features

Wrapped in an attractive exterior of woodlap siding and brick veneer accents, this **compact**, stylish family home is designed for today's housing needs.

Leading from the attractive covered entry, your family and guests will notice the **commodious** living room with heat-circulating fireplace. The sloped ceiling **lends** volume to this area, and is highlighted by the hallway overlook upstairs.

The well-appointed kitchen has lots of built-in storage, and is laid out in the popular "U"-shape. Directly adjacent to the kitchen, the dining area opens to the living room and to the patio outside via a set of French doors.

Finishing off the first floor is the utility room and a half bath. One cost-saving feature is that this area is located directly under the two full baths upstairs. This planning concept will significantly reduce plumbing costs.

Upstairs are two good-sized bedrooms with ample closets. These rooms are separated from the master bedroom suite by a full bath with a large linen closet. The master bedroom is attractively sized and

includes a large walk-in closet and a full bath with shower. This bath boasts its own linen closet.

Affordability is of concern to many families today, and this design will go a long way toward meeting that need. Heating and cooling costs are reduced with all exterior walls insulated to R-23. In addition, the design provides for R-38 ceiling insulation and R-30 insulation in the floors. Attention has been given to the window areas by sizing and positioning to make them as efficient as possible.

In sum, this home will provide a comfortable, efficient and affordable setting for you and your family, while fitting into many varied neighborhoods.

First floor: 853 sq. ft.
Second floor: 900 sq. ft.

Total living area: 1,753 sq. ft.
(Not counting basement or garage)

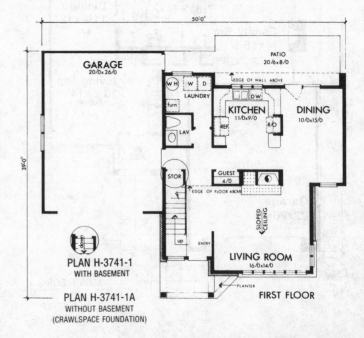

PLAN H-3741-1
WITH BASEMENT

PLAN H-3741-1A
WITHOUT BASEMENT
(CRAWLSPACE FOUNDATION)

Blueprint Price Code B

Plans H-3741-1 & H-3741-1A

Modern Country Cottage for Small Lot

This drive-under garage design is great for smaller lots. But even though the home is relatively compact, it's still loaded with modern features. The deluxe master bedroom has a large bath with garden tub and shower. The country kitchen/dining room combination has access to a deck out back. The large living room with fireplace is accessible from the two story foyer.

The upper floor has two large bedrooms and a full bath, and the large basement

has room for two cars and expandable living areas.

This plan is available with basement foundation only.

Main floor:	1,100 sq. ft.
Second floor:	664 sq. ft.
Total living area: (Not counting basement or garage)	1,764 sq. ft.
Basement:	1,100 sq. ft.

PLAN C-8870
WITH BASEMENT

Blueprint Price Code B

Plan C-8870

**To order blueprints, call
1-800-547-5570** or see order form
and pricing information on pages 220-224.

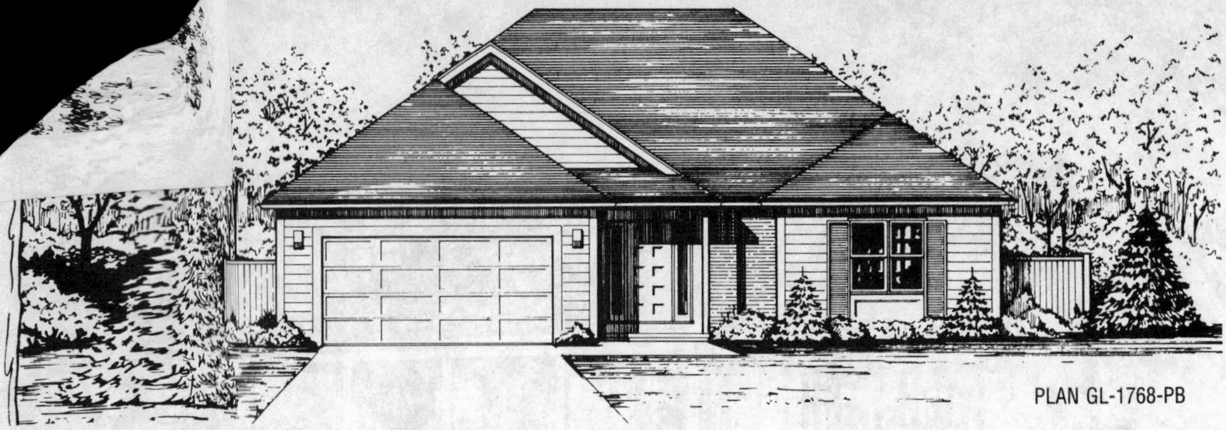

PLAN GL-1768-PB

Choice of Exterior Treatments for Same Floor Plan

Total living area: (Not counting basement or garage)	1,768 sq. ft.

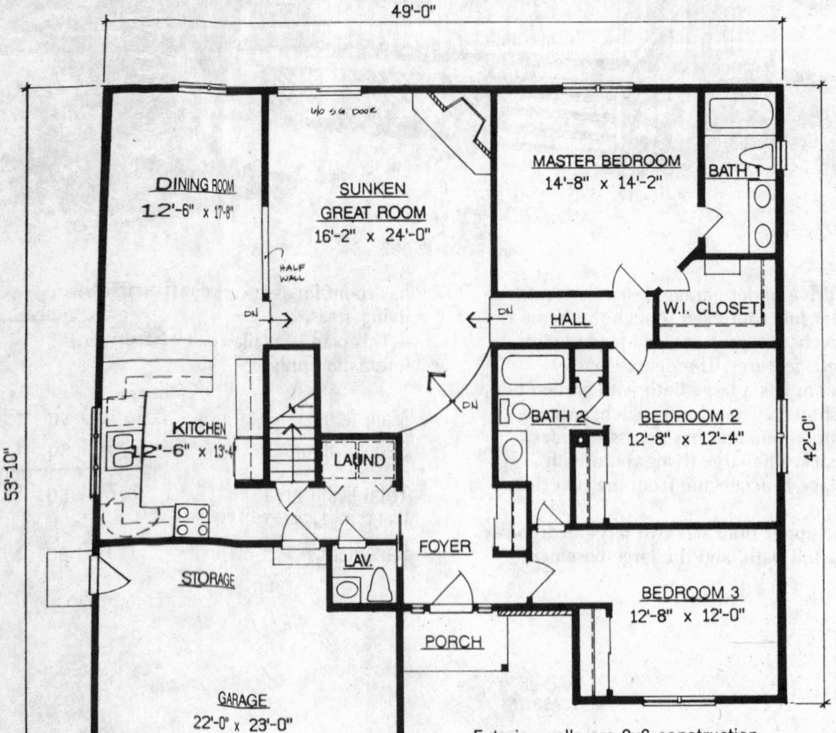

49'-0"
53'-10"
42'-0"
W/O SG. DOOR
DINING ROOM
12'-6" x 17'-8"
SUNKEN
GREAT ROOM
16'-2" x 24'-0"
HALF WALL
MASTER BEDROOM
14'-8" x 14'-2"
BATH 1
W.I. CLOSET
HALL
DN
KITCHEN
12'-6" x 13'-4"
LAUND
BATH 2
BEDROOM 2
12'-8" x 12'-4"
STORAGE
LAV.
FOYER
BEDROOM 3
12'-8" x 12'-0"
PORCH
GARAGE
22'-0" x 23'-0"

Exterior walls are 2x6 construction.

(Both versions include basement.)

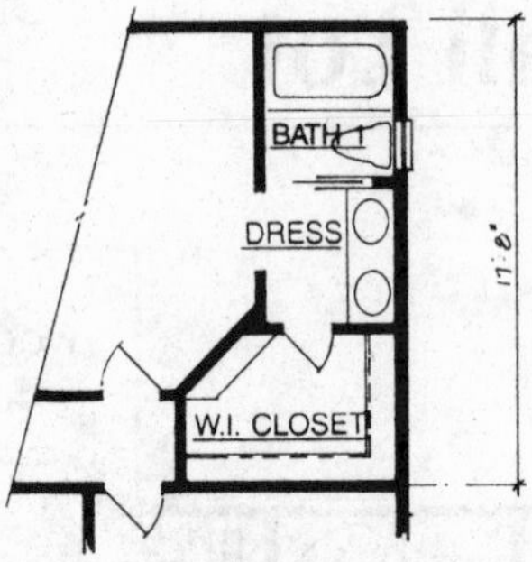

BATH 1
DRESS
W.I. CLOSET
17'-8"

OPT MASTER BATH

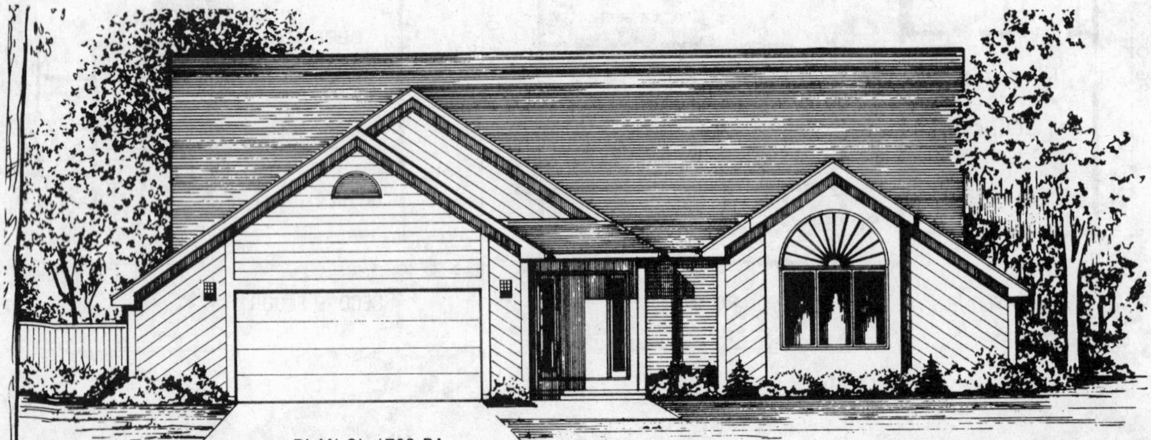

PLAN GL-1768-PA

HomeStyles SOURCE 1 DESIGNERS' NETWORK

Blueprint Price Code B

Plans GL-1768-PA & GL-1768-PB

To order blueprints, call 1-800-547-5570 or see order form and pricing information on pages 220-224.

Expansive Porch Offers Warm Welcome

PLAN J-8895
(Specify basement, crawlspace or slab foundation)

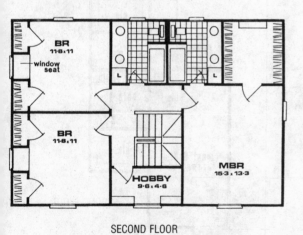

SECOND FLOOR

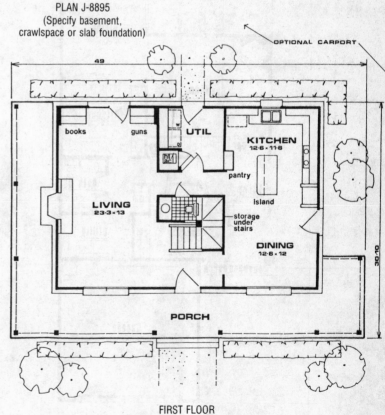

FIRST FLOOR

First floor:	919 sq. ft.
Second floor:	860 sq. ft.
Total living area: (Not counting basement)	1,779 sq. ft.
Porch:	466 sq. ft.
Carport:	462 sq. ft.

Blueprint Price Code B

Plan J-8895

To order blueprints, call
1-800-547-5570 or see order form
and pricing information on pages 220-224.

Creative 3 Bedroom For Small Lots

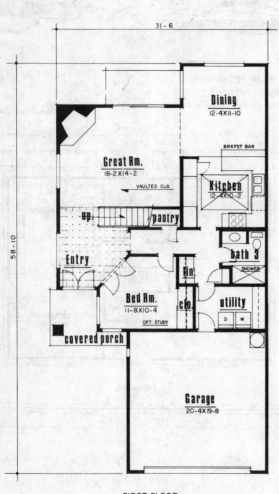

FIRST FLOOR

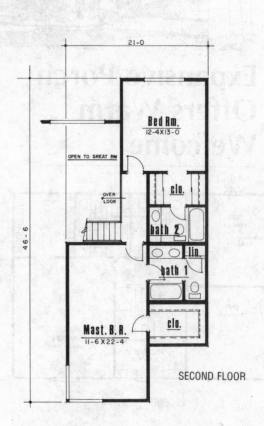

SECOND FLOOR

First floor: 1,066 sq. ft.
Second floor: 718 sq. ft.
Total living area: 1,784 sq. ft.

Blueprint Price Code B

Plan Q-1784-1A

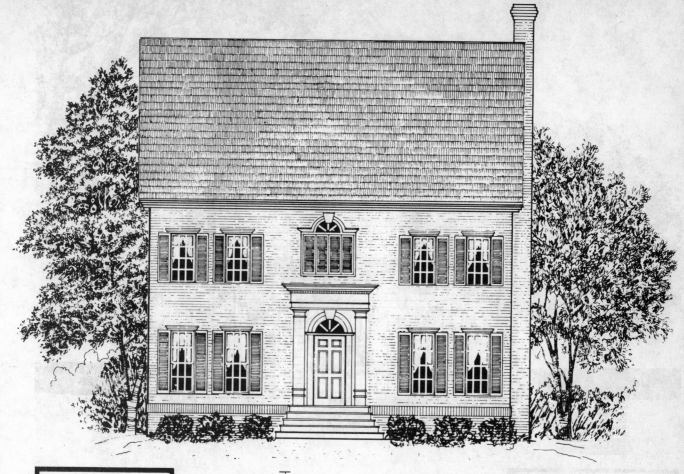

GARAGE
19-6 x 21-0

GREAT ROOM
13-0 x 14-6

KITCHEN

UP

42'

LIVING ROOM
11-0 x 13-0

DINING ROOM
11-0 x 13-0

36'

BATH

MASTER
BEDROOM
12-0 x 13-0

DOWN

BEDROOM
11-0 x 13-0

BATH

BEDROOM
11-0 x 13-0

Ceiling height first floor 9'

Ceiling height second floor 8'

Timeless Georgian Elegance

The timeless elegance of the late Georgian era is captured in this beautifully proportioned house. Its pleasing symmetry will appeal to those who seek a home of enduring and classic lines.

Once inside, the foyer opens onto a formal living room and dining room. Just beyond the cased opening, a beautiful stairway ascends conveniently near the kitchen. A long breakfast bar separates the kitchen from the cozy Great Room.

The second floor bedrooms feature an especially large amount of closet space. The master suite also has separate shower and bath for the owners.

First floor:	932 sq. ft.
Second floor:	869 sq. ft.
Total living area:	1,801 sq. ft.

Blueprint Price Code B

Plan V-1801

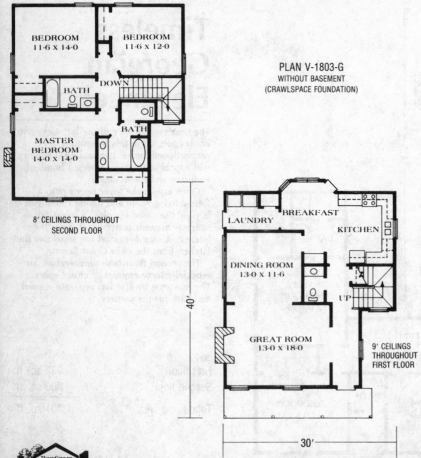

BEDROOM
11-6 x 14-0

BEDROOM
11-6 x 12-0

BATH

DOWN

BATH

MASTER
BEDROOM
14-0 x 14-0

8' CEILINGS THROUGHOUT
SECOND FLOOR

PLAN V-1803-G
WITHOUT BASEMENT
(CRAWLSPACE FOUNDATION)

LAUNDRY

BREAKFAST

KITCHEN

DINING ROOM
13-0 x 11-6

UP

GREAT ROOM
13-0 x 18-0

9' CEILINGS
THROUGHOUT
FIRST FLOOR

40'

30'

Classic Design for Small Lots

The quaint and restful appeal of this peaceful residence makes it appreciated in either urban or rural settings.

The openness of this plan gives those who enter the impression of a house much larger than its square footage indicates.

The stairs are dramatically lit by a double tier of windows. Please note the minimum of hall space when one arrives on the second floor.

First floor:	928 sq. ft.
Second floor:	875 sq. ft.
Total living area:	1,803 sq. ft.

Blueprint Price Code B
Plan V-1803-G

Compact Classic

First floor:	1,265 sq. ft.
Second floor:	571 sq. ft.
Total living area:	1,836 sq. ft.

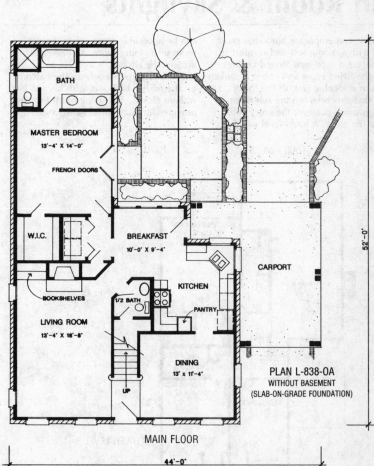

BATH

MASTER BEDROOM
13'-4" X 14'-0"

FRENCH DOORS

W.I.C.

BREAKFAST
10'-0" X 9'-4"

CARPORT

BOOKSHELVES

KITCHEN

1/2 BATH

PANTRY

LIVING ROOM
13'-4" X 18'-8"

DINING
13' X 11'-4"

UP

PLAN L-838-OA
WITHOUT BASEMENT
(SLAB-ON-GRADE FOUNDATION)

MAIN FLOOR

52'-0"

44'-0"

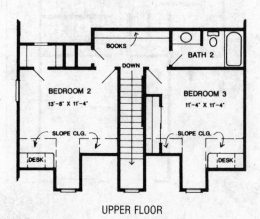

BOOKS

BATH 2

DOWN

BEDROOM 2
13'-8" X 11'-4"

BEDROOM 3
11'-4" X 11'-4"

SLOPE CLG.

SLOPE CLG.

DESK

DESK

UPPER FLOOR

Blueprint Price Code B

Plan L-838-OA

To order blueprints, call
1-800-547-5570 or see order form
and pricing information on pages 220-224.

91

Rustic Contemporary Features Sun Room & Skylights

This rustic contemporary home has great appeal with spaciousness and comfort to rival the great outdoors. Sloped ceilings crown the living room and entry. A sunken sun room is located just off the living room. Skylights brighten the sun room.

A high window above the entry door accents the entry. A multi-level wood deck can be accessible from either the sun room or a dining room. An eating bar accents the kitchen.

You'll love the view from the balcony off the master bedroom with his and her walk-in closets. The living-room fireplace provides for cozy social gatherings.

Total living area: 1,845 sq. ft.

MASTER BEDROOM
13'-4" x 15'-6"

BALCONY

L

LIVING ROOM BELOW

DN

ROOF BELOW

BEDROOM 3
10'-0" x 12'-0"

BEDROOM 2
11'-3" x 12'-0"

ROOF LINE ABOVE

LOWER LEVEL

ROOF BELOW

PLAN N-1270-1
WITH BASEMENT

PLAN N-1270-2
WITHOUT BASEMENT

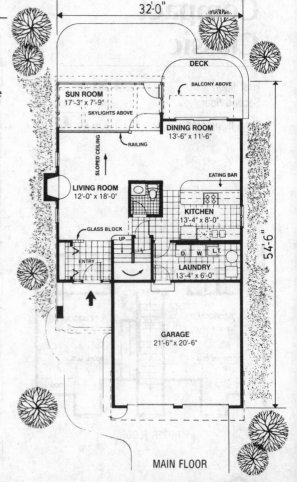

32'-0"

DECK
BALCONY ABOVE

SUN ROOM
17'-3" x 7'-9"
SKYLIGHTS ABOVE

DINING ROOM
13'-6" x 11'-6"

SLOPED CEILING

RAILING

LIVING ROOM
12'-0" x 18'-0"

EATING BAR

KITCHEN
13'-4" x 8'-0"

GLASS BLOCK

UP

ENTRY

D. W. L.T.

LAUNDRY
13'-4" x 6'-0"

GARAGE
21'-6" x 20'-6"

54'-6"

MAIN FLOOR

Blueprint Price Code B

Plans N-1270-1 & N-1270-2

**To order blueprints, call
1-800-547-5570** or see order form
and pricing information on pages 220-224.

Wrap Around Porch Adds Warmth

Undeniably appealing, the wrap-around porch of this engaging dwelling lends additional warmth to a very special house plan. Within, a graceful stairway is brightened by thoughtful window placement.

The formal dining room opens onto a sheltered porch; additional eating space is offered in the large breakfast bay. Nearby, a built-in cabinet provides shelves for cookbooks and cherished serving pieces; here, a desk could also be incorporated.

Upstairs space is particularly well-utilized; note the small amount of hallway. The master suite has a partitioned bath and separate tub and shower.

First floor:	1,005 sq. ft.
Second floor:	846 sq. ft.
Total living area:	1,851 sq. ft.

PLAN V-1851-C
WITHOUT BASEMENT
(CRAWLSPACE FOUNDATION)

First floor ceiling height: 10'
Second floor ceiling height: 9'

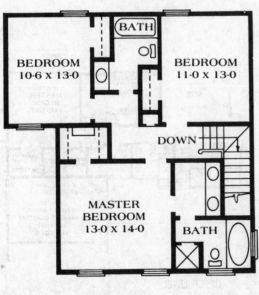

SECOND FLOOR

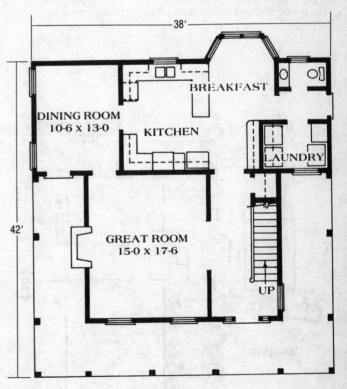

FIRST FLOOR

Blueprint Price Code B

Plan V-1851-C

To order blueprints, call 1-800-547-5570 or see order form and pricing information on pages 220-224.

Contemporary Design with Options Included

In this modern design, the sunken living room with cathedral ceiling is overlooked by a balcony/loft area, and the living areas focus toward the outdoor deck and greenhouse. A separate dining room, convenient to both living room and kitchen, opens to the deck.

The large, sunny greenhouse, functioning as a passive solar element, has a 6' brick thermal storage wall, and includes solar storage underground.

A large family room features a cozy yet functional wood stove with tile hearth.

The master bedroom has vaulted ceiling, walk-in closet and separate bath. (Alternate master bedroom suite plan included.)

A vaulted loft above the garage serves as a recreation area, or can be used for a super-deluxe master bath.

First level has 1,056 sq. ft. (excluding garage); second level, 802 sq. ft.

Main floor:	1,058 sq. ft.
Upper level:	802 sq. ft.
Total living area: (Not counting garage)	1,860 sq. ft.

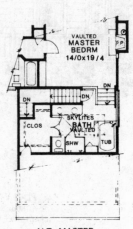

ALT. MASTER BEDRM. SUITE

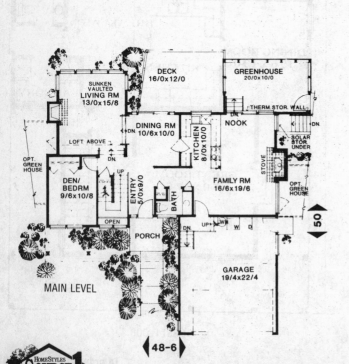

MAIN LEVEL

48-6

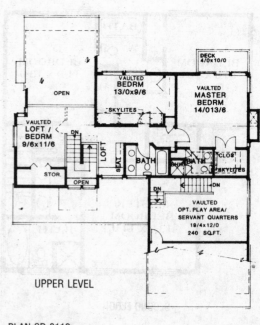

UPPER LEVEL

PLAN SD-8119
WITHOUT BASEMENT
(CRAWLSPACE FOUNDATION)

Blueprint Price Code B
Plan SD-8119

To order blueprints, call 1-800-547-5570 or see order form and pricing information on pages 220-224.

Stunning Split-Level for Sloping Lots

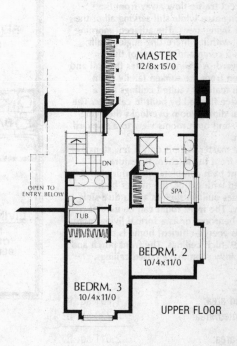

PLAN P-7717-2A

Main floor: 1,096 sq. ft.
Upper floor: 780 sq. ft.

Total living area: 1,876 sq. ft.
(Not counting garage)

MAIN FLOOR

45'-0"

44'-0"

DINING
10/0 x 10/0

KITCHEN
9/0 x 12/8

VAULTED
NOOK
8/0 x 9/2

FAMILY RM.
16/8 x 14/8

PATIO

FLOOR LINE ABOVE

STEP

REF

CEILING LINE

DN
UP

RAIL

VAULTED/SUNKEN
LIVING RM.
17/0 x 18/0

VAULTED
ENTRY

UTIL.

W D

DN

F WH

GARAGE
21/0 x 21/6

UPPER FLOOR

MASTER
12/8 x 15/0

OPEN TO
ENTRY BELOW

DN

SPA

TUB

BEDRM. 2
10/4 x 11/0

BEDRM. 3
10/4 x 11/0

Blueprint Price Code B

Plan P-7717-2A

To order blueprints, call
1-800-547-5570 or see order form
and pricing information on pages 220-224

A Garden Home With A View

This clever design proves that privacy doesn't have to be compromised even in high-density urban neighborhoods. From within, all views are oriented to the sideyard and to a lush entry courtyard. From the outside, the home is sheltered yet maintains a warm, welcoming look.

The centrally located kitchen is designed to direct traffic flow away from the working area while still serving all of the major living areas. The adjacent morning room, with its interesting angled walls, offers a commanding view of the courtyard. A railing separates the hall and kitchen from the sunken family room, which features vaulted ceilings and a fireplace flanked by built-in cabinets. The formal dining room overlooks the living room, and both rooms view to a sideyard porch.

The master suite is only a few steps away from the kitchen. It features an elegant bath complete with whirlpool tub. Packed with extras, the master bath includes built-in shelves and a dual-sink vanity. The front room can be used as a third bedroom or as a formal living room.

This energy-efficient home is designed with 9' high ceilings. The front porch and the family room have raised ceilings.

Heated area:	1,891 sq. ft.
Unheated area:	720 sq. ft.
Total area:	2,611 sq. ft.

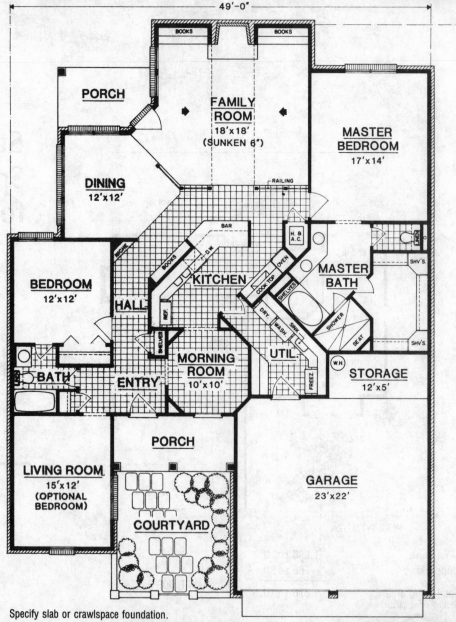

Specify slab or crawlspace foundation.

Blueprint Price Code B

Plan E-1824

To order blueprints, call
1-800-547-5570 or see order form
and pricing information on pages 220-224

Rustic Home with Drive-Under Garage

This 1,760 sq. ft. rustic design includes a two-car garage as part of its full basement. All or part of the basement can be used to supplement the main living area. The master suite features a large walk-in closet and a double vanity in the master bath. An L-shaped kitchen with dining bay, a living room with raised-hearth fireplace and a centrally located utility room complete the 1,100 sq. ft. of heated living area on the main floor.

The open two-story foyer leads to an additional 660 sq. ft. of heated living area on the upper floor, consisting of two bedrooms with walk-in closets and a second full bath with two linen closets.

Front porch, multi-paned windows, shutters and horizontal wood siding combine for a rustic exterior. Basement version only.

First floor: 1,100 sq. ft.
Second floor: 660 sq. ft.

Total living area: 1,760 sq. ft.
(Not counting basement or garage)

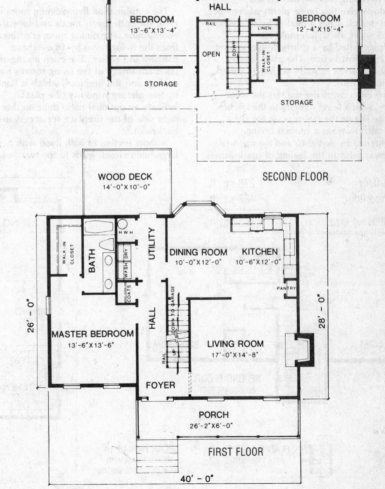

SECOND FLOOR

STORAGE

BEDROOM
13'-6" X 13'-4"

HALL

BATH

BEDROOM
12'-4" X 15'-4"

SLOPED CEILING

WALK-IN CLOSET

LINEN

LINEN

WALK-IN CLOSET

OPEN

DOWN

RAIL

STORAGE

STORAGE

FIRST FLOOR

WOOD DECK
14'-0" X 10'-0"

BATH

UTILITY

DINING ROOM
10'-0" X 12'-0"

KITCHEN
10'-6" X 12'-0"

PANTRY

WALK-IN CLOSET

W/SH DRY

COATS

H W H

MASTER BEDROOM
13'-6" X 13'-6"

HALL

DOWN TO GARAGE

RAIL

LIVING ROOM
17'-0" X 14'-8"

FOYER

26' - 0"

28' - 0"

PORCH
26'-2" X 6'-0"

40' - 0"

Blueprint Price Code B

Plan C-8339

To order blueprints, call
1-800-547-5570 or see order form
and pricing information on pages 220-224.

Stylish Looks, Sturdy Design

The sweeping roofline and arched windows give this home plenty of presence, even though it has a modest living area of 1,765 sq. ft. Its stylish looks are complemented by a sturdy design, calling for 2x6 construction. The plans specify R-19 insulation in walls, with R-38 called for in the roof.

The deep overhang shelters the front entry, which leads directly to the kitchen on the left or the stairway on the right. The entryway has a vaulted ceiling brightened by skylights, and the open-rail stairway adds to the feeling of spaciousness.

The kitchen is large but private, keeping clutter away from the dining and living areas. An abundance of counter and storage space, plus the triangular arrangement of sink, refrigerator and range, add up to a highly efficient work area.

The combination living/dining room is great for both family meals and formal entertaining. The dining room is delineated from the living room by an overhead balcony and railing. The open arrangement takes advantage of the living room's high ceilings and the fireplace, which is flanked by two picture windows (the plans indicate an optional patio door on the right side of the fireplace for access to the backyard).

A short section of hall, lined with a large linen closet, leads to the two

first-floor bedrooms. The smaller bedroom would make an ideal study or a guest room. The second bedroom, with dimensions of 12' x 12', has a large picture window and a walk-in closet. A full bath is at the end of the hall, where it's also handy to the laundry room. The 9 x 8 laundry room is accessible from the two-car garage as well.

The master bedroom suite, taking up the entire second floor, has a walk-in closet and a private bath with corner shower. A cozy loft, for quiet reading or watching TV, looks down to the living room and is brightened by two skylights and a half-round window.

This design is available with basement (plan H-1448-1) or with a crawlspace foundation (plan H-1448-1A). The basement adds another 1,278 sq. ft. of space.

First floor:	1,278 sq. ft.
Second floor:	487 sq. ft.
Total living area:	**1,765 sq. ft.**
(Not counting basement or garage)	

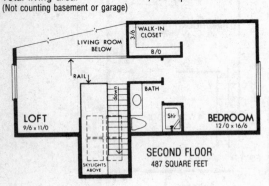

LOFT 9/6 x 11/0

LIVING ROOM BELOW

RAIL

WALK-IN CLOSET 8/0

BATH

Shr

BEDROOM 12/0 x 16/6

SECOND FLOOR
487 SQUARE FEET

PLAN H-1448-1
WITH BASEMENT

PLAN H-1448-1A
WITHOUT BASEMENT
(CRAWLSPACE FOUNDATION)

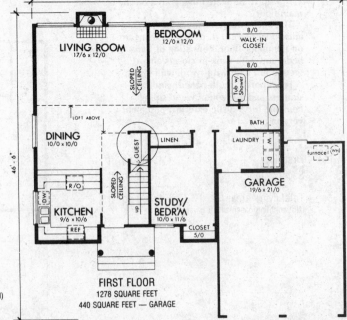

49' - 3"

LIVING ROOM 17/6 x 12/0

BEDROOM 12/0 x 12/0

WALK-IN CLOSET 8/0

SLOPED CEILING

LOFT ABOVE

DINING 10/0 x 10/0

LINEN

GUEST

Tub w/ Shower

BATH

LAUNDRY

W D

furnace WH

SLOPED CEILING

KITCHEN 9/6 x 10/6

DW

R/O

REF

STUDY/ BEDR'M 10/0 x 11/6

CLOSET 5/0

GARAGE 19/6 x 21/0

46' - 6"

FIRST FLOOR
1278 SQUARE FEET
440 SQUARE FEET — GARAGE

Blueprint Price Code B

Plans H-1448-1 & H-1448-1A

To order blueprints, call
1-800-547-5570 or see order form
and pricing information on pages 220-224.

FRONT VIEW

A Bungalow Style for Today

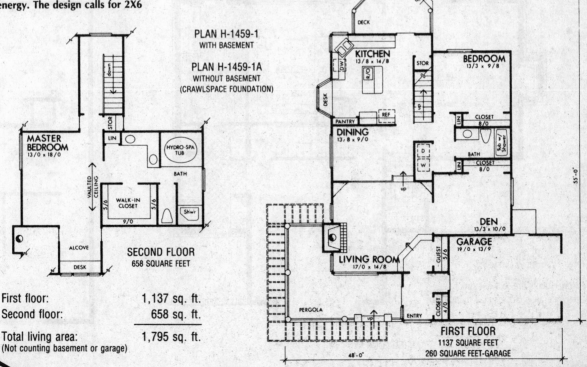

REAR VIEW

After a hiatus of nearly 40 years, the bungalow is back. This plan preserves — and improves upon — many of the features that made the bungalow so popular from the late 1800s to the 1940s.

One such feature is the pergola — a wooden trelliswork attached to the roof of the porch and supported by a set of tapered columns. Other classic touches include the decorative molding around the double louvered vents, deep overhangs, and interesting roofline.

While the exterior remains relatively unchanged, the interior has been updated to incorporate more efficiency in use of space and energy. The design calls for 2X6

construction of exterior walls, with R-30 insulation in the floors, R-38 in the ceilings and R-19 in the walls.

The spacious foyer has doors opening from the porch and the garage. This is actually an energy-saving airlock entry, and with the addition of twin closets, it serves as an excellent mudroom as well.

The foyer leads to the sunken living room, separated from the dining room by a custom-designed handrail. Other extras include built-in shelves in both corners and a fireplace with stone hearth. French doors close off the den from the living

room. The den could be converted into a third bedroom if needed.

The kitchen has undergone dramatic changes, with a desk built into the bay window bump-out, island work center, and pantry closet.

The upstairs is reserved for the master bedroom suite. A dormer-shaped hallway leads to the master bedroom, a cozy retreat complemented by a naturally lighted alcove with desk, a spacious walk-in closet, double-sink vanity, a shower and hydro-spa tub.

PLAN H-1459-1
WITH BASEMENT

PLAN H-1459-1A
WITHOUT BASEMENT
(CRAWLSPACE FOUNDATION)

First floor:	1,137 sq. ft.
Second floor:	658 sq. ft.
Total living area:	1,795 sq. ft.
(Not counting basement or garage)	

SECOND FLOOR
658 SQUARE FEET

FIRST FLOOR
1137 SQUARE FEET
260 SQUARE FEET-GARAGE

Blueprint Price Code B

Plans H-1459-1 & H-1459-1A

To order blueprints, call
1-800-547-5570 or see order form
and pricing information on pages 220-224.

Two-Story Traditional Design

AREAS

Living-Lower	1251 sq. ft.
Living-Upper	576 sq. ft.
Living-Total	1827 sq. ft.
Porches	477 sq. ft.
Sun Garden	80 sq. ft.
Total	2384 sq. ft.

THIS PLAN INCLUDES A SEPARATE GARAGE PLAN FEATURING A 22' x 22' DOUBLE GARAGE AND A 4' x 14' STORAGE AREA.

46'-0"

DINING
14'-0" x 10'-0"

SUN GARDEN
10'-0" x 8'-0"

PORCH

PANTRY
DISHWASHER
REFRIGERATOR

UTILITY
8'-0" x 8'-0"

WASH

DRY

BAR

FREEZ.

W.H.

BEAMS

LIVING
18'-0" x 16'-0"

HALL

KITCHEN
11'-6" x 9'-6"

SINK

RANGE

CLO.

HEAT & AC

46'-0"

FIXED DOOR

UP

STORAGE

LINEN

BATH

PORCH

FIXED DOOR

ENTRY

CLO.

MASTER B. R.
16'-6" x 16'-0"

COURT

PLAN E-1814
(WITHOUT BASEMENT)

Exterior walls are 2x6 construction.
Specify crawlspace or slab foundation.

MAIN FLOOR

BED ROOM
16'-0" x 11'-0"

CLO.

DOWN

HALL

BED ROOM
14'-6" x 10'-4"

BATH

LINEN

SHELVES

CLO.

UPPER FLOOR

HomeStyles
SOURCE 1
DESIGNERS NETWORK

An Energy Efficient Home
Blueprint Price Code B

Plan E-1814

To order blueprints, call
1-800-547-5570 or see order form
and pricing information on pages 220-224

Modern Interior, Traditional Exterior

8' Ceilings Throughout
Unless Otherwise Noted

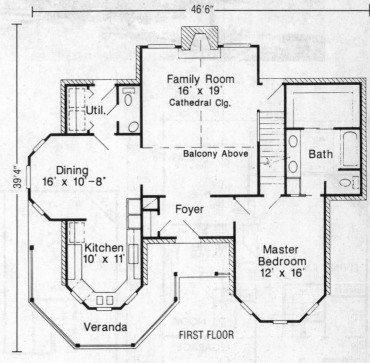

46'6"

39'4"

FIRST FLOOR

Family Room
16' x 19'
Cathedral Clg.

Util.

Balcony Above

Bath

Dining
16' x 10'-8"

Foyer

Kitchen
10' x 11'

Master Bedroom
12' x 16'

Veranda

First floor: 1,201 sq. ft.
Second floor: 647 sq. ft.

Total living area: 1,848 sq. ft.

PLAN L-1848
WITHOUT BASEMENT
(SLAB FOUNDATION)

(Plans for a detached two-car garage included with blueprint.)

Family Room Below

Balcony

Bath 2

Gameroom
14' x 11'-8"

Bedroom 2
10' x 12'-8"

Bedroom 3
13' x 12'

SECOND FLOOR

Blueprint Price Code B

Plan L-1848

FRONT VIEW

Queen Anne with Contemporary Interior

This gracious home offers numerous features for convenience and charm:
- 1,864 sq. ft. of living area.
- 2 bedrooms, plus den.
- Traditional exterior style.
- 30' wide at first floor, 32' wide at second floor.
- Versatile kitchen with range/oven/eating bar combination.
- Practical spice cabinet, pantry and nook.
- Sunken living room with vaulted ceiling, fireplace, French doors, wet bar and built-in shelves.
- Dramatic open staircase.
- Interesting entry open to bridge above.
- 2½ baths.
- Cozy loft open to living area.
- Spacious and elegant master bedroom with bay window, walk-in closet, separate shower, double-sink vanity and window overlooking living/loft area.
- Energy-efficient specifications throughout including 2x6 wall framing.

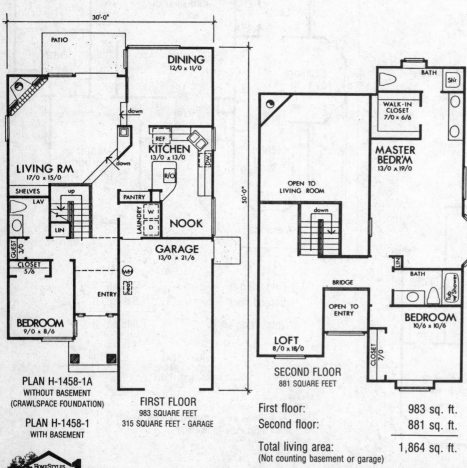

PLAN H-1458-1A
WITHOUT BASEMENT
(CRAWLSPACE FOUNDATION)

PLAN H-1458-1
WITH BASEMENT

FIRST FLOOR
983 SQUARE FEET
315 SQUARE FEET - GARAGE

SECOND FLOOR
881 SQUARE FEET

First floor:	983 sq. ft.
Second floor:	881 sq. ft.
Total living area:	**1,864 sq. ft.**

(Not counting basement or garage)

Blueprint Price Code B

Plans H-1458-1 & H-1458-1A

To order blueprints, call
1-800-547-5570 or see order form
and pricing information on pages 220-224.

Every Room with a View

This unique octagonal design lets almost every part of the house enjoy an exterior wall. The first-floor living area is designed as an open studio. Separate kitchen, laundry, lavatory and entry assure convenience as well as privacy. A massive stone fireplace adds drama to the living room.

Storage is abundant on both levels. Three decks extend the first-level living area even further.

A balcony hallway connects all second-floor bedrooms. Both levels open to a sunny skylight. Access to the first level is via an open staircase. An alternate second-floor plan replaces one bedroom with a viewing deck.

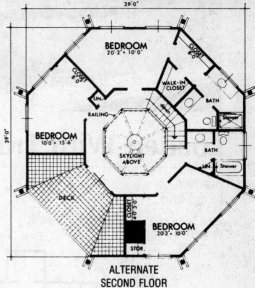

ALTERNATE SECOND FLOOR
960 SQUARE FEET

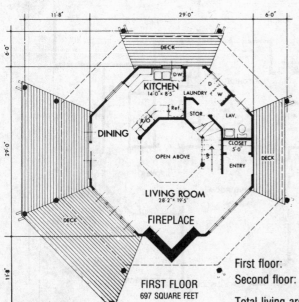

FIRST FLOOR
697 SQUARE FEET

PLAN H-27
WITHOUT BASEMENT
(CRAWLSPACE FOUNDATION)

First floor:	697 sq. ft.
Second floor:	1,167 sq. ft.
Total living area:	1,864 sq. ft.

(Total with alternate second floor: 1,657 sq. ft.)

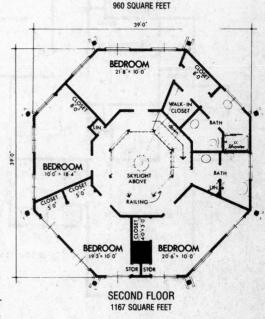

SECOND FLOOR
1167 SQUARE FEET

Blueprint Price Code B

Plan H-27

To order blueprints, call
1-800-547-5570 or see order form
and pricing information on pages 220-224

Loaded With Traditional Charm

First floor: 811 sq. ft.
Second floor: 1,067 sq. ft.

Total living area: 1,878 sq. ft.
(Not counting garage)

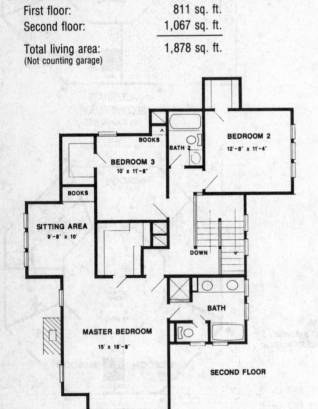

BOOKS
BATH 2
BEDROOM 2
12'-8" x 11'-4"

BEDROOM 3
10' x 11'-8"

BOOKS

SITTING AREA
9'-8" x 10'

DOWN

BATH

MASTER BEDROOM
15' x 18'-8"

SECOND FLOOR

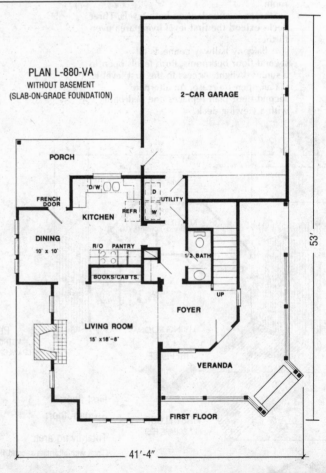

PLAN L-880-VA
WITHOUT BASEMENT
(SLAB-ON-GRADE FOUNDATION)

2-CAR GARAGE

PORCH

FRENCH DOOR

KITCHEN

D/W

REFR

D
W

UTILITY

DINING
10' x 10'

R/O PANTRY

BOOKS/CAB TS.

1/2 BATH

UP

FOYER

LIVING ROOM
15' x 18'-8"

VERANDA

FIRST FLOOR

53'

41'-4"

HomeStyles
SOURCE 1
DESIGNERS NETWORK

Blueprint Price Code B
Plan L-880-VA

Distinctive Charm

Shuttered dormers and traditional detailing add distinctive charm to this three-bedroom home.

The kitchen is illuminated by a large window over the sink and a convenient pantry. A desk is located in the adjoining nook, providing an excellent area for paying bills and organizing household accounts.

Double doors open into a fantastic master bedroom. For those who can never get enough closet space, you'll find plenty here. The walk-in closet is cleverly designed into the dormer with a pleasant window seat.

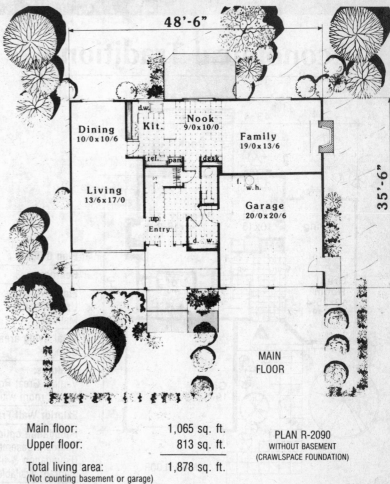

MAIN FLOOR

48'-6"

35'-6"

Dining 10/0 x 10/6
Kit.
Nook 9/0 x 10/0
Family 19/0 x 13/6
Living 13/6 x 17/0
Garage 20/0 x 20/6
Entry
d.w.
f.
w.h.
ref. pan. desk
up

PLAN R-2090
WITHOUT BASEMENT
(CRAWLSPACE FOUNDATION)

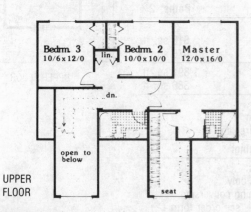

Bedrm. 3 10/6 x 12/0
Bedrm. 2 10/0 x 10/0
Master 12/0 x 16/0
lin.
dn.
open to below
seat

UPPER FLOOR

Main floor:	1,065 sq. ft.
Upper floor:	813 sq. ft.
Total living area:	1,878 sq. ft.
(Not counting basement or garage)	

HomeStyles SOURCE 1 DESIGNERS' NETWORK

Blueprint Price Code B

Plan R-2090

To order blueprints, call
1-800-547-5570 or see order form
and pricing information on pages 220-224.

Economical Traditional

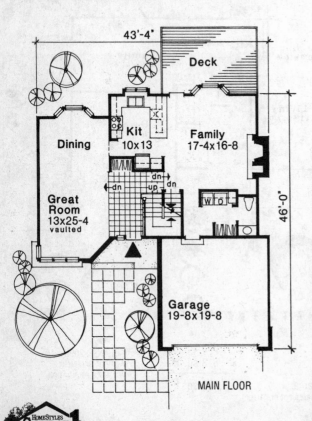

43'-4"

Deck

Dining

Kit
10x13

Family
17-4x16-8

Great
Room
13x25-4
vaulted

dn dn
up dn

w/o

46'-0"

Garage
19-8x19-8

MAIN FLOOR

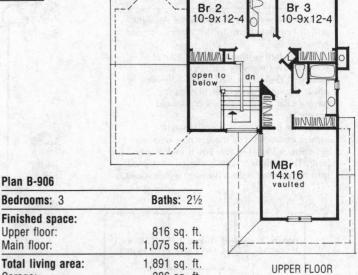

Br 2
10-9x12-4

Br 3
10-9x12-4

open to
below

dn

MBr
14x16
vaulted

UPPER FLOOR

Plan B-906

Bedrooms: 3		**Baths:** 2½

Finished space:

Upper floor:	816 sq. ft.
Main floor:	1,075 sq. ft.

Total living area:	1,891 sq. ft.
Garage:	386 sq. ft.

Features:
Vaulted Great Room.
Family room with fireplace.

Exterior Wall Framing:	2x4

Foundation options:
Standard basement only.
(Foundation & framing conversion
diagram available — see order form.)

Blueprint Price Code:	B

Plan B-906

To order blueprints, call
1-800-547-5570 or see order form
and pricing information on pages 220-224.

Exciting, Economical Design

Exciting but economical, this 1,895 sq. ft., three-bedroom house is arranged carefully for maximum use and enjoyment on two floors, and is only 42 feet wide to minimize lot size requirements. The multi-paned bay windows of the living room and an upstairs bedroom add contrast to the hip rooflines and lead you to the sheltered front entry porch.

The open, vaulted foyer is brightened by a skylight as it sorts traffic to the downstairs living areas or to the upper bedroom level. A few steps to the right puts you in the vaulted living room and the adjoining dining area. Sliding doors in the dining area and the nook, and a pass-through window in the U-shaped kitchen, make the patio a perfect place for outdoor activities and meals.

A large fireplace warms the spacious family room, which has a corner wet bar for efficient entertaining. A utility room leading to the garage and a powder room complete the 1,020 sq. ft. main floor.

An open stairway in the foyer leads to the 875 sq. ft. upper level. The master bedroom has a large walk-in wardrobe, twin vanity, shower and bathroom. The front bedroom has a seat in the bay window and the third bedroom has a built-in seat overlooking the vaulted living room. A full bath with twin vanity serves these bedrooms.

The daylight basement version of the plan adds 925 sq. ft. of living space.

Main floor:	1,020 sq. ft.
Upper floor:	875 sq. ft.
Total living area:	1,895 sq. ft.
(Not counting basement or garage)	

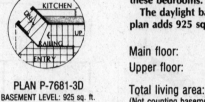

PLAN P-7681-3D
BASEMENT LEVEL: 925 sq. ft.

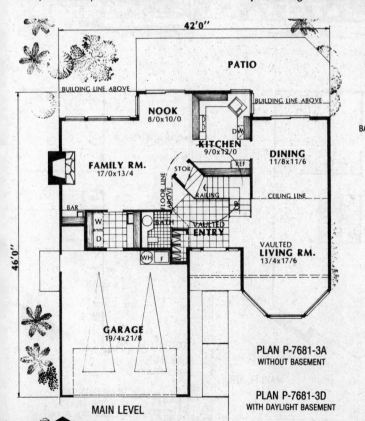

PLAN P-7681-3A
WITHOUT BASEMENT

PLAN P-7681-3D
WITH DAYLIGHT BASEMENT

MAIN LEVEL

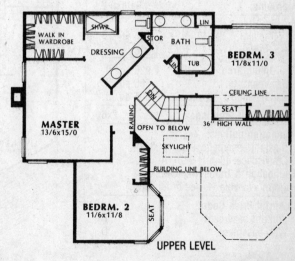

UPPER LEVEL

Blueprint Price Code B

Plans P-7681-3A & P-7681-3D

To order blueprints, call
1-800-547-5570 or see order form and pricing information on pages 220-224.

Soaring Design Lifts the Human Spirit

- Striking design is a favorite for year-round or vacation home living.
- Prow-shaped Great Room design includes the kitchen as a part of the living room area, which features a fireplace and a soaring wall of windows.

- The second floor includes two bedrooms and a balcony room which overlooks the living room — in addition to another full bath.
- Optional basement includes rec room, garage and space for a shop and storage.

UPPER FLOOR

Plans H-930-1 & H-930-1A

Bedrooms: 3	Baths: 2

Space:

Upper floor:	710 sq. ft.
Main floor:	1,210 sq. ft.

Total living area:	**1,920 sq. ft.**
Basement:	605 sq. ft.
Garage/shop:	605 sq. ft.

Exterior Wall Framing:	2x6

Foundation options:
Daylight basement, Plan H-930-1
Crawlspace, Plan H-930-1A
(Foundation & framing conversion diagram available — see order form.)

Blueprint Price Code:

Without basement:	B
With basement:	D

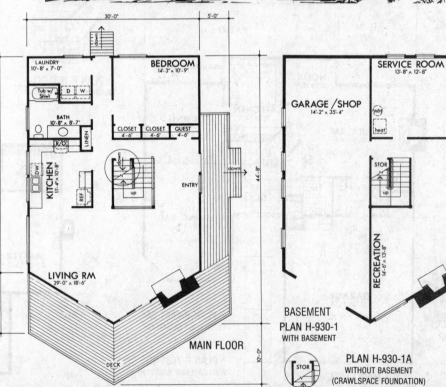

MAIN FLOOR

BASEMENT
PLAN H-930-1
WITH BASEMENT

PLAN H-930-1A
WITHOUT BASEMENT
(CRAWLSPACE FOUNDATION)

Plans H-930-1 & H-930-1A

To order blueprints, call
1-800-547-5570 or see order form
and pricing information on pages 220-224.

Decked-Out for Fun

A spacious deck surrounds this unique residence. The covered deck at the entrance blends with the design.

Sliding glass doors and windows in the living-dining room occupy an entire wall to provide additional access to the deck.

The breakfast bar acts as a serviceable buffer between the dining room and the compact kitchen. In consideration of household duties, the laundry room adjoins the kitchen.

The second floor primarily serves as a private sleeping wing. An impressive balcony room for recreation overlooks the dining room. Attractive exposed beams provide a finishing touch.

Exterior walls are framed with 2x6 studs.

First floor:	1,064 sq. ft.
Second floor:	869 sq. ft.
Basement:	475 sq. ft.
Total living area with basement: (Not counting garage)	2,408 sq. ft.

FIRST FLOOR
1064 SQUARE FEET

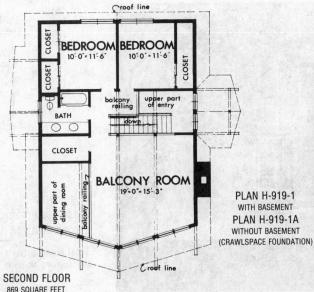

PLAN H-919-1
WITH BASEMENT
PLAN H-919-1A
WITHOUT BASEMENT
(CRAWLSPACE FOUNDATION)

SECOND FLOOR
869 SQUARE FEET

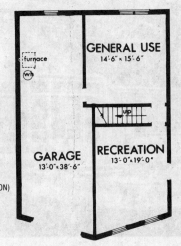

BASEMENT
475 SQUARE FEET

Blueprint Price Code C With Basement
Blueprint Price Code B Without Basement

Plans H-919-1 & H-919-1A

To order blueprints, call
1-800-547-5570 or see order form and pricing information on pages 220-224.

FRONT VIEW

Sun Chaser

A passive sun room with two fully glazed walls and an all-glass roof offers leeway when siting this comfortable, contemporary leisure home. Orientation is towards the south to capture maximum solar warmth. The window wall in the living room and a bank of clerestory windows high on the master bedroom wall soak up the winter rays for direct heat gain, yet are shaded with overhangs to block out the higher sun in the summer.

The 165 sq. ft. sun room is a focal point from the living and family rooms, through windows and sliding glass doors between these rooms. A dining table in the family room would command a sweeping view, or meals could be enjoyed in the sun room.

Sloping ceilings in the living and sun rooms allow balcony railings to open the master bedroom partially for a view down to these rooms, and let warm air flow up from the masonry storage floor of the sun room.

Accent walls of solid board paneling add visual warmth and texture to the rooms. Western cedar bevel siding adds beauty and individuality to the exterior. Exterior walls are of 2x6 construction.

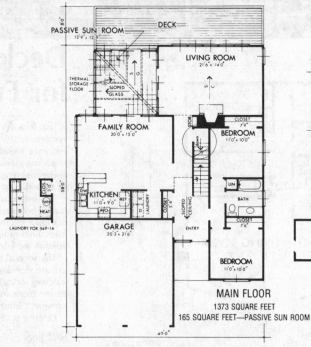

MAIN FLOOR
1373 SQUARE FEET
165 SQUARE FEET—PASSIVE SUN ROOM

LAUNDRY FOR 949-1A

SECOND FLOOR
428 SQUARE FEET

PLAN H-949-1A
WITHOUT BASEMENT
(CRAWLSPACE FOUNDATION)

PLAN H-949-1B
DAYLIGHT BASEMENT

PLAN H-949-1
STANDARD BASEMENT

First floor:	1,373 sq. ft.
Passive sun room:	165 sq. ft.
Second floor:	428 sq. ft.
Total living area:	1,966 sq. ft.

(Not counting basement or garage)

Blueprint Price Code B

To order blueprints, call
1-800-547-5570 or see order form
and pricing information on pages 220-224.

Plans H-949-1, H-949-1A & H-949-1B

Contemporary Elegance

A "street appeal" contemporary with traditional overtones, this home is finished in cedar siding applied vertically. Rough-sawn trim and corner boards are indicated at key points to give the home a look of solid, lasting endurance.

The two-story vaulted sunspace located

First floor:	1,248 sq. ft.
Second floor:	723 sq. ft.
Total living area:	**1,971 sq. ft.**
(Not counting basement, garage or bonus room)	
Bonus area:	225 sq. ft.

Exterior walls are 2x6 construction.

at the rear of the home may be added while under construction or provided at a later date. The space is accessible from both the family room and the second-floor master bedroom.

The main interior staircase to the upper level is designed partially open to the living room on two sides.

A separate hallway offers privacy to the two downstairs bedrooms from the activity areas.

The upstairs master suite has all the amenities of much larger homes. Access to

the bonus room over the garage is from the study area.

The amply designed kitchen is just a short step away from the utility room, which also offers a separate ironing area and a clothes-sorting counter with deep sink.

Total square footage of this home, not including the bonus space, is 1,971. The garage bonus space is an additional 225 sq. ft. Width of home is 46'6", with depth at 57'.

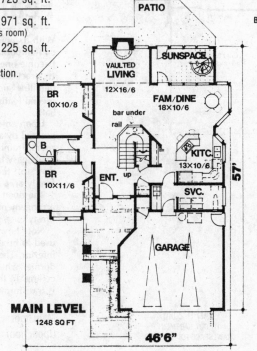

PLAN S-1971
BASEMENT OPTION INCLUDED WITH BLUEPRINT

PATIO

VAULTED LIVING 12×16/6

SUNSPACE

FAM/DINE 18×10/6

BR 10×10/8

bar under rail

B

KITC. 13×10/6

BR 10×11/6

ENT. up

SVC.

GARAGE

57'

MAIN LEVEL
1248 SQ FT

46'6"

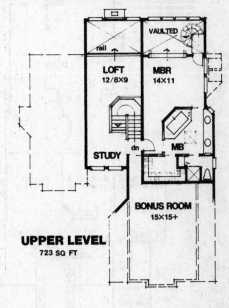

VAULTED

rail

LOFT 12/8×9

MBR 14×11

STUDY

dn

MB

BONUS ROOM 15×15+

UPPER LEVEL
723 SQ FT

Blueprint Price Code B

Plan S-1971

To order blueprints, call
1-800-547-5570 or see order form
and pricing information on pages 220-224.

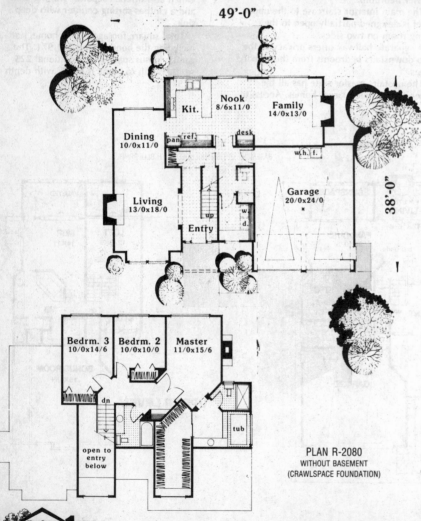

49'-0"

38'-0"

Kit.

Nook
8/6x11/0

Family
14/0x13/0

Dining
10/0x11/0

pan. ref. desk

w.h. f.

Living
13/0x18/0

Garage
20/0x24/0

up

Entry

w.
d.

Bedrm. 3
10/0x14/6

Bedrm. 2
10/0x10/0

Master
11/0x15/6

dn

tub

open to
entry
below

PLAN R-2080
WITHOUT BASEMENT
(CRAWLSPACE FOUNDATION)

Practical Home with Popular Features

With its unique blend of traditional and contemporary styling, this plan has fast become one of our most popular designs. Its practical layout is complemented by rich detailing such as arched doorways and special features in the luxurious master bath.

Upon entering the house, visitors are greeted by an arched entry into the living room, framing the fireplace. Entertaining is made easy by simply using the double doors off the nook to close off the informal family area to the rear of the house.

The open kitchen, nook and family room arrangement allows for a simple, relaxed lifestyle.

Note how the dormers are creatively used to brighten and visually enlarge the interior. The entry features an overhead dormer which emphasizes the vaulted ceiling. In the master bedroom the dormer is transformed into a walk-in closet.

Main floor:	1,093 sq. ft.
Upper floor:	905 sq. ft.
Total living area: (Not counting garage)	1,998 sq. ft.

To order blueprints, call
1-800-547-5570 or see order form and pricing information on pages 220-224.

Blueprint Price Code B

Plan R-2080

Sleek
Contemporary
Lines

Sleek, contemporary lines and natural vertical wood siding combine to create an appealing exterior for this exciting two-story four-bedroom home. Inside, the open plan boasts many amenities, including a dramatic two-level reception hall. A stone-finished, wood-burning fireplace adorns the living area. An expansive bay window in the dining room stretches down to the floor, bringing in natural light.

The kitchen, dinette and family room serve as a focal point and a comfortable family gathering space. Wide sliding glass doors in the family room and dinette lead to separate terraces.

The upper level, brightened by a large skylight, includes four bedrooms and two full baths. The master bedroom features ample closet space and a private bath with a whirlpool tub.

Living area is 1,894 sq. ft. — with 922 sq. ft. on the first floor and 972 sq. ft. at the second. Garage, mud room, etc. come to 532 sq. ft. Optional basement is 922 sq. ft.

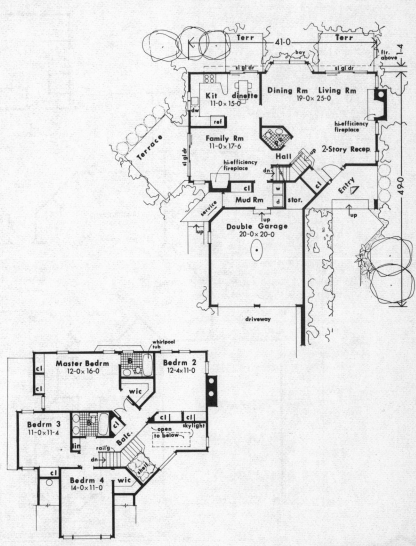

First floor:	922 sq. ft.
Second floor:	972 sq. ft.
Total living area:	1,894 sq. ft.

(Not counting basement or garage)

Blueprint Price Code B

Plan K-652-U

Spacious One-Story

Total living area: 1,935 sq. ft.
(Not counting garage)

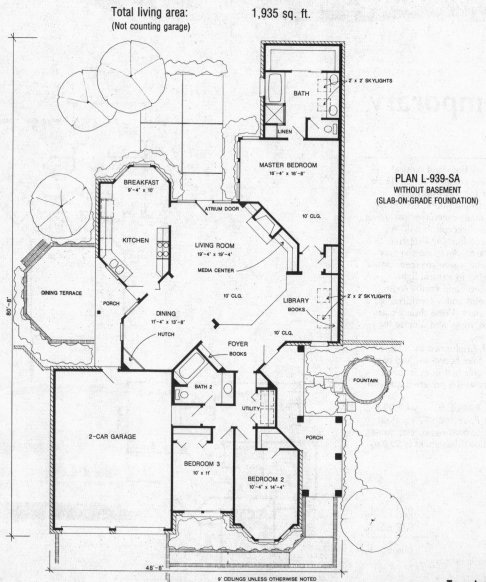

PLAN L-939-SA
WITHOUT BASEMENT
(SLAB-ON-GRADE FOUNDATION)

Floor plan labels:
- BATH
- 2' x 2' SKYLIGHTS
- LINEN
- MASTER BEDROOM 16'-4" x 16'-8"
- 10' CLG.
- BREAKFAST 9'-4" x 10'
- ATRIUM DOOR
- KITCHEN
- LIVING ROOM 19'-4" x 19'-4"
- MEDIA CENTER
- 10' CLG.
- LIBRARY BOOKS
- 2' x 2' SKYLIGHTS
- DINING TERRACE
- PORCH
- DINING 11'-4" x 13'-8"
- HUTCH
- 10' CLG.
- FOYER BOOKS
- FOUNTAIN
- BATH 2
- UTILITY
- 2-CAR GARAGE
- PORCH
- BEDROOM 3 10' x 11'
- BEDROOM 2 10'-4" x 14'-4"
- 80'-8"
- 48'-8"
- 9' CEILINGS UNLESS OTHERWISE NOTED

HomeStyles
SOURCE 1
DESIGNERS' NETWORK

Blueprint Price Code B
Plan L-939-SA

An Octagonal Home with a Lofty View

There's no better way to avoid the ordinary than by building an octagonal home and "escaping" from rigid rooms with four square corners. This variation adds a six-window, 355 sq. ft. loft for a family or recreation room, while the 1,567 sq. ft. main floor offers plenty of room for full-time family living or for a comfortable second-home retreat. An optional daylight basement adds a fourth bedroom and a bath, a two-car garage and storage/work place.

This contemporary octagon with vertical siding has a vaulted entry hall brightened by a skylight and two octagonal windows along the stairs leading to the loft room. To the right of the entry lie the master bedroom and two smaller bedrooms with bump-out window seats. The master bath has a spa bathtub. The other bedrooms share the hall bathroom.

To the left of the entry is the utility room, the spacious U-shaped kitchen, and the great room, warmed by a woodstove. Sliding glass doors open onto a wide wood deck, also accessible from the master bedroom.

The vaulted-ceiling loft has a woodstove or pre-fab fireplace and a wet bar for entertaining. The loft also can be used for a den or crafts room.

FRONT VIEW

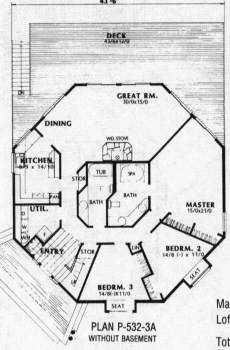

PLAN P-532-3A
WITHOUT BASEMENT

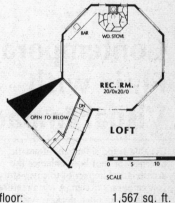

LOFT

SCALE

Main floor:	1,567 sq. ft.
Loft:	355 sq. ft.
Total living area: (Not counting basement or garage)	1,922 sq. ft.
Basement:	350 sq. ft.
Total with basement:	2,272 sq. ft.

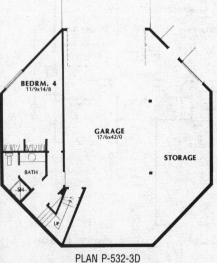

PLAN P-532-3D
WITH DAYLIGHT BASEMENT
350 SQUARE FEET

REAR VIEW

Blueprint Price Code C With Basement
Blueprint Price Code B Without Basement

To order blueprints, call
1-800-547-5570 or see order form and pricing information on pages 220-224.

Plans P-532-3A & P-532-3D

Contemporary Flair with Visual Impact

Durable wood siding and dramatic interplay of roof lines enhance the architectural impact of this two-story contemporary design. A main feature of the plan is an open deck, carved into the roof, as an extension of the master suite. At the entry, double doors lead into a sloped-ceilinged reception hall. Open planning throughout creates interesting spatial relationships.

Formal living and dining rooms, with Cathedral ceilings, are warmed by a woodburning fireplace. The informal area, with U-shaped kitchen, cheerful dinette and bright family room, is graced by a second fireplace.

Four bedrooms are tucked away on the upper level. The master suite is a self-contained retreat that features luxury amenities and an open deck over the garage.

SECOND FLOOR

- Bedrm 3 · 12-0 × 10-0
- wic
- lin
- Bedrm 2 · 13-0 × 12-0
- Hall
- operable skylight above
- Bedrm 4 · 10-0 × 10-4
- cl
- B
- operable clerestory window above
- vanity
- dn
- dras'g
- cl
- cl
- attic cl.
- whirlpool tub
- B
- Master Suite · 13-0 × 15-0
- Deck

First floor:	1,025 sq. ft.
Second floor:	873 sq. ft.
Total living area: (Not counting basement or garage)	1,898 sq. ft.
Optional basement:	1,000 sq. ft.
Garage, mud room, etc.:	578 sq. ft.

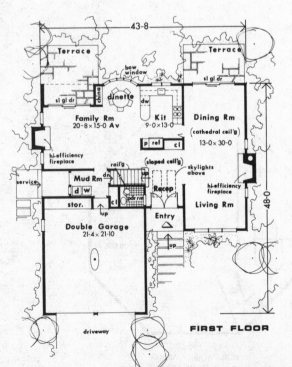

FIRST FLOOR

43-8 · 48-0

- Terrace
- bow window
- Terrace
- sl gl dr
- china
- dinette
- dw
- sl gl dr
- Family Rm · 20-8 × 15-0 Av
- Kit · 9-0 × 13-0
- Dining Rm (cathedral ceil'g) · 13-0 × 30-0
- hi-efficiency fireplace
- p ref cl
- service
- Mud Rm
- dn
- rail'g
- up
- skylights above
- (sloped ceil'g)
- hi-efficiency fireplace
- d w
- cl
- pdr rm
- Recep
- Living Rm
- stor.
- up
- Entry
- Double Garage · 21-4 × 21-10
- up
- driveway

SECTION

- attic
- sl gl dr
- rail'g
- Deck
- Master Suite
- Bedrm 4
- Bedrm 3
- driveway
- Double Garage
- stor.
- Mud Rm
- Family Rm
- sl gl dr
- Terrace
- wall insul.
- Bsmt.

Blueprint Price Code B

Plan K-647-P

To order blueprints, call
1-800-547-5570 or see order form and pricing information on pages 220-224.

Bay Window in Master Bedroom

- Compact two-story design makes best use of a small lot.
- Living room includes a fireplace, vaulted ceiling and sunny bay window.
- Master suite includes deluxe bath and large closet.
- Efficient family room/nook/kitchen combination is great for family life and informal entertaining.
- Dining and living rooms combine to create space for formal parties or large family gatherings.

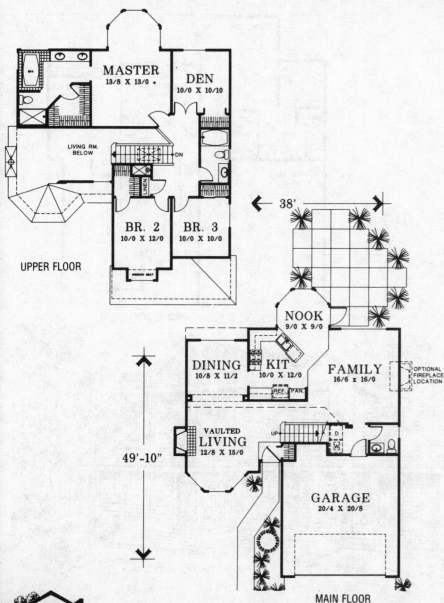

MASTER
13/8 X 13/0 +

DEN
10/0 X 10/10

LIVING RM.
BELOW

DN

BR. 2
10/0 X 12/0

BR. 3
10/0 X 10/0

LINEN

WINDOW SEAT

UPPER FLOOR

← 38' →

NOOK
9/0 X 9/0

DINING
10/8 X 11/2

KIT
10/0 X 12/0

FAMILY
16/6 x 16/0

OPTIONAL
FIREPLACE
LOCATION

REF. PAN.

49'-10"

VAULTED
LIVING
12/8 X 15/0

UP

GARAGE
20/4 X 20/8

MAIN FLOOR

Plan AM-2147

Bedrooms: 3	Baths: 2½

Space:

Upper floor:	1,019 sq. ft.
Main floor:	935 sq. ft.

Total living area:	1,954 sq. ft.
Garage:	420 sq. ft.

Exterior Wall Framing:	2x4

Foundation options:
Crawlspace only.
(Foundation & framing conversion diagram available — see order form.)

Blueprint Price Code:	B

HomeStyles
SOURCE 1
DESIGNERS NETWORK

Plan AM-2147

FRONT

Traditional Two-Story with Modern Touch

First floor:	1,300 sq. ft.
Second floor:	660 sq. ft.
Total living area:	1,960 sq. ft.
(Not counting basement or garage)	
Garage:	483 sq. ft.

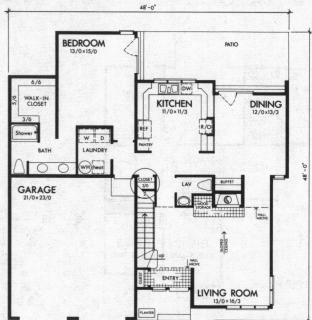

BEDROOM
13/0 x 15/0

PATIO

6/6

5/6

WALK-IN CLOSET

3/6

Shower

BATH

W D

LAUNDRY

WH heat

KITCHEN
11/0 x 11/3

DW

REF

R/O

PANTRY

DINING
12/0 x 13/3

GARAGE
21/0 x 23/0

CLOSET
3/0

LAV

BUFFET

WOOD STORAGE

WALL ABOVE

SLOPED CEILING

GUEST

UP

ENTRY

WALL ABOVE

PLANTER

LIVING ROOM
13/0 x 16/3

48'-0"

48'-0"

FIRST FLOOR

BEDROOM
13/0 x 12/0

CLOSET
7/4

LIN

BATH

Tub w/ Shower

CLOSET
7/4

LIN

WALL ABOVE

LOFT
12/9 x 9/6

SLOPED CEILING

ATTIC

3/0 h. wall

OPEN TO BELOW

SLOPED CEILING

down

down

BEDROOM
13/0 x 12/0

SECOND FLOOR

PLAN H-3744-1
WITH BASEMENT

PLAN H-3744-1A
WITHOUT BASEMENT
(CRAWLSPACE FOUNDATION)

REAR

Blueprint Price Code B

Plans H-3744-1 & H-3744-1A

To order blueprints, call
1-800-547-5570 or see order form
and pricing information on pages 220-224.

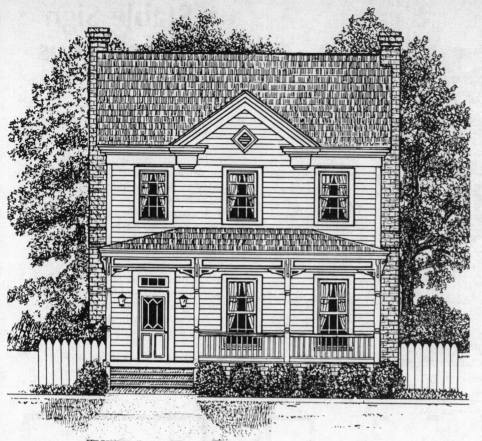

Inviting Porch Welcomes Guests

The inspiration for this charming turn-of-the-century house is found in Natchez, Mississippi. The inviting porch extends a gracious invitation to friends and neighbors.

Once inside, a very impressive foyer leads to the living room or the great room. A formal dining room, located conveniently between the kitchen and the living room, lends itself to easy entertaining.

The master bedroom has a bath with a separate shower stall, as well as an oversized tub. A large walk-in closet completes the amenities of this spacious room. The other bedrooms share a compartmentalized bath.

This plan is especially well-suited for a narrow lot.

First floor:	1,066 sq. ft.
Second floor:	913 sq. ft.
Total living area:	1,979 sq. ft.

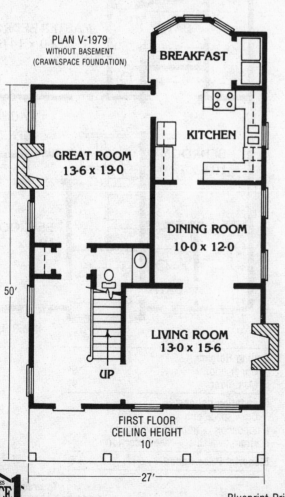

PLAN V-1979
WITHOUT BASEMENT
(CRAWLSPACE FOUNDATION)

BREAKFAST

KITCHEN

GREAT ROOM
13-6 x 19-0

DINING ROOM
10-0 x 12-0

LIVING ROOM
13-0 x 15-6

UP

50'

27'

FIRST FLOOR
CEILING HEIGHT
10'

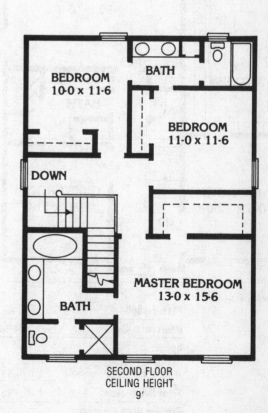

BEDROOM
10-0 x 11-6

BATH

BEDROOM
11-0 x 11-6

DOWN

MASTER BEDROOM
13-0 x 15-6

BATH

SECOND FLOOR
CEILING HEIGHT
9'

Blueprint Price Code B

Plan V-1979

A Stable Sign of Prosperous Times

- The timeless appeal of Georgian architecture is captured in this entrancing design.
- This plan maintains the flavor of the original Colonial dwellings on the exterior, while including modern features inside.
- A spacious kitchen opens to a sunny breakfast nook.
- A large Great Room with fireplace provides wonderful space for family living or entertaining.
- The master suite boasts a dazzling bath with whirlpool tub and double vanities, plus a large walk-in closet.
- Two secondary bedrooms share a connecting bath with separate vanity areas.
- The laundry area is conveniently located upstairs by the bedrooms.

BREAKFAST

GREAT ROOM
14-0 x 18-0

KITCHEN

BATH

DINING ROOM
10-6 x 12-0

GUEST ROOM
10-6 x 11-0

UP

36'

30'

MAIN FLOOR

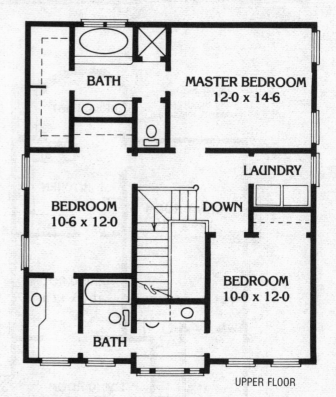

BATH

MASTER BEDROOM
12-0 x 14-6

LAUNDRY

BEDROOM
10-6 x 12-0

DOWN

BEDROOM
10-0 x 12-0

BATH

UPPER FLOOR

Plan V-1986	
Bedrooms: 3-4	**Baths:** 3
Space:	
Upper floor:	958 sq. ft.
Main floor:	1,028 sq. ft.
Total living area:	1,926 sq. ft.
Exterior Wall Framing:	2x6

Ceiling Heights:	
Upper floor:	8'
Main floor:	9'
Foundation options:	
Crawlspace only.	
(Foundation & framing conversion diagram available — see order form.)	
Blueprint Price Code:	B

Plan V-1986

To order blueprints, call
1-800-547-5570 or see order form
and pricing information on pages 220-224.

Stylish Four-Bedroom Home

First floor: 1,020 sq. ft.
Second floor: 1,020 sq. ft.

Total living area: 2,040 sq. ft.
(Not counting garage)

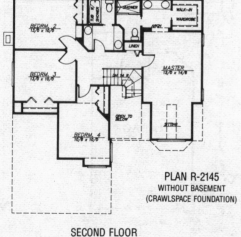

PLAN R-2145
WITHOUT BASEMENT
(CRAWLSPACE FOUNDATION)

SECOND FLOOR

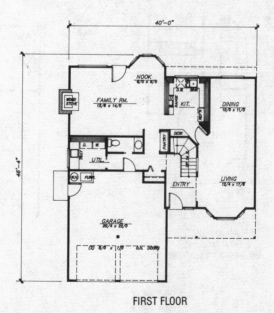

FIRST FLOOR

Blueprint Price Code C

Plan R-2145

To order blueprints, call
1-800-547-5570 or see order form
and pricing information on pages 220-224.

Small-Lot Design Offers Four Bedrooms

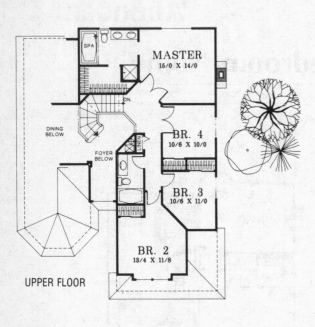

MASTER
15/0 X 14/0

SPA

DN.

DINING
BELOW

BR. 4
10/6 X 10/0

FOYER
BELOW

LINEN

BR. 3
10/6 X 11/0

BR. 2
13/4 X 11/8

UPPER FLOOR

PLAN AM-2247
WITHOUT BASEMENT
(CRAWLSPACE FOUNDATION)

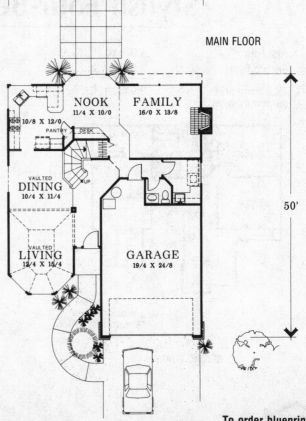

38'

MAIN FLOOR

NOOK
11/4 X 10/0

FAMILY
16/0 X 13/8

10/8 X 12/0

PANTRY

DESK

UP

VAULTED
DINING
10/4 X 11/4

50'

VAULTED
LIVING
12/4 X 15/4

GARAGE
19/4 X 24/8

Main floor:	1,094 sq. ft.
Upper floor:	956 sq. ft.
Total living area:	2,050 sq. ft.
(Not counting garage)	

Blueprint Price Code C

Plan AM-2247

To order blueprints, call
1-800-547-5570 or see order form
and pricing information on pages 220-224.

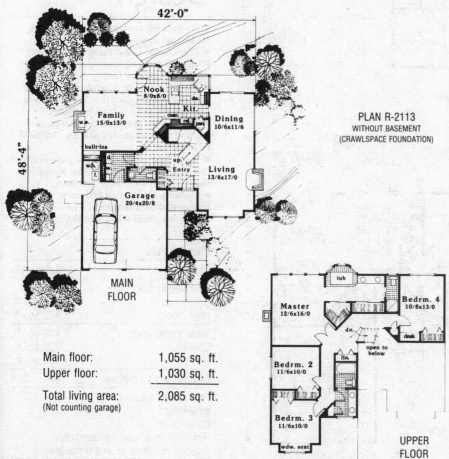

PLAN R-2113
WITHOUT BASEMENT
(CRAWLSPACE FOUNDATION)

42'-0"

Nook
8/0x8/0

Family
15/0x13/0

Kit.

Dining
10/6x11/6

built-ins

up.
Entry

Living
13/4x17/0

48'-4"

Garage
20/4x20/8

MAIN FLOOR

Master
12/6x16/0

Bedrm. 4
10/8x13/0

dn.

open to below

Bedrm. 2
11/6x10/0

Bedrm. 3
11/6x10/0

wdw. seat

desk

UPPER FLOOR

Main floor:	1,055 sq. ft.
Upper floor:	1,030 sq. ft.
Total living area: (Not counting garage)	2,085 sq. ft.

Abundant Living Space

Notice how the delightful arched windows add an appealing touch to this contemporary home, in addition to bringing more light into the interior. Even the entry door reflects the line of the arched windows.

You will find abundant living space in this charming four-bedroom home, and all in less than 2,100 sq. ft.

The vaulted living room, with its stately fireplace, merges with the lofty foyer to create a voluminous space which is accented by the open stairway. A powder room is conveniently located off the foyer.

A graceful arch helps define the entry into the spacious country kitchen, which is graced by such features as a wood stove, bar, French door access to a covered patio, corner kitchen sink, and a handy walk-in pantry.

The second story is devoted to bedroom space. Notice how the main bath is divided so that two or more people can use the space at the same time.

Entering through double doors, you will find yourself in the generously sized master bedroom. Opening off the master bedroom is a roomy dressing/bathing area with amenities that include mirrored closet doors, twin vanities, and a luxurious whirlpool tub nestled in a windowed bay.

Blueprint Price Code C
Plan R-2113

To order blueprints, call
1-800-547-5570 or see order form and pricing information on pages 220-224.

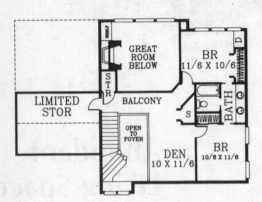

UPPER FLOOR

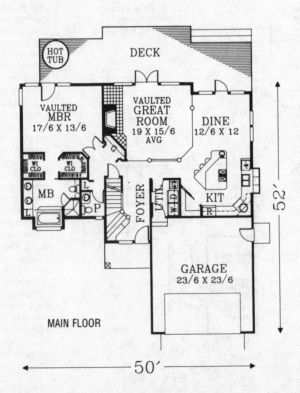

MAIN FLOOR

Traditional Overtones in Modern Design

- An exciting contemporary home with traditional overtones.
- The vaulted Great Room with adjacent kitchen and dining room give the home an open and spacious feeling.
- The master suite is located on the first floor away from the other bedrooms and features his and her walk-in closets.
- The custom master bath has a jacuzzi tub and double vanities plus an additional linen closet.
- A hot tub is located on the patio and can be reached from the Great Room or directly from the master bedroom.
- Upstairs are the two bedrooms with a continental bath between them.
- The den views down into the vaulted foyer.

Plan S-81189

Bedrooms: 3	Baths: 2½

Finished space:	
Upper floor:	660 sq. ft.
Main floor:	1,440 sq. ft.

Total living area:	2,100 sq. ft.
Bonus area:	220 sq. ft.
Garage:	552 sq. ft.

Exterior Wall Framing:	2x6

Foundation options:
Basement.
Crawlspace.
(Foundation & framing conversion diagram available — see order form.)

Blueprint Price Code:	C

To order blueprints, call
1-800-547-5570 or see order form
and pricing information on pages 220-224.

Vaulted Great Room Opens to Large Deck

- An exciting contemporary home with traditional overtones.
- Vaulted Great Room with adjacent kitchen and dining room give the home an open and spacious feeling.
- Master suite on the first floor is away from the other bedrooms.
- Master bath has a jacuzzi tub and

- double vanities plus an additional linen closet.
- A hot tub on the patio can be reached from the Great Room or master bedroom.
- Two bedrooms upstairs share continental bath.
- The den, which views down into the vaulted foyer, is also located upstairs.

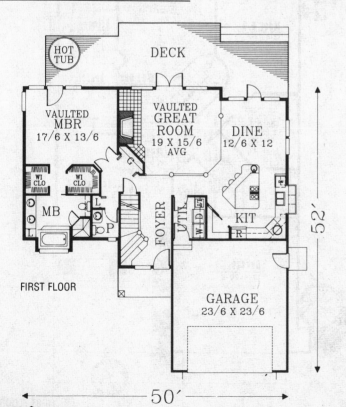

FIRST FLOOR

First floor:	1,440 sq. ft.
Second floor:	660 sq. ft.
Total living area: (Not counting garage)	2,100 sq. ft.
Bonus room:	220 sq. ft.

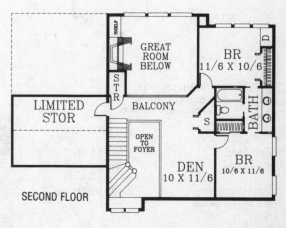

SECOND FLOOR

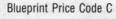

HomeStyles SOURCE 1 DESIGNERS NETWORK

Blueprint Price Code C

Plan S-2100

To order blueprints, call 1-800-547-5570 or see order form and pricing information on pages 220-224

Interior Angles Add to Excitement of Dramatic Design

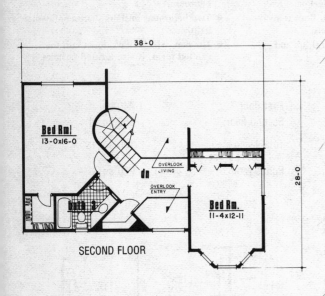

SECOND FLOOR

PLAN Q-2107-1A
WITHOUT BASEMENT
(SLAB-ON-GRADE FOUNDATION)

First floor: 1,507 sq. ft.
Second floor: 600 sq. ft.

Total living area: 2,107 sq. ft.
(Not counting garage)

FIRST FLOOR

Blueprint Price Code C

Plan Q-2107-1A

To order blueprints, call
1-800-547-5570 or see order form
and pricing information on pages 220-224.

Cozy Home with Secluded Entry

The elegance of a brick front, hipped roof and special window treatments give this home the high curb appeal that today's homeowner is looking for.

Upon entering through the angled double doors, you are welcomed by the elegantly arched entry of the dining room and the inviting step down into the living room. Both rooms are enhanced with a vaulted ceiling. To your left are double doors that lead to an optional fourth bedroom or den.

Moving through the house, a spacious kitchen with island and lots of cupboard space await you. The nook and family room are open to the kitchen, with all three rooms sharing a vaulted ceiling. Once inside the family room, a brick fireplace, lots of glass and double French doors leading to a covered patio make this room truly a place to relax.

Just off the kitchen is the utility room. Notice the unique placement of the walk-in closet to act as a buffer for the bedrooms. The main bathroom is centrally located between the generously sized bedrooms. The master bedroom is complemented with coved ceiling, double French doors and large walk-in closet. Open to the bedroom is the vaulted bath, complete with a large vanity, oversized spa tub, shower and linen closet.

Throughout this 2,137 sq. ft. home, the angled walls, well placed windows and outstanding design make this home a welcomed part of any neighborhood.

Total living area: 2,137 sq. ft.
(Not counting garage)

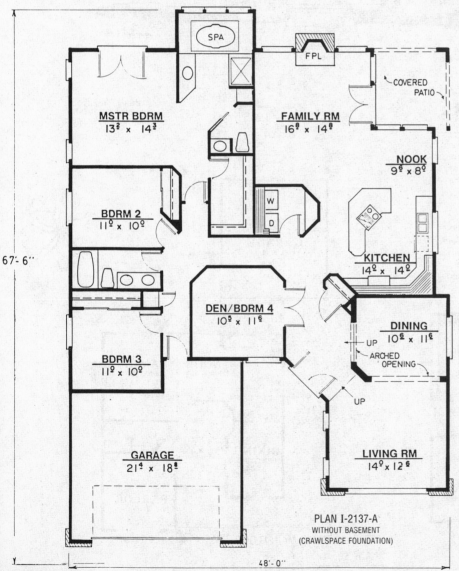

MSTR BDRM
13² x 14³

BDRM 2
11⁰ x 10⁰

BDRM 3
11⁰ x 10⁰

GARAGE
21⁴ x 18⁸

DEN/BDRM 4
10⁰ x 11⁶

FAMILY RM
16⁸ x 14⁰

SPA

FPL

COVERED PATIO

NOOK
9⁰ x 8⁰

KITCHEN
14⁰ x 14⁰

DINING
10⁰ x 11⁶

UP
ARCHED OPENING
UP

LIVING RM
14⁰ x 12⁸

67'-6"

48'-0"

PLAN I-2137-A
WITHOUT BASEMENT
(CRAWLSPACE FOUNDATION)

HomeStyles
SOURCE 1
DESIGNERS NETWORK

Blueprint Price Code C

Plan I-2137-A

To order blueprints, call
1-800-547-5570 or see order form
and pricing information on pages 220-224

127

Front Porch Invites Guests

This great-looking farmhouse features a cozy front porch outside and a modern floor plan inside. The dramatic two-story foyer with its angled stairway forms the circulation hub for this efficient home.

The upstairs features a large master bedroom with spa tub, large shower, double vanity and walk-in closet. Three additional bedrooms are provided making this a perfect home for the larger family.

A flexible rear- or side-entry garage works well for corner lots or lots served by a lane.

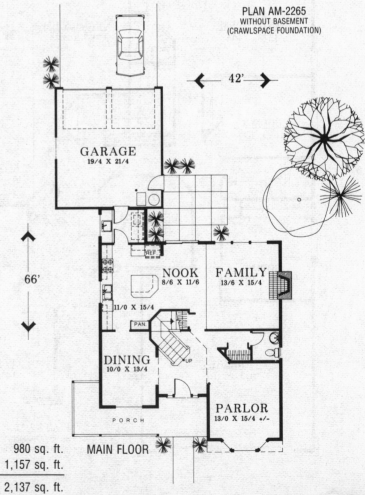

PLAN AM-2265
WITHOUT BASEMENT
(CRAWLSPACE FOUNDATION)

42'

66'

GARAGE
19/4 X 21/4

NOOK
8/6 X 11/6

FAMILY
13/6 X 15/4

11/0 X 15/4

DINING
10/0 X 13/4

PARLOR
13/0 X 15/4 +/-

PORCH

MAIN FLOOR

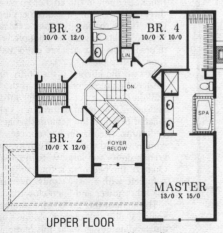

BR. 3
10/0 X 12/0

BR. 4
10/0 X 10/0

LIN.

DN.

SPA

BR. 2
10/0 X 12/0

FOYER
BELOW

MASTER
13/0 X 15/0

UPPER FLOOR

Upper floor:	980 sq. ft.
Main floor:	1,157 sq. ft.
Total living area: (Not counting garage)	2,137 sq. ft.

Blueprint Price Code C

Plan AM-2265

Cozy Look for Spacious Design

Gable ends with round-top windows, cedar siding and a tasteful use of brick give this home the high curb appeal that today's buyer is looking for.

Upon entering through the angled double doors, you are welcomed by the elegantly arched entry of the dining room and the inviting step down into the living room. Both rooms are enhanced with a vaulted ceiling. To your left are double doors that lead to an optional fourth bedroom or den. Notice the arched top window above, giving the vaulted entry plenty of natural light.

Moving through the house, a spacious kitchen with island and lots of cupboard space awaits you. The nook and family room are open to the kitchen, with all three rooms sharing a vaulted ceiling. Once inside the family room, a brick fireplace, lots of glass and double French doors leading to a covered patio make this room truly a place to relax.

Just off the kitchen is the utility room. Notice the unique placement of the walk-in closet to act as a buffer for the bedrooms. The main bathroom is centrally located between the generously sized bedrooms. The master bedroom is complemented with coved ceiling, double French doors and large walk-in closet. Open to the bedroom is the vaulted bath, complete with a large vanity, oversized spa tub, shower and linen closet. Throughout this 2,153 square foot home, the angled walls, well placed windows and outstanding design make this home a welcomed part of any neighborhood.

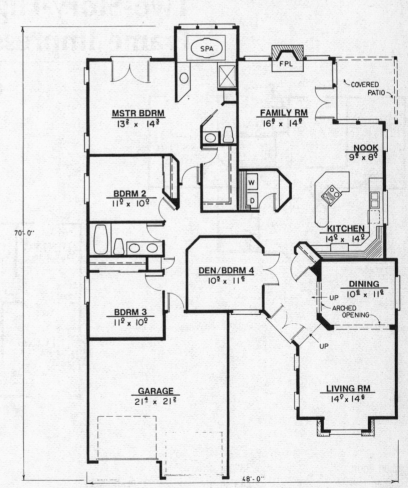

PLAN I-2153-A
WITHOUT BASEMENT
(CRAWLSPACE FOUNDATION)

Total living area: 2,153 sq. ft.

Blueprint Price Code C

Plan I-2153-A

To order blueprints, call
1-800-547-5570 or see order form
and pricing information on pages 220-224

Two-Story-High Brick Columns Frame Impressive Entry

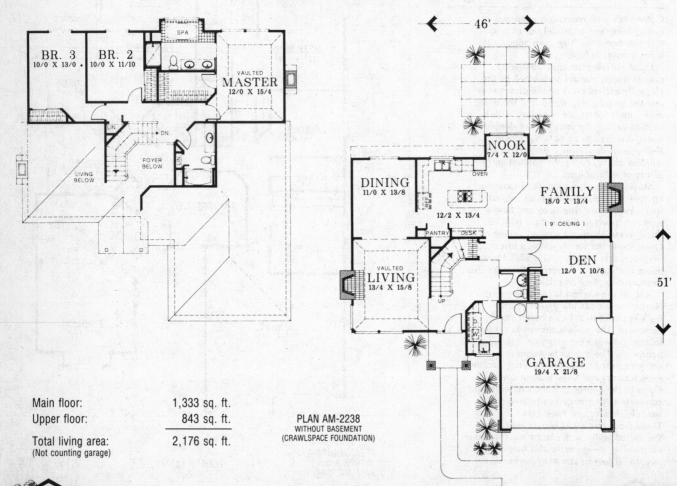

BR. 3
10/0 X 13/0

BR. 2
10/0 X 11/10

SPA

VAULTED
MASTER
12/0 X 15/4

LIN

DN.

LIVING
BELOW

FOYER
BELOW

LIN

← 46' →

NOOK
7/4 X 12/0

DINING
11/0 X 13/8

OVEN

REF

FAMILY
18/0 X 13/4

(9' CEILING)

12/2 X 13/4

PANTRY

DESK

VAULTED
LIVING
13/4 X 15/8

UP

DEN
12/0 X 10/8

51'

GARAGE
19/4 X 21/8

Main floor:	1,333 sq. ft.
Upper floor:	843 sq. ft.
Total living area: (Not counting garage)	2,176 sq. ft.

PLAN AM-2238
WITHOUT BASEMENT
(CRAWLSPACE FOUNDATION)

HomeStyles
SOURCE 1
DESIGNERS NETWORK

Blueprint Price Code C

Plan AM-2238

To order blueprints, call
1-800-547-5570 or see order form
and pricing information on pages 220-224.

Deluxe Master Suite on Second Floor

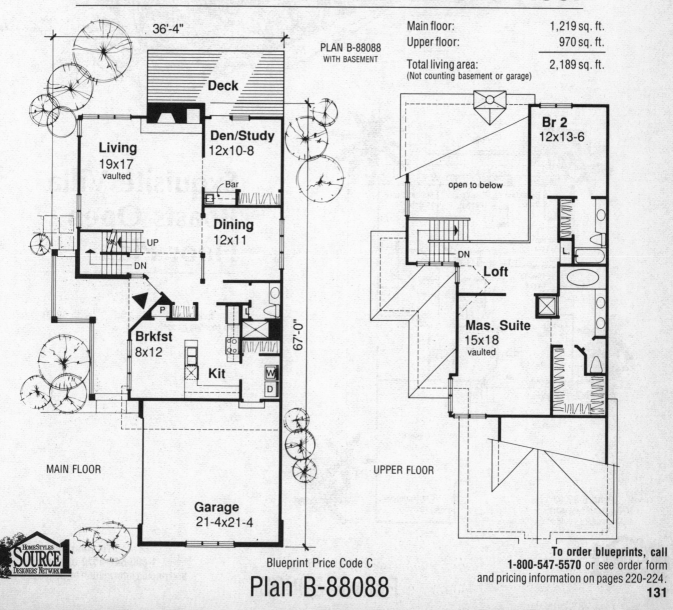

PLAN B-88088
WITH BASEMENT

Main floor:	1,219 sq. ft.
Upper floor:	970 sq. ft.
Total living area: (Not counting basement or garage)	**2,189 sq. ft.**

36'-4"

Deck

Living
19x17
vaulted

Den/Study
12x10-8

Bar

Dining
12x11

UP

DN

P

Brkfst
8x12

Kit

W
D

67'-0"

MAIN FLOOR

Garage
21-4x21-4

Br 2
12x13-6

open to below

DN

Loft

Mas. Suite
15x18
vaulted

UPPER FLOOR

Blueprint Price Code C

Plan B-88088

To order blueprints, call
1-800-547-5570 or see order form
and pricing information on pages 220-224.

HomeStyles
SOURCE 1
DESIGNERS NETWORK

Floor Plan

50'-0"

Pool

| Breakfast 9x10 | Family 18x17-2 | Master Suite 14-6x15-6 |

Kitchen 16x11-4

Bar

Dining 14x11

Garden

Mech

Living 12-8x16

Den/Br 3 10-8x13

Br 2 12-9x13

83'-0"

Garage 23-6x24

1 Car (optional) 20x10

PLAN B-89003
WITHOUT BASEMENT
(SLAB-ON-GRADE FOUNDATION)

Exquisite Villa Boasts Open Floor Plan

Total living area: 2,235 sq. ft.
(Not counting garage)

HomeStyles SOURCE 1 DESIGNERS' NETWORK

Blueprint Price Code C

Plan B-89003

To order blueprints, call
1-800-547-5570 or see order form
and pricing information on pages 220-224

Big Space for Small Lot

- Simplicity and construction economy are benefits of this classic design.
- From the impressive foyer to the spacious master bedroom, this home gives the impression of being much larger than it actually is.
- The master bath features a step-up tub and separate shower.
- Note the second-floor laundry area and convenient entry to second bath from both secondary bedrooms.
- A downstairs guest bedroom with bath would also serve nicely as a home office.
- Kitchen and breakfast nook combine for a 'country kitchen' effect.
- Large Great Room includes a fireplace.

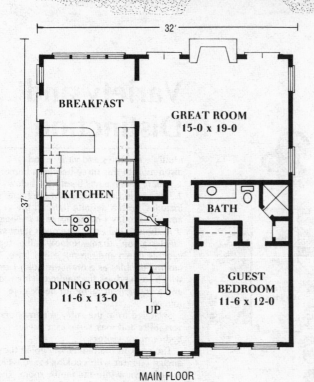

BREAKFAST

GREAT ROOM
15-0 x 19-0

KITCHEN

BATH

DINING ROOM
11-6 x 13-0

UP

GUEST BEDROOM
11-6 x 12-0

32'

37'

MAIN FLOOR

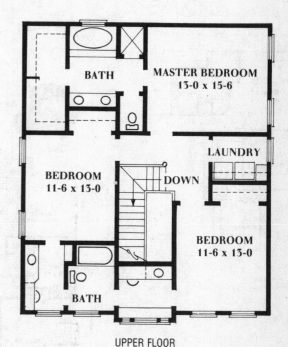

BATH

MASTER BEDROOM
13-0 x 15-6

BEDROOM
11-6 x 13-0

DOWN

LAUNDRY

BATH

BEDROOM
11-6 x 13-0

UPPER FLOOR

Plan V-2240-C

Bedrooms: 3-4	Baths: 3

Space:

Upper floor:	1,080 sq. ft.
Main floor:	1,160 sq. ft.
Total living area:	2,240 sq. ft.
Exterior Wall Framing:	2x6

Ceiling Heights:

Upper floor:	8'
Main floor:	9'

Foundation options:
Crawlspace only.
(Foundation & framing conversion diagram available — see order form.)

Blueprint Price Code:	C

HomeStyles **SOURCE 1** DESIGNERS NETWORK

To order blueprints, call
1-800-547-5570 or see order form
and pricing information on pages 220-224.

Plan V-2240-C

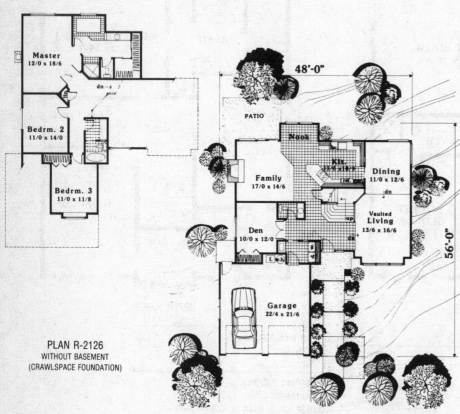

Master
12/0 x 18/6

Bedrm. 2
11/0 x 14/0

Bedrm. 3
11/0 x 11/8

dn

PATIO

48'-0"

Nook

Kit.
11/6 x10/9

Family
17/0 x 14/6

Dining
11/0 x 12/6

dn

up

Vaulted Living
13/6 x 16/6

Den
10/0 x 12/0

56'-0"

Garage
22/4 x 21/6

PLAN R-2126
WITHOUT BASEMENT
(CRAWLSPACE FOUNDATION)

Variety and Distinction

Multiple rooflines add variety and distinction to this three-bedroom home.

Square footage has been kept below 2,300 feet in this design. But the home still includes, with a definite flair, all the amenities today's home buyer is seeking.

In the vaulted entry, the open staircase creates a bold, dramatic look as the steps cascade down and fan out at the base. The landing doubles as a dramatic point from which to overlook the vaulted living room and a convenient niche for decorative foliage.

Secluded from the entry, a den offers versatility and may serve as a guest bedroom for visitors.

The cook in the family will enjoy the angled counter with cooking range which affords a view into the family room. The fireplace with raised hearth can be enjoyed from the kitchen and the nook.

Upstairs, the master bedroom includes a great bath with tiled spa tub and shower, plus a large wardrobe closet with mirrored bypass doors.

Main floor:	1,298 sq. ft.
Upper floor:	964 sq. ft.
Total living area:	2,262 sq. ft.
(Not counting garage)	

Blueprint Price Code C
Plan R-2126

To order blueprints, call
1-800-547-5570 or see order form
and pricing information on pages 220-224

Chalet Style for Town or Country

Exposed wooden beams and vertical board siding, viewing decks with cut-out railings, and an expansive great room lend a chalet feeling to this multi-level home. This home is especially suited for a sloping lot with a view — in an urban neighborhood or on a country site.

A flight of stairs leads to the raised wood deck surrounding two sides of the house, and to the dormer sheltered front door. The entry hall sorts traffic to the 1,103 sq. ft. main floor, and stairs lead to the 665 sq. ft. upper level or the 532 sq. ft. lower floor.

To the left of the entry, the exposed beam great room encompasses the open ceiling dining area and the spacious kitchen, all warmed with a large, masonry fireplace. A window wall overlooks the deck, reached through sliding glass doors. Two bedrooms share the full bath on this floor.

The master bedroom suite has a wall-length closet and skylit bath. It and the loft share the beamed ceiling upper floor, and both rooms have viewing decks. The recreation room on the daylight basement level has a woodstove and sliding glass doors leading to a patio, plus a three-quarters bath and doors to the garage.

PLAN P-531-2D
WITH DAYLIGHT BASEMENT

UPPER FLOOR

MASTER SUITE 15/3x13/0
DN
GUN RACK
OPEN TO BELOW
LOFT 12/0x15/0

MAIN FLOOR

28'-0"
BEDRM.2 11/0x10/8
BEDRM.3 10/0x14/0
D W
UTIL.
SKI RACK
LINEN
ENTRY
KITCHEN 9/9x11/6
DN UP
EXP. BMS.
DINING
GREAT RM. 27/0x15/0
DN
40'-0"
DECK 32/0x10/0
10'-0"

LOWER FLOOR

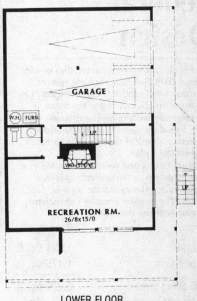

GARAGE
W.H. FURN
UP
WD-STOVE
RECREATION RM. 26/8x15/0
UP

Main floor:	1,103 sq. ft.
Upper floor:	665 sq. ft.
Lower floor:	532 sq. ft.
Total living area: (Not counting garage)	2,300 sq. ft.

Blueprint Price Code C
Plan P-531-2D

Modern Interior in Classic Federal Design

Two of the primary characteristics of the Federal (late Georgian) era are splayed keystone lintels and intricate fanlights. Our version carefully maintains the flavor of the original dwelling on the exterior, yet such a modern amenity as the spacious kitchen is a radical departure from the original floor plan!

A first-floor guest room can double as a study. Upstairs, a particularly spacious master suite offers separate walk-in closets. The laundry room is conveniently located near the bedrooms.

9' CEILINGS THROUGHOUT BOTH FLOORS

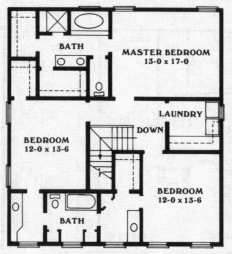

SECOND FLOOR

BATH

MASTER BEDROOM
13-0 x 17-0

LAUNDRY

DOWN

BEDROOM
12-0 x 13-6

BEDROOM
12-0 x 13-6

BATH

FIRST FLOOR

34'

GARAGE
23-0 x 24-0

BREAKFAST

GREAT ROOM
16-0 x 20-6

KITCHEN

BATH

DINING ROOM
12-0 x 14-0

GUEST BEDROOM
12-0 x 13-0

UP

60'

First floor:	1,224 sq. ft.
Second floor:	1,175 sq. ft.
Total living area:	2,399 sq. ft.
(Not counting garage)	

PLAN V-2399-C
WITHOUT BASEMENT
(CRAWLSPACE FOUNDATION)

Blueprint Price Code C
Plan V-2399-C

To order blueprints, call
1-800-547-5570 or see order form
and pricing information on pages 220-224.

Solid, Permanent, Classic Design

First floor:	1,549 sq. ft.
Second floor:	1,059 sq. ft.
Total living area:	2,608 sq. ft.

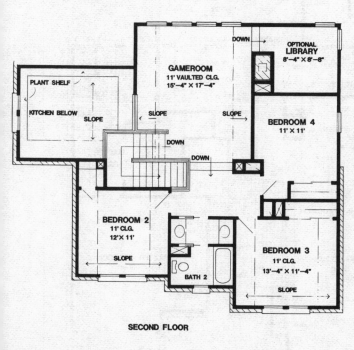

SECOND FLOOR

PLANT SHELF
KITCHEN BELOW
SLOPE

GAMEROOM
11' VAULTED CLG.
15'-4" × 17'-4"

OPTIONAL LIBRARY
8'-4" × 8'-8"

DOWN

SLOPE SLOPE SLOPE

BEDROOM 4
11' × 11'

DOWN
DOWN

BEDROOM 2
11' CLG.
12'× 11'
SLOPE

BATH 2

BEDROOM 3
11' CLG.
13'-4" × 11'-4"
SLOPE

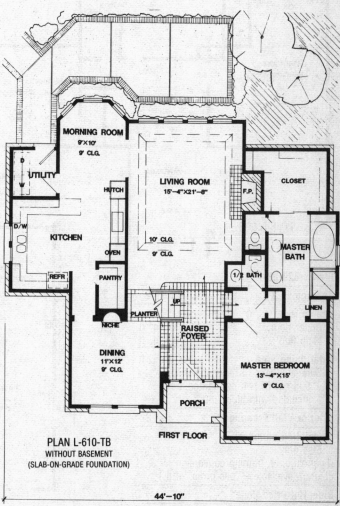

MORNING ROOM
9'×10'
9' CLG.

UTILITY

LIVING ROOM
15'-4"×21'-6"

CLOSET

F.P.

HUTCH

D/W

KITCHEN

10' CLG.
9' CLG.

MASTER BATH

OVEN

1/2 BATH

REFR

PANTRY

LINEN

NICHE

PLANTER

UP

RAISED FOYER

DINING
11'×12'
9' CLG.

MASTER BEDROOM
13'-4" × 15'
9' CLG.

PORCH

FIRST FLOOR

PLAN L-610-TB
WITHOUT BASEMENT
(SLAB-ON-GRADE FOUNDATION)

44'–10"

Blueprint Price Code D
Plan L-610-TB

To order blueprints, call
1-800-547-5570 or see order form
and pricing information on pages 220-224.

Super Kitchen, Deluxe Master Bedroom Suite

- This elegant home looks compact and cozy but is actually quite spacious — from its raised foyer to a big upstairs game room.
- A huge living/dining room combination provides a magnificent space for entertaining, especially with the 14' ceiling over the living room.
- An expansive kitchen/breakfast area gives plenty of elbow room for an active family.
- A lavish master suite includes a superb bath and huge closets.

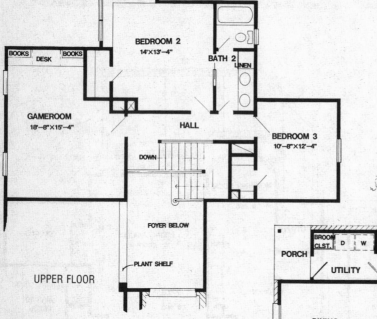

UPPER FLOOR

Plan L-629-EB

Bedrooms: 3	**Baths:** 2½

Space:
Upper floor: 832 sq. ft.
Main floor: 1,795 sq. ft.

Total living area: 2,627 sq. ft.
Garage: (Plans for a detached 505 sq. ft. two-car garage are included with blueprints.)

Exterior Wall Framing: 2x4

Foundation options:
Slab only.
(Foundation & framing conversion diagram available — see order form.)

Blueprint Price Code: D

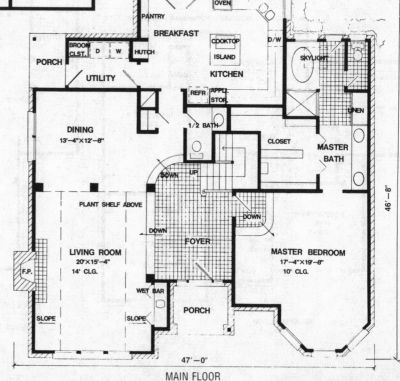

MAIN FLOOR

Plan L-629-EB

138

To order blueprints, call
1-800-547-5570 or see order form and pricing information on pages 220-224.

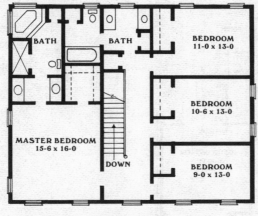

PLAN V-2724-C
WITHOUT BASEMENT
(CRAWLSPACE FOUNDATION)

BATH

BATH

BEDROOM
11-0 x 13-0

BEDROOM
10-6 x 13-0

MASTER BEDROOM
15-6 x 16-0

DOWN

BEDROOM
9-0 x 13-0

SECOND FLOOR

(9' CEILINGS THROUGHOUT BOTH FLOORS)

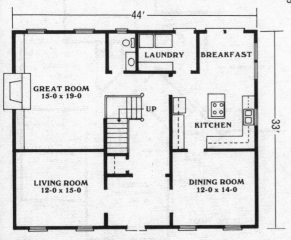

44'

LAUNDRY   BREAKFAST

GREAT ROOM
15-0 x 19-0

UP

KITCHEN

33'

LIVING ROOM
12-0 x 15-0

DINING ROOM
12-0 x 14-0

FIRST FLOOR

Designed for Formal or Casual Living

This imposing residence was inspired by the General Leavenworth mansion in Syracuse, New York. Appearing much larger than its square footage indicates, our rendition of this impressive house contains formal areas as well as family rooms. The beautiful staircase descends conveniently between the kitchen and the Great Room, only a few steps away from the walk-in laundry room.

The second floor contains a luxurious master suite, with an oversized shower and a corner whirlpool surrounded by windows. Three bedrooms share a divided bath.

First floor:	1,386 sq. ft.
Second floor:	1,338 sq. ft.
Total living area:	2,724 sq. ft.

Blueprint Price Code D

Plan V-2724-C

To order blueprints, call
1-800-547-5570 or see order form
and pricing information on pages 220-224.

139

Stately Outside, Comfortable Inside

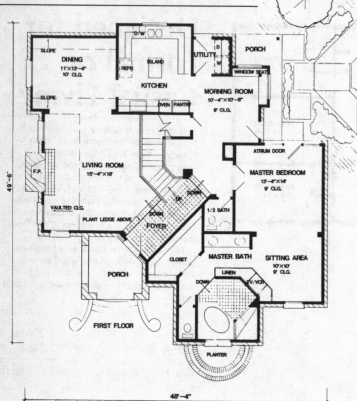

First floor:	1,695 sq. ft.
Second floor:	1,033 sq. ft.
Total living area:	2,728 sq. ft.

(Plans for a detached two-car garage are included with blueprints.)

PLAN L-730-EM-2B
WITHOUT BASEMENT
(SLAB-ON-GRADE FOUNDATION)

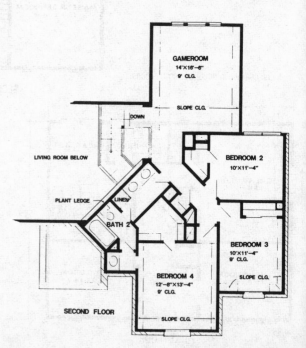

Blueprint Price Code D
Plan L-730-EM-2B

To order blueprints, call
1-800-547-5570 or see order form
and pricing information on pages 220-224.

Victorian Surprise & Whimsy

Collectors of Victorian furniture and ornament will find this house an irresistible backdrop for displaying their carefully

acquired objects. The high-ceilinged rooms, with their many angles and bays, accurately reflect the Victorian love of surprise and whimsy. And the abundance of windows in this irresistible plan echoes the Victorian reverence for light and ventilation.

On the second floor, two of the three hall bedrooms share a compartmentalized bath, while the third bedroom has its own. The luxurious master suite contains a spectacular whirlpool tub.

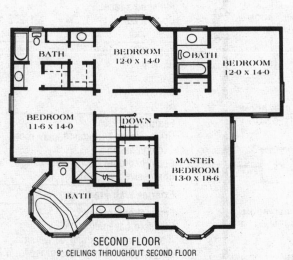

SECOND FLOOR
9' CEILINGS THROUGHOUT SECOND FLOOR

BATH
BEDROOM 12-0 x 14-0
BATH
BEDROOM 12-0 x 14-0
BEDROOM 11-6 x 14-0
DOWN
MASTER BEDROOM 13-0 x 18-6
BATH

First floor: 1,417 sq. ft.
Second floor: 1,380 sq. ft.

Total living area: 2,797 sq. ft.

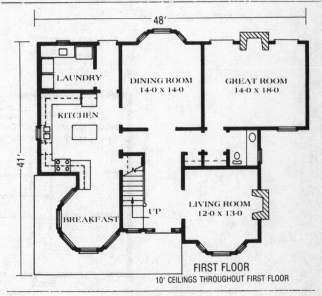

48'
41'
LAUNDRY
DINING ROOM 14-0 x 14-0
GREAT ROOM 14-0 x 18-0
KITCHEN
BREAKFAST
UP
LIVING ROOM 12-0 x 13-0

FIRST FLOOR
10' CEILINGS THROUGHOUT FIRST FLOOR

PLAN V-2797-C
WITHOUT BASEMENT
(CRAWLSPACE FOUNDATION)

HomeStyles **SOURCE 1** DESIGNERS' NETWORK

Blueprint Price Code D

Plan V-2797-C

To order blueprints, call
1-800-547-5570 or see order form
and pricing information on pages 220-224.

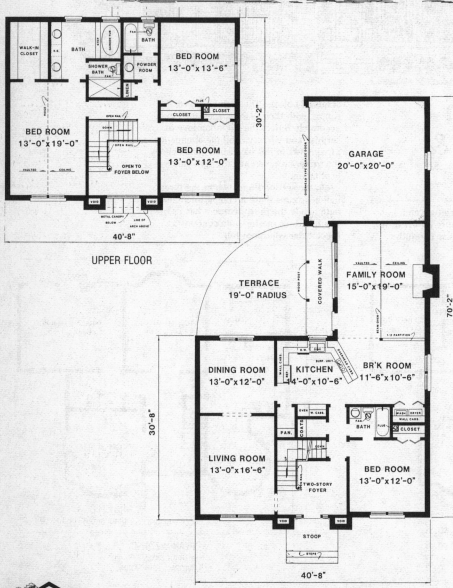

UPPER FLOOR

Walk-In Closet · Bath · Bath · Powder Room · Shower Bath · Linen · Closet · Closet
BED ROOM 13'-0" x 13'-6"
BED ROOM 13'-0" x 19'-0"
BED ROOM 13'-0" x 12'-0"
Open To Foyer Below · Open Rail · Down
30'-2"
40'-8"
Vaulted Ceiling · Void · Void · Metal Canopy Below · Line Of Arch Above

MAIN FLOOR

GARAGE 20'-0" x 20'-0"
Overhead Type Garage Door
FAMILY ROOM 15'-0" x 19'-0" · Vaulted Ceiling
TERRACE 19'-0" RADIUS
COVERED WALK · Wood Post
70'-2"
DINING ROOM 13'-0" x 12'-0"
KITCHEN 14'-0" x 10'-6"
BR'K ROOM 11'-6" x 10'-6"
LIVING ROOM 13'-0" x 16'-6"
Bath
BED ROOM 13'-0" x 12'-0"
TWO-STORY FOYER
30'-8"
Wash · Dryer · Closet · Pan. · Coats · Down
Void · Void
STOOP · Steps
40'-8"

The Solid, Substantial Look of Brick

Plan W-2839

Bedrooms: 4	Baths: 3

Finished space:

Upper floor:	1,252 sq. ft.
Main floor:	1,570 sq. ft.

Total living area:	**2,822 sq. ft.**
Basement:	1,246 sq. ft.
Garage:	452 sq. ft.
Covered walk:	95 sq. ft.
Stoop:	47 sq. ft.

Features:
Great kitchen/breakfast/family room combination.
Guest bedroom downstairs with full bath.
Impressive two-story foyer.

Exterior Wall Framing:	2x4

Foundation options:
Standard basement only.
(Foundation & framing conversion diagram available — see order form.)

Blueprint Price Code:	D

Plan W-2839

Separate Family and Formal Zones

Here's a home you'll never outgrow. It has all the ingredients of a true classic — an efficient floor plan for day-to-day living complemented by a light and open interior.

This plan is particularly well suited for families with children who enjoy entertaining and prefer to keep their formal living area well away from the family room and kitchen. Just off the entry, double doors usher you into the kitchen/nook and family room area which can be completely closed off.

The kitchen is highlighted by a spacious walk-in pantry for extra storage space and a bright, cheerful corner window. Note that the family room is heightened by a vaulted ceiling and is overlooked by the upstairs hallway and den.

You'll find your own secluded hide-a-way upstairs. The master suite comes complete with a sunny alcove and French doors that open on to a private deck. Illuminated by a skylight, the master bath boasts a luxurious whirlpool tub and spacious closet.

Main floor:	1,525 sq. ft.
Upper floor:	1,367 sq. ft.
Total living area: (Not counting garage)	2,892 sq. ft.

PLAN R-2025
WITHOUT BASEMENT
(CRAWLSPACE FOUNDATION)

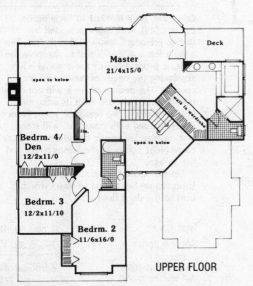

UPPER FLOOR

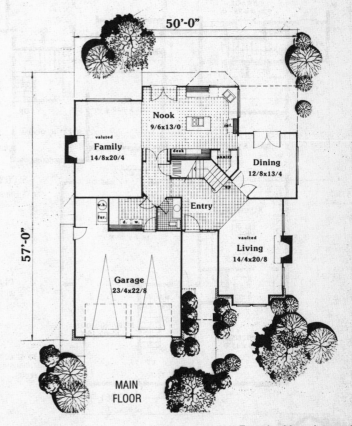

MAIN FLOOR

Blueprint Price Code D

Plan R-2025

To order blueprints, call
1-800-547-5570 or see order form
and pricing information on pages 220-224

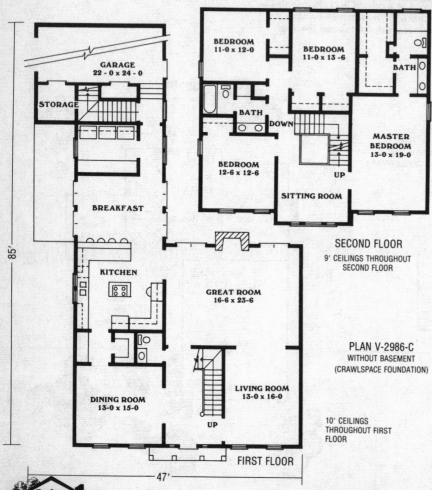

GARAGE
22 - 0 x 24 - 0

STORAGE

BREAKFAST

KITCHEN

GREAT ROOM
16-6 x 23-6

DINING ROOM
13-0 x 15-0

LIVING ROOM
13-0 x 16-0

UP

UP

FIRST FLOOR

10' CEILINGS
THROUGHOUT FIRST
FLOOR

85'

47'

BEDROOM
11-0 x 12-0

BEDROOM
11-0 x 13 -6

BATH

BATH

DOWN

MASTER
BEDROOM
13-0 x 19-0

BEDROOM
12-6 x 12-6

SITTING ROOM

UP

SECOND FLOOR

9' CEILINGS THROUGHOUT
SECOND FLOOR

PLAN V-2986-C
WITHOUT BASEMENT
(CRAWLSPACE FOUNDATION)

Historic Design Adapted to Today's Needs

Old Gate, built in 1781 in Farmington, Connecticut, with labor provided by British prisoners, inspired this design. This adaptation was developed to preserve the historic proportions of the original while answering the needs of contemporary couples. The dedicated cook will appreciate the oversized kitchen with its adjacent butler's pantry. The breakfast room French doors, topped with transoms, will stand ajar on fragrant spring mornings. Note the convenient access to the bonus room and the garage.

On the second floor, the light-filled sitting room has access to stairs which lead to the third floor attic.

First floor:	1,680 sq. ft.
Second floor:	1,306 sq. ft.
Total living area: (Not counting garage)	2,986 sq. ft.

Blueprint Price Code D

Plan V-2986-C

To order blueprints, call
1-800-547-5570 or see order form
and pricing information on pages 220-224.

A Glorious Blend of New and Old

This three-bedroom, two and one-half-bath home is a glorious blend of contemporary and traditional lines. Inside, its 2,035 sq. ft. are wisely distributed among amply proportioned, practically appointed rooms. A vaulted entry gives way to a second reception area bordering on a broad, vaulted living room nearly 20' long.

With its walls of windows overlooking the back yard, this grand room's centerpiece is a massive woodstove, whose central location contributes extra energy efficiency to the home — upstairs as well as down. The dining room offers quiet separation from the living room, while still enjoying the warmth from its woodstove. Its sliding door accesses a large wraparound covered patio to create a cool, shady refuge.

For sun-seeking, another wraparound patio at the front is fenced but uncovered, and elegantly accessed by double doors from a well-lighted, vaulted nook.

Placed conveniently between the two dining areas is a kitchen with all the trimmings: pantry, large sink window, and an expansive breakfast bar.

A stylish upstairs landing overlooks the living room on one side and the entry on the other, and leads to a master suite that rambles over fully half of the second floor.

Adjacent to the huge bedroom area is a spacious dressing area bordered by an abundance of closet space and a double-sink bath area. Unusual extras include walk-in wardrobe in the third bedroom and the long double-sink counter in the second upstairs bath.

Note also the exceptional abundance of closet space on both floors, and the separate utility room that also serves as a clean-up room connecting with the garage.

Main floor:	950 sq. ft.
Upper floor:	1,085 sq. ft.
Total living area:	2,035 sq. ft.
(Not counting basement or garage)	

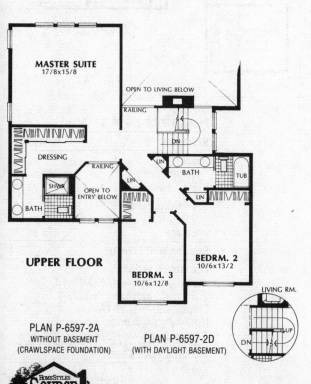

MASTER SUITE 17/8x15/8

OPEN TO LIVING BELOW

RAILING

DRESSING

RAILING

SHWR

OPEN TO ENTRY BELOW

BATH

DN

LIN

BATH

TUB

LIN

LIN

UPPER FLOOR

BEDRM. 3 10/6x12/8

BEDRM. 2 10/6x13/2

LIVING RM.

UP

DN

PLAN P-6597-2A
WITHOUT BASEMENT
(CRAWLSPACE FOUNDATION)

PLAN P-6597-2D
(WITH DAYLIGHT BASEMENT)

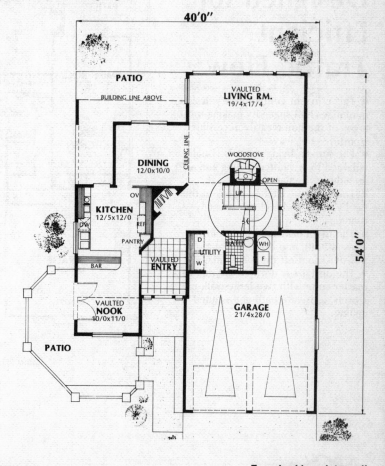

40'0"

PATIO

BUILDING LINE ABOVE

VAULTED LIVING RM. 19/4x17/4

CEILING LINE

DINING 12/0x10/0

WOODSTOVE

OPEN

UP

OV

KITCHEN 12/5x12/0

DW

REF

PANTRY

D

W

UTILITY

BATH

WH

F

BAR

VAULTED ENTRY

54'0"

VAULTED NOOK 10/0x11/0

GARAGE 21/4x28/0

PATIO

Blueprint Price Code C

Plans P-6597-2A & P-6597-2D

Carefully Designed for Efficient Traffic Flow

- This efficient contemporary design minimizes hall space by making most areas of the home easily accessible from the entryway.
- The sunken living room is visually enlarged by a vaulted ceiling and also includes a fireplace.
- The spacious kitchen opens to the family room and includes a handy island.
- The two downstairs bedrooms share a bath, and there is also a powder room off the main entry.
- The upstairs is devoted entirely to a master suite with two large walk-in closets, a private bath and vaulted ceiling.

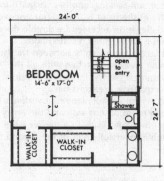

UPPER FLOOR

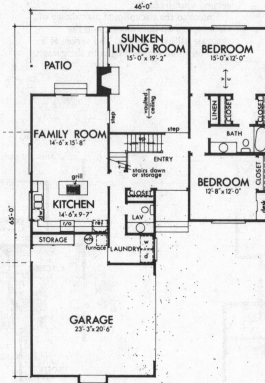

MAIN FLOOR

Plans H-3709-1, -1A & -1B

Bedrooms: 3	Baths: 2½
Space:	
Upper floor:	497 sq. ft.
Main floor:	1,545 sq. ft.
Total living area:	2,042 sq. ft.
Basement:	± 1,545 sq. ft.
Garage:	476 sq. ft.
Exterior Wall Framing:	2x4

Foundation options:
Daylight basement, H-3709-1B.
Standard basement, H-3709-1.
Crawlspace, H-3709-1A.
(Foundation & framing conversion diagram available — see order form.)

Blueprint Price Code:	C

To order blueprints, call
1-800-547-5570 or see order form
and pricing information on pages 220-224.

146

Plan H-3709-1, -1A & -1B

Space and Luxury

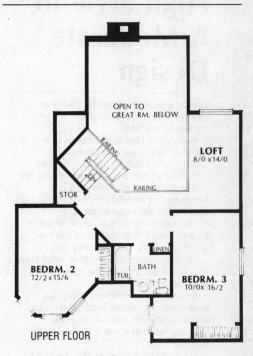

40'0"

DECK

SUNKEN TUB

BATH

PATIO

VAULTED
GREAT RM.
15/4 x 21/0

DINING
10/0 x 14/0

SKYLIGHTS

RAILING UP

MASTER
12/0 x 16/0

ENTRY

BATH

KITCHEN
11/6 x 11/0

DW

NOOK
13/0 x 8/0

REF

PANTRY

STORAGE

72'0"

PATIO

COURTYARD

UTILITY

D   W

FENCE

F

WH

GARAGE
21/4 x 20/6

MAIN FLOOR
PLAN P-6593-3A
WITHOUT BASEMENT
(CRAWLSPACE FOUNDATION)

Main floor: 1,427 sq. ft.
Upper floor: 707 sq. ft.
Total living area: 2,134 sq. ft.
(Not counting garage)

OPEN TO
GREAT RM. BELOW

LOFT
8/0 x 14/0

RAILING

DN

RAILING

STOR.

BEDRM. 2
12/2 x 15/6

TUB

LINEN

BATH

BEDRM. 3
10/0 x 16/2

UPPER FLOOR

DN

UP

PLAN P-6593-3D
WITH DAYLIGHT BASEMENT

Basement level: 1,427 sq. ft.

Blueprint Price Code C

To order blueprints, call
1-800-547-5570 or see order form
and pricing information on pages 220-224.

Plans P-6593-3A & P-6593-3D

High Style in A Moderate Design

Sweeping roof lines amplify the clean exterior of this wood-finished contemporary home.

Majority of glass is positioned at rear of home for maximum solar benefit. A sunspace may also be added if desired.

Interior of home is designed around the "open plan concept," allowing free movement of air while visually borrowing space from the adjacent areas.

The vaulted entry features a clerestory located over the second-floor balcony, which overlooks the first floor spaces.

Kitchen, family and breakfast nook areas may be zoned off from the more formal areas of the home.

A large master bedroom features a walk-in closet, master bath, shower, tub and a deck to the rear of the home.

Living room of home is vaulted to the balcony level.

Total square footage of this residence is 2,139. Building dimensions are 50' wide by 52' deep. Please specify type of basement version desired.

Total living area: 2,139 sq. ft.
(Not counting basement or garage)

Exterior walls are 2x6 construction.

SECOND LEVEL

PLAN S-2001
WITHOUT BASEMENT
(CRAWLSPACE FOUNDATION)

PLAN S-2001-FB
FULL BASEMENT VERSION

PLAN S-2001-DB
DAYLIGHT BASEMENT VERSION

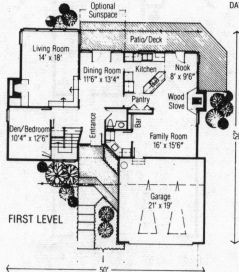

FIRST LEVEL

HomeStyles
SOURCE 1
DESIGNERS NETWORK

Blueprint Price Code C

Plans S-2001, S-2001-FB & S-2001-DB

To order blueprints, call
1-800-547-5570 or see order form
and pricing information on pages 220-224.

REAR VIEW

A Striking Contemporary

A multiplicity of decks and outcroppings along with unusual window arrangements combine to establish this striking contemporary as a classic type of architecture. To adapt to the sloping terrain, the structure has three levels of living space on the downhill side. As one moves around the house from the entry to the various rooms and living areas, both the appearance and function of the different spaces change, as do the angular forms and cutouts that define the floor plan arrangement. Almost all the rooms are flooded with an abundance of daylight, yet are shielded by projections of wing walls and roof surfaces to assure privacy as well as to block undesirable direct rays of sunshine.

The design projects open planning of a spacious living room that connects with the dining and kitchen area. The home features four large bedrooms, two of which have walk-in closets and private baths. The remaining two bedrooms also have an abundance of wardrobe space, and the rooms are of generous proportions.

For energy efficiency, exterior walls are framed with 2x6 studs.

First floor:	1,216 sq. ft.
Second floor:	958 sq. ft.
Total living area: (Not counting basement or garage)	2,174 sq. ft.
Basement:	1,019 sq. ft.

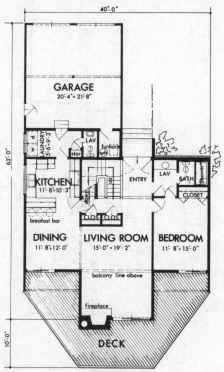

FIRST FLOOR
1216 SQUARE FEET

PLAN H-914-1A
WITHOUT BASEMENT
(CRAWLSPACE FOUNDATION)

PLAN H-914-1
WITH BASEMENT

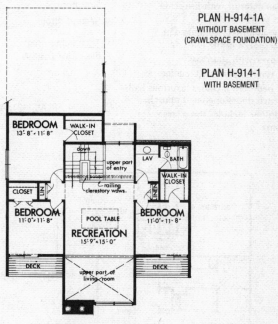

SECOND FLOOR
958 SQUARE FEET

HomeStyles SOURCE 1 DESIGNERS NETWORK

Blueprint Price Code C

Plans H-914-1 & H-914-1A

To order blueprints, call
1-800-547-5570 or see order form and pricing information on pages 220-224.
149

Open Interior in Victorian Home

- Victorian exterior with fish-scale shingles on gable.
- Wide wrap-around veranda with optional piazza at the left side.
- Open foyer with staircase.
- Dining room features 13' ceiling.
- Master bedroom includes luxurious bath and French doors opening to porch.
- Second floor includes three large bedrooms.

First floor: 1,351 sq. ft.
Second floor: 862 sq. ft.

Total living area: 2,213 sq. ft.
(Not counting garage)

PLAN L-215-VSB
WITHOUT BASEMENT
(SLAB-ON-GRADE FOUNDATION)

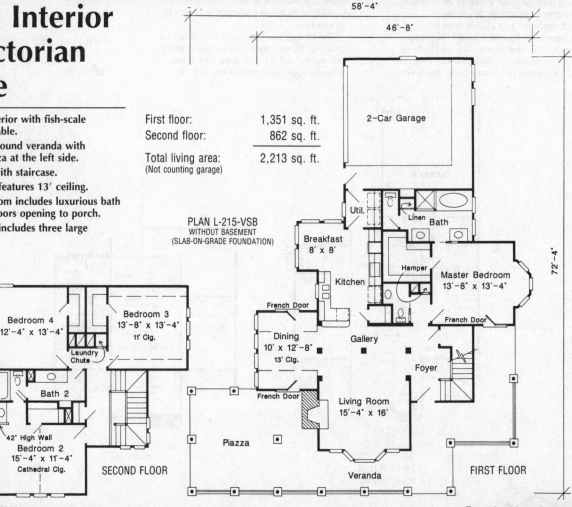

Blueprint Price Code C

Plan L-215-VSB

To order blueprints, call
1-800-547-5570 or see order form and pricing information on pages 220-224.

Cozy & Stylish

First floor:	1,290 sq. ft.
Second floor:	932 sq. ft.
Total living area:	**2,222 sq. ft.**
(Not counting basement or garage)	
Bonus room:	228 sq. ft.

Exterior walls are 2x6 construction.

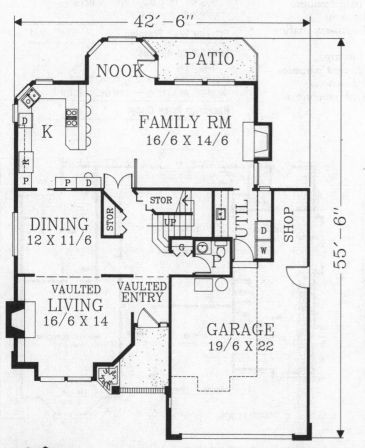

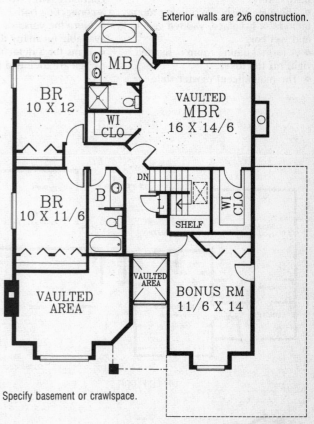

Specify basement or crawlspace.

Blueprint Price Code C

Plan S-70989

To order blueprints, call
1-800-547-5570 or see order form
and pricing information on pages 220-224.

Deluxe Master Bedroom, Spacious Kitchen

- Time-tested traditional design combines brick and wood for an attractive facade.
- A vast kitchen/breakfast area provides abundant space for a large, busy family.
- The generously sized living room includes a fireplace, vaulted ceiling and wet bar.
- A formal dining room is located right off the foyer.
- The magnificent master suite includes bay window at the front, a 10' ceiling, a large walk-in closet and a superb master bath with separate tub and shower plus twin vanities.
- Upstairs, the spaciousness continues, with two bedrooms sharing a connecting bath.
- Note the versatile loft area, available for many different purposes.
- Plans for a detached two-car garage are included with blueprints.

Plan L-2247-C

Bedrooms: 3	**Baths:** 2½

Space:
Upper floor:	735 sq. ft.
Main floor:	1,512 sq. ft.

Total living area: 2,247 sq. ft.
Garage: (Plans for a detached two-car, 505 sq. ft. garage are included with blueprints.)

Exterior Wall Framing: 2x4

Foundation options:
Slab only.
(Foundation & framing conversion diagram available — see order form.)

Blueprint Price Code: C

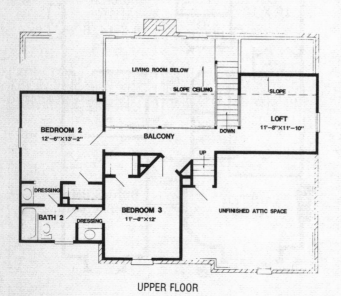

UPPER FLOOR

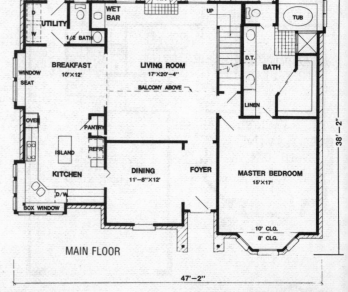

MAIN FLOOR

Plan L-2247-C

Four-Bedroom Contemporary Style

Steeply pitched, multi-level gable rooflines accented by diagonal board siding and tall windows add imposing height to this contemporary, 2,289 sq. ft. home. With most of the 1,389 sq. ft. main floor devoted to the living, dining and family rooms, and a long patio or wood deck accessible off the nook, the home lends itself ideally to family activities and gracious entertaining.

Directly off the spacious foyer is the vaulted-ceiling living room and dining area, brightened with high windows and warmed by a log-sized fireplace. The wide U-shaped kitchen, nook and family room, with wood stove, join and extend across the back half of the main floor. With doors off the nook and utility room leading to a large patio, this area combines for large, informal activities. Also off the front entry hall is a full bathroom, a den or fourth bedroom, and the open stairway, brightened by a skylight, leading to the upper floor.

The master bedroom suite, occupying about half of the upper floor, has a wide picture window, walk-in dressing room/wardrobe, and a skylighted bathroom with sunken tub and separate shower. The other two bedrooms share the hall bathroom. A daylight basement version of the plan further expands the family living and recreation areas of this home.

Main floor:	1,389 sq. ft.
Upper floor:	900 sq. ft.
Total living area: (Not counting basement or garage)	2,289 sq. ft.
Basement level:	1,389 sq. ft.

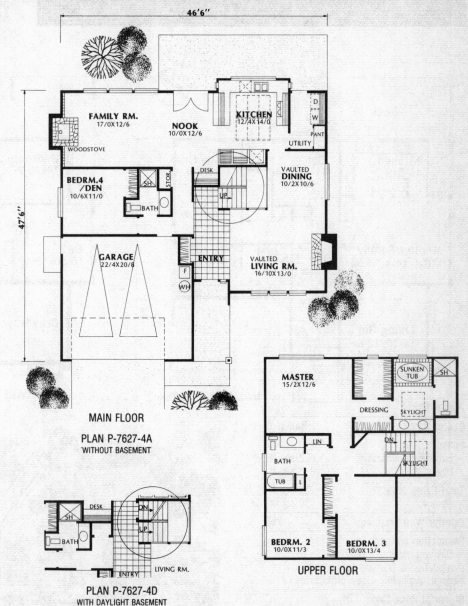

MAIN FLOOR

PLAN P-7627-4A
WITHOUT BASEMENT

PLAN P-7627-4D
WITH DAYLIGHT BASEMENT

UPPER FLOOR

Blueprint Price Code C

Plans P-7627-4A & P-7627-4D

To order blueprints, call
1-800-547-5570 or see order form
and pricing information on pages 220-224.

Charming Design for Hillside Site

- Split-level design puts living room on entry level, other rooms up or down a half-flight of steps.
- Upper level kitchen includes work/eating island and combines with dining/family room for informal living.
- Vaulted master suite includes private bath and large closet.
- Lower level includes two bedrooms, bath, utility area and a rec room.

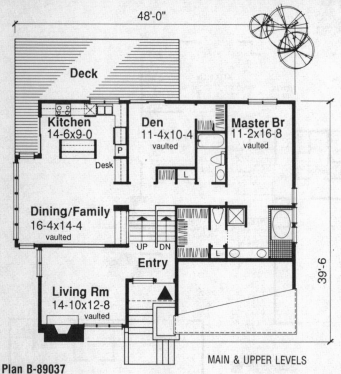

48'-0"

Deck

Kitchen
14-6x9-0

Den
11-4x10-4
vaulted

Master Br
11-2x16-8
vaulted

Desk

P

L

Dining/Family
16-4x14-4
vaulted

UP   DN

Entry

L

Living Rm
14-10x12-8
vaulted

39'-6

MAIN & UPPER LEVELS

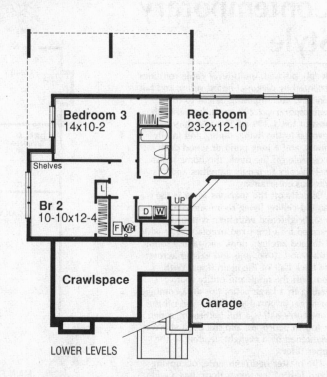

Bedroom 3
14x10-2

Rec Room
23-2x12-10

Shelves

Br 2
10-10x12-4

L

D   W

F

UP

Crawlspace

Garage

LOWER LEVELS

Plan B-89037

Bedrooms: 3	**Baths:** 3

Space:

Entry & upper levels:	1,422 sq. ft.
Lower level:	913 sq. ft.

Total living area:	**2,335 sq. ft.**
Garage:	480 sq. ft.

Exterior Wall Framing:	2x6

Foundation options:
Daylight basement only.
(Foundation & framing conversion diagram available — see order form.)

Blueprint Price Code:	C

Plan B-89037

Gracious Veranda

First floor: 1,357 sq. ft.

Second floor: 1,079 sq. ft.

Total living area: 2,436 sq. ft.
(Not counting garage)

PLAN L-438-VSB
WITHOUT BASEMENT
(SLAB-ON-GRADE FOUNDATION)

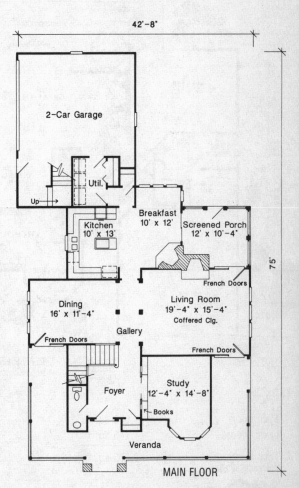

Incline Ladder

Bath Below

Exercise Loft
15 x 13

Optional Exercise Loft
228 Sq. Ft.

Office
16'-4" x 17'

**Optional Second Floor
At Garage**
167 Sq. Ft.

Deck

French Doors

Bedroom 2
12' x 11'-4"

Bath 2

Bath

Bedroom 3
12' x 11'-4"
Cathedral Clg.

Up

Master Bedroom
12'-4" x 15'

Foyer Below

Seat Books

Balcony

Sitting Area
12' Clg.

SECOND FLOOR

42'-8"

2-Car Garage

Up

Util.

Kitchen
10' x 13'

Breakfast
10' x 12'

Screened Porch
12' x 10'-4"

French Doors

Dining
16' x 11'-4"

Living Room
19'-4" x 15'-4"
Coffered Clg.

Gallery

French Doors

French Doors

Foyer

Study
12'-4" x 14'-8"

Books

75'

Veranda

MAIN FLOOR

9' ceilings throughout first and second floors unless otherwise noted.

HomeStyles **SOURCE 1** DESIGNERS NETWORK

Blueprint Price Code C

Plan L-438-VSB

To order blueprints, call
1-800-547-5570 or see order form
and pricing information on pages 220-224.

Simple Exterior, Luxurious Interior

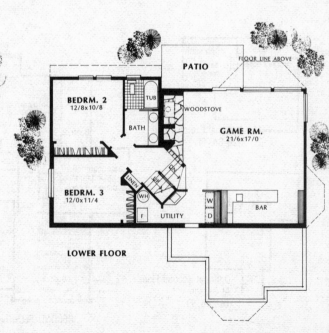

PLAN P-6595-3D
WITH DAYLIGHT BASEMENT

49'3"
50'8"

RAILING
DECK
HOT TUB
MASTER
19/0x14/0
VAULTED GREAT RM.
21/6x17/6
PLNTR.
SUNKEN TUB
DRESSING
LIN
RAIL
VAULTED DINING
14/4x10/6
WALK IN WARDROBE
BATH
SKYLIGHT
PANTRY
REF
VAULTED ENTRY
KITCHEN
13/6x10/6
GARAGE
21/4x21/8
NOOK
10/0x10/0
DW

LOWER FLOOR
PATIO
FLOOR LINE ABOVE
BEDRM. 2
12/8x10/8
TUB
BATH
WOODSTOVE
GAME RM.
21/6x17/0
BEDRM. 3
12/0x11/4
LINEN
REF
WH
UTILITY
F
W D
BAR

Main floor:	1,530 sq. ft.
Lower floor:	1,145 sq. ft.
Total living area: (Not counting garage)	**2,675 sq. ft.**

Blueprint Price Code D

Plan P-6595-3D

To order blueprints, call
1-800-547-5570 or see order form
and pricing information on pages 220-224.

Tomorrow's Interior in Classic Exterior Design

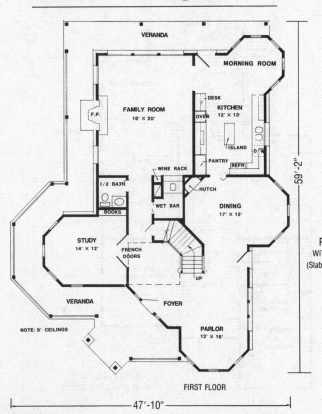

VERANDA

MORNING ROOM

FAMILY ROOM
16' X 20'

F.P.

DESK
OVEN
KITCHEN
12' X 13'

ISLAND
D/W

WINE RACK
PANTRY
REFR

1/2 BATH
HUTCH

BOOKS
WET BAR
DINING
17' X 12'

STUDY
14' X 12'

FRENCH DOORS
UP

VERANDA
FOYER

NOTE: 9' CEILINGS

PARLOR
12' X 16'

FIRST FLOOR

59'-2"

47'-10"

PLAN L-3163
WITHOUT BASEMENT
(Slab-on-grade foundation)

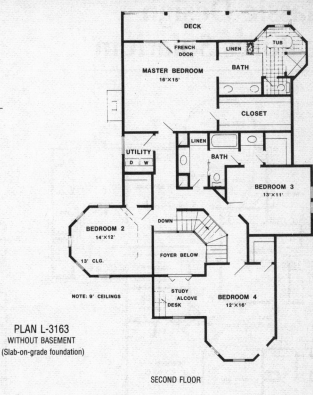

DECK

FRENCH DOOR
LINEN
TUB

MASTER BEDROOM
16' X 15'

BATH

CLOSET

UTILITY
LINEN
D W
BATH

BEDROOM 3
13' X 11'

BEDROOM 2
14' X 12'

DOWN

13' CLG.

FOYER BELOW

NOTE: 9' CEILINGS

STUDY ALCOVE
DESK
BEDROOM 4
12' X 16'

SECOND FLOOR

First floor: 1,565 sq. ft.
Second floor: 1,598 sq. ft.
Total living area: 3,163 sq. ft.
(Plans for a detached two-car garage are included with blueprints)

HomeStyles SOURCE 1
DESIGNERS NETWORK

Blueprint Price Code E
Plan L-3163

To order blueprints, call
1-800-547-5570 or see order form
and pricing information on pages 220-224.

Classic Design
Features Solarium

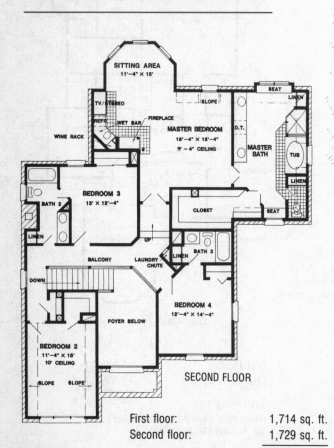

SITTING AREA
11'-4" X 15'

TV/STEREO
SLOPE
SEAT
LINEN

WET BAR
FIREPLACE
REFR.
D.T.

WINE RACK
MASTER BEDROOM
18'-4" X 15'-4"
9'-4" CEILING
MASTER BATH

TUB
BEDROOM 3
13' X 12'-4"

BATH 2
LINEN
CLOSET
SEAT
LINEN

UP
BALCONY
LAUNDRY CHUTE
LINEN
BATH 3
DOWN
BEDROOM 4
12'-4" X 14'-4"

FOYER BELOW

BEDROOM 2
11'-4" X 18'
10' CEILING

SLOPE   SLOPE

SECOND FLOOR

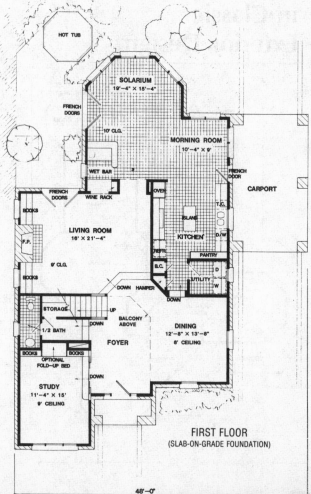

HOT TUB

SOLARIUM
19'-4" X 15'-4"

FRENCH DOORS
10' CLG.
MORNING ROOM
10'-4" X 9'

WET BAR
FRENCH DOOR
OVEN
CARPORT

FRENCH DOORS
WINE RACK
ISLAND
T.C.

BOOKS
LIVING ROOM
16' X 21'-4"
KITCHEN
D/W

F.P.
9' CLG.
REFR.
PANTRY
B.C.
D
UTILITY
W

BOOKS
DOWN HAMPER
DOWN

STORAGE
DOWN
UP
BALCONY ABOVE
DINING
12'-8" X 13'-8"
8' CEILING

1/2 BATH
FOYER

BOOKS
BOOKS
OPTIONAL FOLD-UP BED
DOWN

STUDY
11'-4" X 15'
9' CEILING

FIRST FLOOR
(SLAB-ON-GRADE FOUNDATION)

48'-0"

First floor: 1,714 sq. ft.
Second floor: 1,729 sq. ft.
Total living area: 3,443 sq. ft.

Blueprint Price Code E
Plan L-3443-C

FRONT VIEW

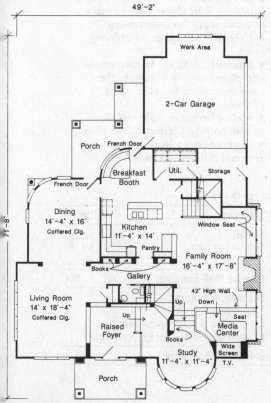

REAR VIEW

Romantic Round Turret

- This shingle-exterior design is reminiscent of the East Coast summer homes of the late 18th Century, the last years of the Victorian Era.
- Exterior detailing includes decorative brackets and numerous windows.
- Other features include the front porch,

round turret, a rear porch and a rear deck above the porch.
- Media center in family room has built-in seating.
- Breakfast area features curved-glass windows and a built-in booth.

First floor: 1,812 sq. ft.
Second floor: 1,997 sq. ft.

Total living area: 3,809 sq. ft.
(Not counting garage)

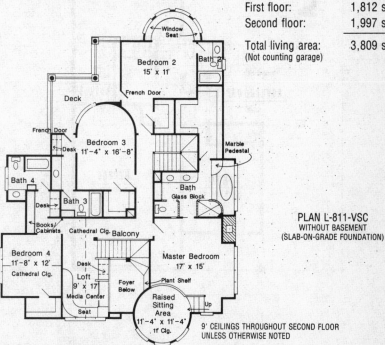

FIRST FLOOR
9' CEILING THROUGHOUT FIRST FLOOR

SECOND FLOOR

PLAN L-811-VSC
WITHOUT BASEMENT
(SLAB-ON-GRADE FOUNDATION)

9' CEILINGS THROUGHOUT SECOND FLOOR
UNLESS OTHERWISE NOTED

Blueprint Price Code E

Plan L-811-VSC

To order blueprints, call
1-800-547-5570 or see order form
and pricing information on pages 220-224.

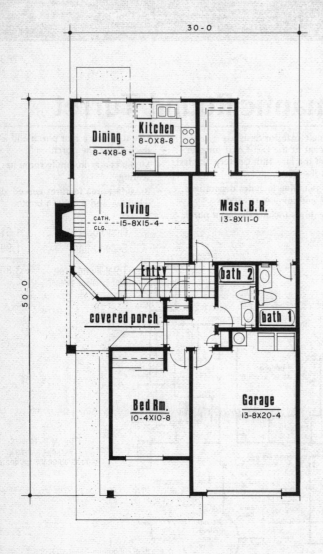

Compact Two-Bedroom Home

- Designed for narrow lots or Zero-lot-line situations.
- Living room with cathedral ceiling combines with dining area to make a pleasant space for entertaining.
- Fireplace is focal point of living room.
- Efficient U-shaped kitchen opens into dining area to eliminate the confined feeling found in many kitchens.
- Master bedroom suite includes private bath and large walk-in closet.
- Covered porch leads into entry area and efficient hallway.

Plan Q-911-1A

Bedrooms: 2	Baths: 2

Space:	
Total living area:	911 sq. ft.
Garage:	278 sq. ft.

Exterior Wall Framing:	2x4

Foundation options:
Slab only.
(Foundation & framing conversion diagram available — see order form.)

Blueprint Price Code:	A

To order blueprints, call 1-800-547-5570 or see order form and pricing information on pages 220-224.

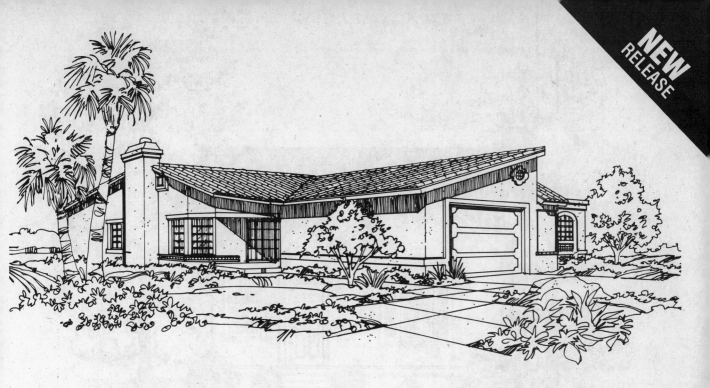

Cozy Home with Spanish Touch

- Cathedral ceiling in living room makes for a feeling of more space.
- Living and dining areas flow together to create space for entertaining and family gatherings.
- Master bedroom has its own bath and a roomy walk-in closet.
- An inviting covered porch with built-in planter leads visitors into a space-saving, efficient entryway.
- Living room includes cozy fireplace.

Plan Q-950-1A

Bedrooms: 2	**Baths:** 2

Total living area: 950 sq. ft.
  Garage: 287 sq. ft.

Exterior Wall Framing: 2x4

Foundation options:
  Slab.
(Foundation & framing conversion diagram available — see order form.)

Blueprint Price Code: A

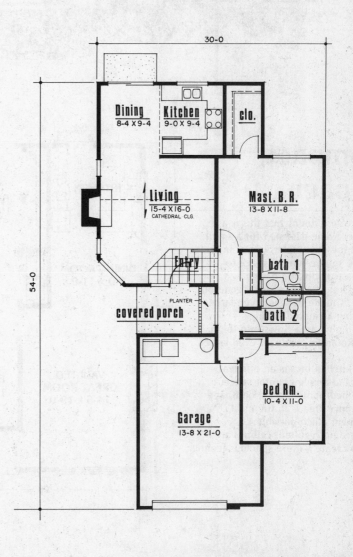

Plan Q-950-1A

To order blueprints, call
1-800-547-5570 or see order form
and pricing information on pages 220-224.

161

Compact Impact

- There's no doubt that this is a compact home designed for a small lot, yet the plan makes use of every possible square foot of space to create a truly livable design.
- The Great Room, already generous in size, is made to seem even larger by adding a vaulted ceiling.
- The dining area flows into the Great Room to create an even larger space.
- The kitchen boasts an efficient design and ample counter space.
- Two bedrooms share a bath, and the laundry area is in the most convenient place possible.
- Where not vaulted, ceilings are 9' high to create a more spacious feeling.

KITCHEN

MASTER BEDROOM
10-6 x 12-0

DINING ROOM
9-0 x 11-0

BATH

VAULTED GREAT ROOM
14-6 x 19-0

BEDROOM
10-0 x 10-0

39'

28'

Plan V-984	
Bedrooms: 2	Baths: 1
Total living area:	984 sq. ft.
Exterior Wall Framing:	2x6
Ceiling Height:	9'

Foundation options:
Crawlspace only.
(Foundation & framing conversion diagram available — see order form.)

Blueprint Price Code:	A

Plan V-984

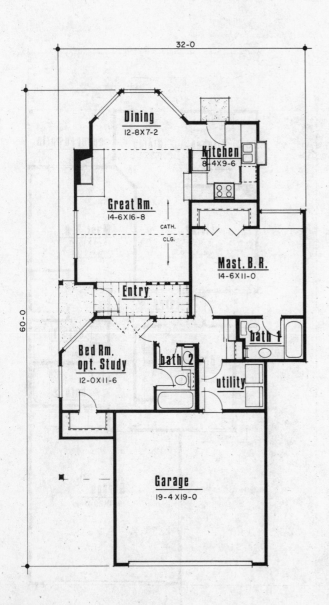

Plan Q-1017-1A

Compact Home Offers Great Room

- A large Great Room combines with a sunny, bay-windowed dining area to create a space much larger than one might expect in a home of this modest size.
- Efficient use of space also makes it possible to include a nice-sized master bedroom with private bath and large walk-in closet.
- A side entry eliminates the need for long hallways by directing traffic into the Great Room or into the optional study, which would make a great home office.
- Note the utility space in the passageway leading to the two-car garage.

Plan Q-1017-1A

Bedrooms: 1-2	Baths: 2
Total living area:	1,017 sq. ft.
Garage:	367 sq. ft.
Exterior Wall Framing:	2x4

Foundation options:
  Slab only.
(Foundation & framing conversion diagram available — see order form.)

Blueprint Price Code:	A

HomeStyles
SOURCE 1
DESIGNERS' NETWORK

To order blueprints, call
1-800-547-5570 or see order form and pricing information on pages 220-224.

163

Vaulted Ceilings Create More Space

- Vaulted ceilings in both the living room and master suite create a feeling of spaciousness in this compact home.
- Efficient U-shaped kitchen opens to the dining area, to reduce the closed-in feeling found in many kitchens.
- Master suite includes a private bath, large walk-in closet and access to a covered patio.
- Second bedroom would make a great home office if not needed for a sleeping room.

Plan Q-1034-1A

Bedrooms: 1-2	Baths: 2

Space:

Total living area:	1,034 sq. ft.
Garage:	387 sq. ft.

Exterior Wall Framing:	2x4

Foundation options:
Slab.
(Foundation & framing conversion diagram available — see order form.)

Blueprint Price Code:	A

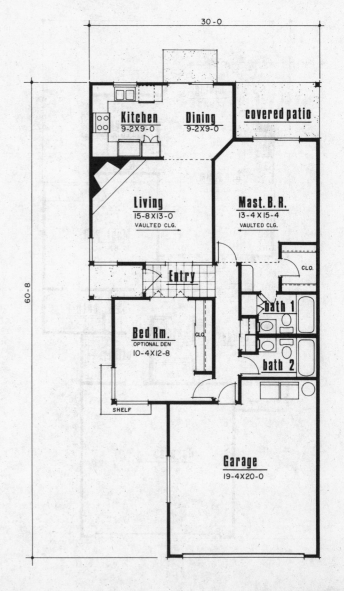

Kitchen
9-2X9-0

Dining
9-2X9-0

covered patio

Living
15-8X13-0
VAULTED CLG.

Mast. B. R.
13-4X15-4
VAULTED CLG.

CLO.

Entry

bath 1

Bed Rm.
OPTIONAL DEN
10-4X12-8

CLO.

bath 2

SHELF

Garage
19-4X20-0

30-0

60-8

HomeStyles SOURCE 1 DESIGNERS' NETWORK

Plan Q-1034-1A

Economical Contemporary

- This clean-lined, basically simple contemporary design is easy and economical to build.
- The roomy living room features an impressive corner fireplace.
- The efficient kitchen includes a handy work island and convenient utility area.
- Bathroom includes two vanities.
- Master bedroom includes large walk-in closet.
- Kitchen opens to dining area to eliminate the confined feeling found in many kitchens.
- Dining area opens onto patio.
- Three bedrooms are more or less isolated from the busier portions of the home.
- This design could be built in multiples for duplex or four-plex developments.

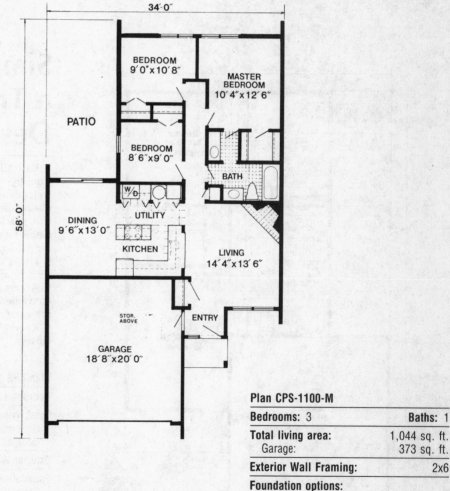

Plan CPS-1100-M

Bedrooms: 3	Baths: 1
Total living area:	1,044 sq. ft.
Garage:	373 sq. ft.
Exterior Wall Framing:	2x6

Foundation options:
Crawlspace.
(Foundation & framing conversion diagram available — see order form.)

Blueprint Price Code: A

Plan CPS-1100-M

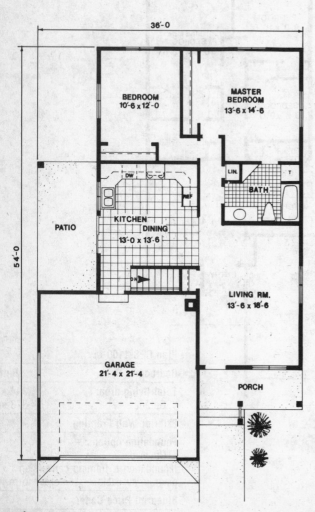

Simplicity in a Traditional Design

- Basically simple design is rescued from the ordinary by a warm, welcoming front porch and distinguished roof lines.
- A spacious kitchen/dining area meets family needs for casual space for eating and other activities.
- Living room is larger than average for a home of this size.
- Access to full basement is convenient to both the kitchen and the garage.
- Roomy bedrooms include large closets.

Plan CPS-1130-B

Bedrooms: 2	Baths: 1
Total living area:	1,055 sq. ft.
Basement:	1,055 sq. ft.
Garage:	455 sq. ft.

Exterior Wall Framing:	2x6

Foundation options:
  Standard basement only.
(Foundation & framing conversion diagram available — see order form.)

Blueprint Price Code:	A

To order blueprints, call
1-800-547-5570 or see order form and pricing information on pages 220-224.

Plan CPS-1130-B

Cozy and Charming

- This compact two-bedroom home offers economical shelter and pleasant styling for a small family.
- A spacious kitchen/dining combination offers ample space for family dining and food preparation.
- Both bedrooms offer large closets plus convenient access to the bathroom.

- The large living room boasts large windows and an energy-efficient heat-circulating fireplace.
- The small but functional foyer is reached via an attractive oval-windowed front door.
- The basement doubles the size of the home.

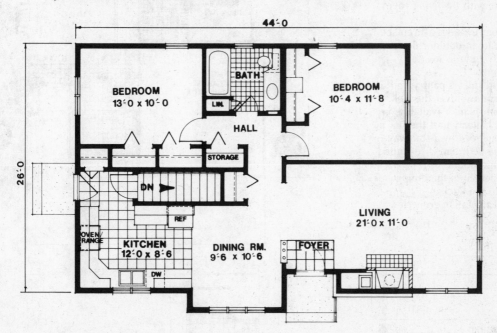

Plan CPS-1112-B

Bedrooms: 2	Baths: 1

Total living area:	1,059 sq. ft.
Basement:	1,059 sq. ft.

Exterior Wall Framing:	2x6

Foundation options:
Standard basement only.
(Foundation & framing conversion diagram available — see order form.)

Blueprint Price Code: A

To order blueprints, call
1-800-547-5570 or see order form
and pricing information on pages 220-224

Plan CPS-1112-B

167

Practicality and Style

- This very practical home still offers a stylish exterior and interior to suit the needs of many families.
- The kitchen and dining room flow together in a large open space, which visually connects with the living room beyond.
- The living room includes a fireplace and easy access to an outdoor deck.
- A handy utility room is located near the bedrooms.
- The kitchen includes a pantry and sunny corner windows over the sink.
- A full basement plan is available, in which the short hallway past the living room is replaced by a stairway and traffic to the bedroom is re-routed through the living room.
- The garage opens into the dining area, just next to the kitchen, convenient for carrying in groceries.

Plan U-87-104

Bedrooms: 3	Baths: 1
Total living area:	1,072 sq. ft.
Basement:	1,072 sq. ft.
Garage:	481 sq. ft.

Exterior Wall Framing:	2x4/2x6

Foundation options:
Standard basement.
Crawlspace.
(Foundation & framing conversion diagram available — see order form.)

Blueprint Price Code:	A

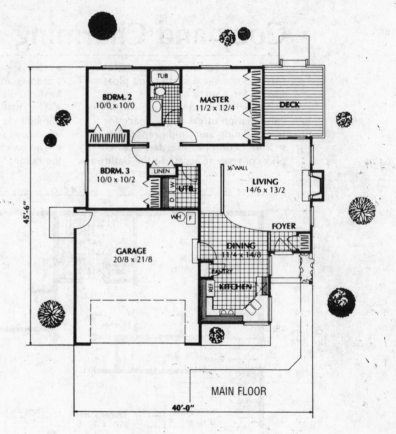

MAIN FLOOR

BDRM. 2
10/0 x 10/0

MASTER
11/2 x 12/4

DECK

BDRM. 3
10/0 x 10/2

LINEN

36" WALL

LIVING
14/6 x 13/2

UTIL.

FOYER

GARAGE
20/8 x 21/8

DINING
11/4 x 14/8

PANTRY

KITCHEN

REF

45'-6"

40'-0"

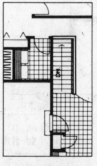

BASEMENT

HomeStyles
SOURCE
DESIGNERS NETWORK

Plan U-87-104

Efficient Side-Entry Design

- Side entry eliminates need for space-wasting hallway to take visitors from the front to the rear.
- Living and dining areas are put together to produce a respectable space for gatherings of family and friends.
- Master bedroom suite includes a private bath and ample closet space.
- Optional third bedroom could be convenient home office.
- Living/dining area sports an impressive cathedral ceiling.

Plan Q-1125-1A

Bedrooms: 2-3	Baths: 2

Space:

Total living area:	1,125 sq. ft.
Garage:	314 sq. ft.

Exterior Wall Framing:	2x4

Foundation options:
Slab only.
(Foundation & framing conversion diagram available — see order form.)

Blueprint Price Code:	A

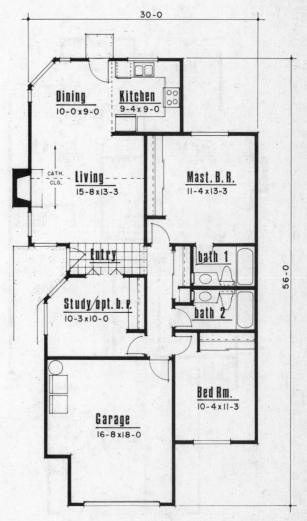

HomeStyles
SOURCE 1
DESIGNERS NETWORK

Plan Q-1125-1A

To order blueprints, call
1-800-547-5570 or see order form and pricing information on pages 220-224.

169

NEW RELEASE

Spanish Look for Narrow Lot

- Modest-sized one-story home offers traditional Spanish style and grace.
- Great Room angles out to an impressive fireplace and is covered by a vaulted ceiling.
- Sunny, bay-windowed dining area serves for both casual and formal meals.
- Kitchen offers easy access to outdoors.
- Master bedroom suite includes private bath and large walk-in closet.
- Front bedroom, off the entry, would make a nice home office if not needed for sleeping.
- Handy utility area located in garage entryway.

Plan Q-1179-1A

Bedrooms: 2-3	Baths: 2
Total living area:	1,179 sq. ft.
Garage:	374 sq. ft.
Exterior Wall Framing:	2x4

Foundation options:
Slab only.
(Foundation & framing conversion diagram available — see order form.)

Blueprint Price Code:	A

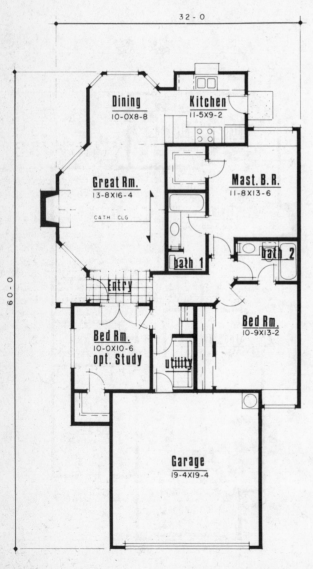

32 - 0

60 - 0

Dining
10-0X8-8

Kitchen
11-5X9-2

Great Rm.
13-8X16-4

C4TH CLG

Mast. B.R.
11-8X13-6

bath 1

bath 2

Entry

Bed Rm.
10-0X10-6
opt. Study

utility

Bed Rm.
10-9X13-2

Garage
19-4X19-4

HomeStyles
SOURCE 1
DESIGNERS NETWORK

To order blueprints, call
1-800-547-5570 or see order form
and pricing information on pages 220-224.

Plan Q-1179-1A

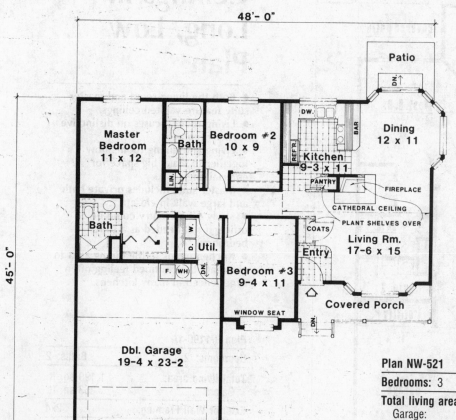

48'- 0"

45'- 0"

Patio

DN.

Master Bedroom
11 x 12

Bath

Bedroom #2
10 x 9

DW.

Kitchen
9-3 x 11

REF'R

BAR

Dining
12 x 11

PANTRY

FIREPLACE

Bath

LIN.

D. W.

Util.

CATHEDRAL CEILING

PLANT SHELVES OVER

COATS

Living Rm.
17-6 x 15

F.

WH

DN.

Bedroom #3
9-4 x 11

Entry

WINDOW SEAT

Covered Porch

DN.

Dbl. Garage
19-4 x 23-2

Classic One-Story Farmhouse

- This classic farmhouse design features a shady and inviting front porch.
- Inside, vaulted ceilings in the living and dining rooms make the home seem larger than it really is.
- An abundance of windows brightens up the living room and dining area.
- The functional kitchen includes a pantry and plenty of cabinet space.
- The master bedroom boasts a mirrored dressing area, private bath and abundant closet space.
- Bedroom 3 includes a cozy window seat.

Plan NW-521

Bedrooms: 3	Baths: 2
Total living area:	1,187 sq. ft.
Garage:	448 sq. ft.
Exterior Wall Framing:	2x6

Foundation options:
Crawlspace only.
(Foundation & framing conversion diagram available — see order form.)

Blueprint Price Code: A

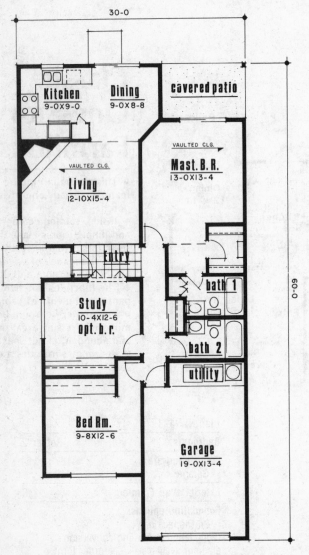

30-0

Kitchen
9-0X9-0

Dining
9-0X8-8

covered patio

VAULTED CLG.

Mast. B. R.
13-0X13-4

VAULTED CLG.

Living
12-10X15-4

60-0

entry

bath 1

Study
10-4X12-6
opt. b. r.

bath 2

utility

Bed Rm.
9-8X12-6

Garage
19-0X13-4

Vaulted Ceilings in Long, Low Plan

- Both the living room and master suite feature vaulted ceilings.
- Living room focuses on distinctive corner fireplace.
- Living and dining rooms flow together to make big space for entertaining.
- Master suite includes private bath and large walk-in closet.
- Study off the entry could be an office, if not needed as a third bedroom.
- Kitchen opens to the dining area to eliminate the confined feeling often experienced in many kitchens.

Plan Q-1190-1A

Bedrooms: 2-3	Baths: 2
Total living area:	1,190 sq. ft.
Garage:	253 sq. ft.
Exterior Wall Framing:	2x4

Foundation options:
  Slab only.
(Foundation & framing conversion diagram available — see order form.)

Blueprint Price Code:	A

To order blueprints, call
1-800-547-5570 or see order form and pricing information on pages 220-224.

Plan Q-1190-1A

Affordable Amenities

- An excellent design for a young family or an empty-nest couple.
- This design is an economical, affordable size, but includes the amenities today's homeowners are looking for.
- The large country-style kitchen includes a sunny breakfast nook, garden window over the sink and a pantry.
- The master bedroom includes a private bath and large walk-in closet.
- Living and dining rooms flow together to make an impressive open space for family gatherings or entertaining.
- Living room boasts an impressive fireplace and a vaulted ceiling.
- Optional third bedroom would make a convenient home office.

Plan CDG-1001

Bedrooms: 2-3	Baths: 2
Total living area:	1,199 sq. ft.
Garage:	494 sq. ft.
Exterior Wall Framing:	2x4

Foundation options:
Crawlspace only.
(Foundation & framing conversion diagram available — see order form.)

Blueprint Price Code:	A

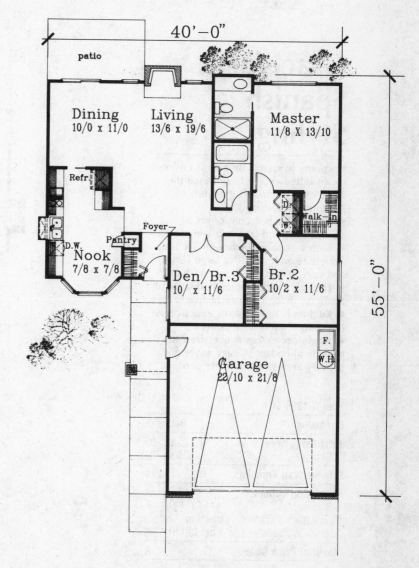

HomeStyles SOURCE 1 DESIGNERS' NETWORK

Graceful Spanish Styling

- Roomy living-dining area is covered by a vaulted ceiling to enhance the sense of space in this graceful, economical design.
- The master bedroom offers a private bath and large walk-in closet.
- Both secondary bedrooms are the same size and also offer large closets and easy access to the second bath.
- The side entry efficiently distributes traffic to living room or bedroom area.
- Kitchen is designed for easy access to outdoor patio or deck area.
- Single-car garage is oversized to provide abundant storage space and laundry area where climate permits.

Plan Q-1226-1A

Bedrooms: 3	Baths: 2
Total living area:	1,226 sq. ft.
Garage:	306 sq. ft.
Exterior Wall Framing:	2x4

Foundation options:
Slab only.
(Foundation & framing conversion diagram available — see order form.)

Blueprint Price Code: A

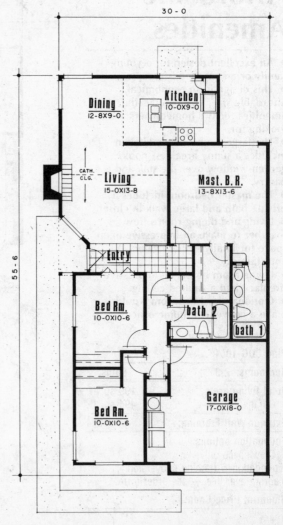

Dining
12-8X9-0

Kitchen
10-0X9-0

Living
15-0X13-8

CATH.
CLG.

Mast. B.R.
13-8X13-6

Entry

Bed Rm.
10-0X10-6

bath 2

bath 1

Bed Rm.
10-0X10-6

Garage
17-0X18-0

30-0

55-6

Plan Q-1226-1A

Stylish Design in Stucco or Wood

- This plan gives you a choice of wood or stucco exteriors.
- Either way, you get a stylish design that will meet the needs of many family units.
- Living and dining areas flow together to create a spacious area for entertaining and for family activities.
- The living room includes a fireplace and an impressive front window arrangement.
- A large family room provides more space for casual living.
- The master suite includes a private bath and ample-sized closet.
- A fence-enclosed front courtyard adds an extra touch of class to the entry area.

Plans SD-9006 (stucco) & SD-9012 (wood)

Bedrooms: 3	Baths: 2

Total living area:	1,229 sq. ft.
Basement:	1,229 sq. ft.
Garage:	419 sq. ft.

Exterior Wall Framing:	2x6

Foundation options:
Standard basement.
Crawlspace.
(Foundation & framing conversion diagram available — see order form.)

Blueprint Price Code:	A

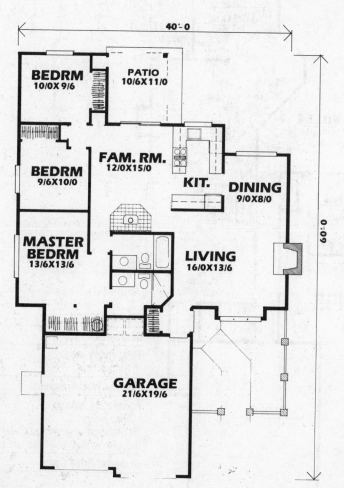

40'-0

60'-0

BEDRM
10/0X 9/6

PATIO
10/6X11/0

BEDRM
9/6X10/0

FAM. RM.
12/0X15/0

KIT.

DINING
9/0X8/0

MASTER BEDRM
13/6X13/6

LIVING
16/0X13/6

GARAGE
21/6X19/6

 HomeStyles SOURCE 1 DESIGNERS' NETWORK

Plans SD-9006 & SD-9012

To order blueprints, call
1-800-547-5570 or see order form and pricing information on pages 220-224.

175

Unique Design for Narrow Corner Lot

● Interesting and different design inside and out.
● Unique dining area angles off the living room.
● Living room provides fireplace and easy access to a covered porch.
● Note that the living room and master suite also include vaulted ceilings.
● The master suite is unusually large for a home of this size and includes a luxurious master bath and large walk-in closet.
● Stucco finish provides a low-maintenance exterior in any climate.

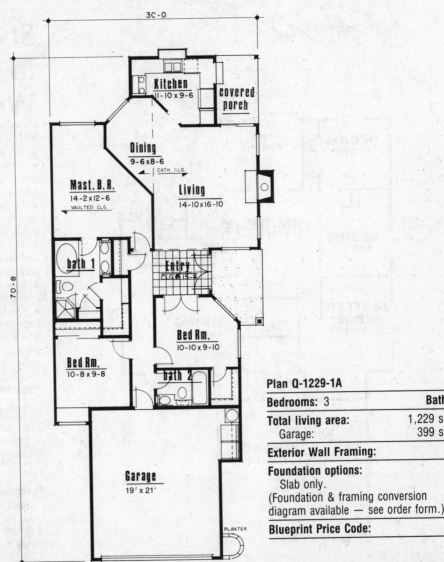

Kitchen 11-10 x 9-6

covered porch

Dining 9-6x8-6 CATH. CLG.

Mast. B.R. 14-2 x 12-6 VAULTED CLG.

Living 14-10x16-10

bath 1

Entry CLG @ 15-4

Bed Rm. 10-10x9-10

Bed Rm. 10-8 x 9-8

bath 2

Garage 19' x 21'

PLANTER

30-0

70-8

Plan Q-1229-1A

Bedrooms: 3	Baths: 2
Total living area:	1,229 sq. ft.
Garage:	399 sq. ft.
Exterior Wall Framing:	2x4

Foundation options:
Slab only.
(Foundation & framing conversion diagram available — see order form.)

Blueprint Price Code:	A

HomeStyles **Source 1** DESIGNERS NETWORK

Plan Q-1229-1A

Quiet Good Taste on a Small Lot

- The proud owners of this home will appreciate the handsome detailing of the porch columns and window caps, all of which support the classic beauty of this solid, time-tested design.
- The thoroughly modern interior starts off with the generously sized Great Room with its impressive corner fireplace.
- The master suite boasts a bath which is exceptionally luxurious for a house of this size.
- The efficient U-shaped kitchen boasts plenty of counter space and flows into the bay windowed dining room.
- A convenient closet hides the washer and dryer off the dining room.
- A hallway helps isolate the bedrooms from the rest of the house.

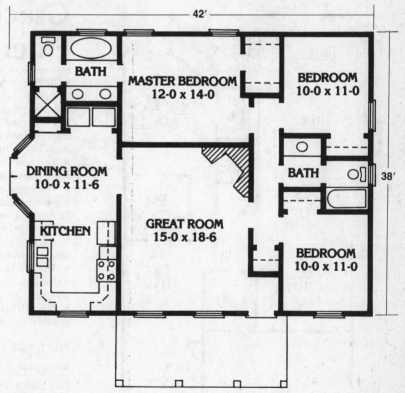

Plan V-1294

Bedrooms: 3	Baths: 2
Total living area:	1,294 sq. ft.
Exterior Wall Framing:	2x6
Ceiling Height:	9'

Foundation options:
Crawlspace only.
(Foundation & framing conversion diagram available — see order form.)

Blueprint Price Code: A

HomeStyles
SOURCE 1
DESIGNERS NETWORK

To order blueprints, call
1-800-547-5570 or see order form and pricing information on pages 220-224.

Plan V-1294

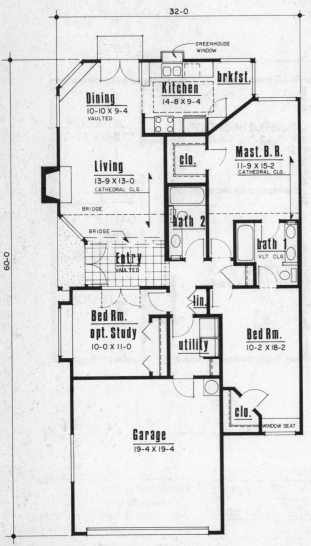

GREENHOUSE WINDOW

Dining
10-10 X 9-4
VAULTED

Kitchen
14-8 X 9-4

brkfst.

clo.

Mast. B.R.
11-9 X 15-2
CATHEDRAL CLG.

Living
13-9 X 13-0
CATHEDRAL CLG.

BRIDGE

BRIDGE

bath 2

bath 1
VLT. CLG.

Entry
VAULTED

lin.

Bed Rm.
opt. Study
10-0 X 11-0

utility

Bed Rm.
10-2 X 18-2

clo.

WINDOW SEAT

Garage
19-4 X 19-4

32-0

60-0

Space for Gracious Entertaining

- Although relatively modest in size, this plan contains abundant space for a fair-sized party or family gathering.
- Combined living/dining area creates a large open space, made to seem even larger by the vaulted ceiling.
- The entry area is also impressive for a home of this size.
- The large master suite includes a big walk-in closet and vaulted ceiling, as does the second bedroom.
- The third bedroom makes a nice home office if not needed for a sleeping room.
- The utility area is conveniently tucked away in the garage entry passage.
- The kitchen includes a cozy, sunny breakfast nook.

Plan Q-1300-1A

Bedrooms: 2-3	Baths: 2
Total living area:	1,300 sq. ft.
Garage:	374 sq. ft.

Exterior Wall Framing:	2x4

Foundation options:
Slab only.
(Foundation & framing conversion diagram available — see order form.)

Blueprint Price Code:	A

To order blueprints, call
1-800-547-5570 or see order form
and pricing information on pages 220-224.

Plan Q-1300-1A

Impressive Great Room Space

● The large open space devoted to the living and dining areas, plus the open-style kitchen, make an impressive Great Room, suitable for both family living and entertaining guests.
● A cozy fireplace is also included in the living room area.
● The large master bedroom suite includes a private bath with two vanities and a huge walk-in closet.
● Both secondary bedrooms also include walk-in closets.

Plan Q-1340-1A

Bedrooms: 3	Baths: 2
Total living area:	1,340 sq. ft.
Garage:	270 sq. ft.
Exterior Wall Framing:	2x4

Foundation options:
Slab only.
(Foundation & framing conversion diagram available — see order form.)

Blueprint Price Code:	A

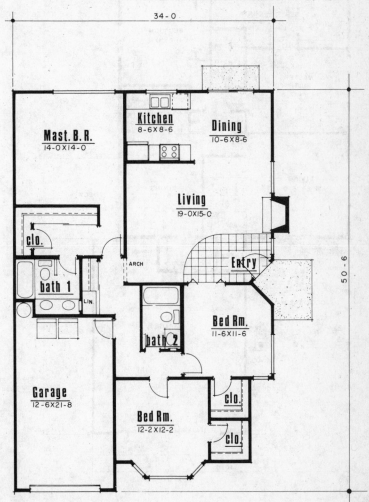

HomeStyles
SOURCE1
DESIGNERS' NETWORK

To order blueprints, call
1-800-547-5570 or see order form
and pricing information on pages 220-224.
179

Plan Q-1340-1A

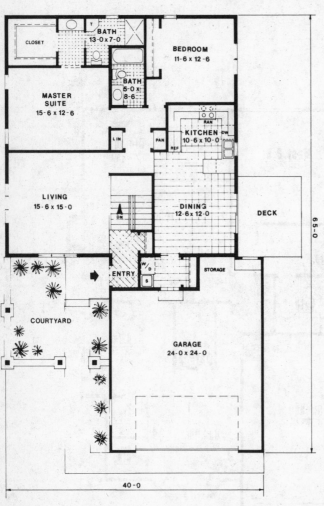

Shaded Courtyard Welcomes Guests

● A classy shaded courtyard takes this basically simple design out of the ordinary and makes it into something special.

● Master suite includes private bath and large walk-in closet.

● Kitchen and dining room combine to create a feeling of spaciousness.

● Note convenient laundry area in garage entryway.

● Dining area opens to outside deck.

● Garage includes storage area, and a full basement doubles the floor space available.

Plan CPS-1143-B

Bedrooms: 2	Baths: 2
Total living area:	1,366 sq. ft.
Basement:	1,366 sq. ft.
Garage:	576 sq. ft.

Exterior Wall Framing:	2x6

Foundation options:
Standard basement only.
(Foundation & framing conversion diagram available — see order form.)

Blueprint Price Code:	A

To order blueprints, call
1-800-547-5570 or see order form
and pricing information on pages 220-224.

Plan CPS-1143-B

Great Kitchen is Focus of Family Life

- In this compact but creative design, the huge kitchen area is the major highlight that sets this home apart from the ordinary.
- Areas for food preparation, sunny eating nook, large island and patio access are all combined into one big casual living space.
- The kitchen area also includes a pantry, built-in desk and garden window.
- In the more formal portion of the plan, the dining and living rooms flow together to make space for entertaining.
- The living room features a sunken floor, vaulted ceiling and fireplace.
- The master suite includes a vaulted ceiling, private bath and large walk-in closet.
- Skylights brighten both the master and main bathrooms.
- Washer and dryer are conveniently located in the garage entry area.

40'-0"

54'-0"

Patio

Pantry

vaulted Nook
9/6 x 8/6

Garden Window

D.W.

Desk

Lin.

vaulted Master
12/0 x 13/6

Arch

Skylight

Walk-in

Linen

Refr.

Pass-Thru

Shlvs.

Dining
13/4 x 10/4

Arch

vaulted Entry

Arch

Dn.

Br. 2
10/8 x 10/2

F. W.H.

Sunken/ Vaulted Living
13/4 x 15/8

Garage
19/0 x 23/6

Plan CDG-1006

Bedrooms: 2	Baths: 2

| **Total living area:** | 1,385 sq. ft. |
| Garage: | 446 sq. ft. |

| **Exterior Wall Framing:** | 2x4 |

Foundation options:
Crawlspace only.
(Foundation & framing conversion diagram available — see order form.)

Blueprint Price Code: A

HomeStyles SOURCE 1 DESIGNERS NETWORK

Plan CDG-1006

To order blueprints, call
1-800-547-5570 or see order form and pricing information on pages 220-224.

Impressive Front Elevation

- **This striking two-story can serve equally well as a permanent home or recreational hide-away.**
- **A cavernous Great Room with a high vaulted ceiling is bound to impress visitors and family alike.**
- **The efficient kitchen opens onto the Great Room to eliminate the closed-in feeling often found in kitchens.**
- **Upstairs, the private master suite includes a vaulted ceiling, impressive bath with spa tub and large closet.**
- **Plans for a large detached two-car, two-story garage with a studio upstairs are included.**

Plan NW-599

Bedrooms: 2	Baths: 2

Space:	
Upper floor:	384 sq. ft.
Main floor:	1,014 sq. ft.

Total living area:	**1,398 sq. ft.**
Garage:	625 sq. ft.
Studio (over garage):	625 sq. ft.

Exterior Wall Framing:	2x6

Foundation options:
Crawlspace only.
(Foundation & framing conversion diagram available — see order form.)

Blueprint Price Code:	A

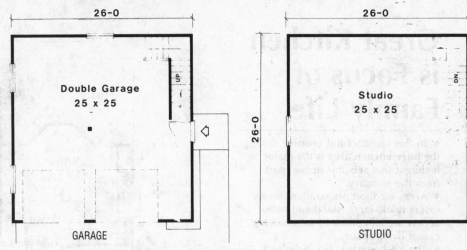

GARAGE — Double Garage 25 x 25

STUDIO — Studio 25 x 25

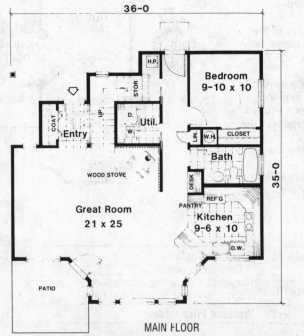

MAIN FLOOR — Great Room 21 x 25, Entry, Wood Stove, Pantry, Kitchen 9-6 x 10, Bath, Bedroom 9-10 x 10, Util., Patio

UPPER FLOOR — Spa Tub, Bath, Closet, Open to Living Room, Master Bedroom 12-3 x 13

To order blueprints, call
1-800-547-5570 or see order form and pricing information on pages 220-224.

Plan NW-599

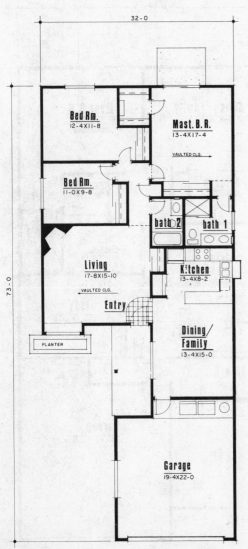

Economical Space

- Protected entry leads into spacious living room with vaulted ceiling and fireplace.
- A roomy dining/family room adjoins the kitchen, which offers an abundance of counter space.
- The master suite includes a private bath and two large closets.
- Note the storage closets also in the kitchen and off the living room.
- Built-in planter near the entry adds an extra touch of class.

Plan Q-1398-1A

Bedrooms: 3	**Baths:** 2
Total living area:	1,398 sq. ft.
Garage:	425 sq. ft.
Exterior Wall Framing:	2x4

Foundation options:
Slab only.
(Foundation & framing conversion diagram available — see order form.)

Blueprint Price Code: A

To order blueprints, call
1-800-547-5570 or see order form
and pricing information on pages 220-224.

Plan Q-1398-1A

183

Atrium Adds Unusual Touch

- An interior atrium adds a touch of class to a basically economical, easy-to-build plan.
- The living room includes a fireplace and vaulted ceiling.
- A large dining/family area adjoins the kitchen and offers easy access to an outdoor patio or deck.
- The study would make a great home office.
- Master suite is comprised of a roomy sleeping area, private bath and large walk-in closet.
- The spacious kitchen offers ample counter space and an efficient design.

Plan Q-1424-1A

Bedrooms: 2	Baths: 2

Total living area:	1,424 sq. ft.
Garage:	444 sq. ft.

Exterior Wall Framing:	2x4

Foundation options:
Slab only.
(Foundation & framing conversion diagram available — see order form.)

Blueprint Price Code:	A

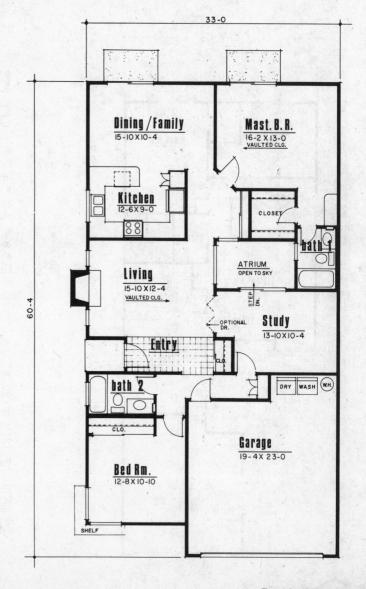

Dining / Family
15-10 X 10-4

Mast. B. R.
16-2 X 13-0
VAULTED CLG.

Kitchen
12-6 X 9-0

CLOSET

bath

Living
15-10 X 12-4
VAULTED CLG.

ATRIUM
OPEN TO SKY

STEP DN.

OPTIONAL DR.

Study
13-10 X 10-4

Entry

CLO.

DRY WASH WH

bath 2

CLO.

Bed Rm.
12-8 X 10-10

Garage
19-4 X 23-0

SHELF

33-0

60-4

Plan Q-1424-1A

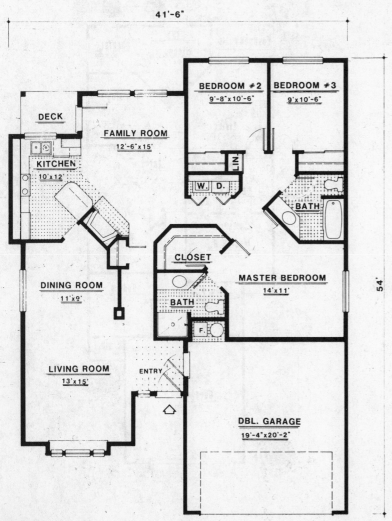

41'-6"

DECK

FAMILY ROOM
12'-6"x15'

KITCHEN
10'x12'

BEDROOM #2
9'-8"x10'-6"

BEDROOM #3
9'x10'-6'

LIN.

W. D.

BATH

DINING ROOM
11'x9'

CLOSET

MASTER BEDROOM
14'x11'

BATH

F.

54'

LIVING ROOM
13'x15'

ENTRY

DBL. GARAGE
19'-4"x20'-2"

Angles Add Interior Excitement

- Eye-catching exterior leads into exciting interior.
- You'll find cathedral ceilings throughout the living and dining area.
- Angular kitchen includes eating bar, plenty of cabinet and counter space.
- Master suite includes angled double-door entry, private bath and large walk-in closet.
- Family room and kitchen join together to make large casual family area.
- Main bathroom continues the angled motif, and the washer and dryer are conveniently located in the bedroom hallway.

Plan NW-864

Bedrooms: 3	Baths: 2
Total living area:	1,449 sq. ft.
Garage:	390 sq. ft.
Exterior Wall Framing:	2x6

Foundation options:
Crawlspace only.
(Foundation & framing conversion diagram available — see order form.)

Blueprint Price Code: A

To order blueprints, call
1-800-547-5570 or see order form
and pricing information on pages 220-224.

Plan NW-864

Angular Interior Adds Spark

- Mediterranean-style exterior encloses a creatively modern interior.
- Living and dining rooms form a "V", with the kitchen at the center.
- Master suite includes a triangular bath with separate tub and shower, which is in a five-sided enclosure.
- The study is also angled, and would make a great home office if needed for that purpose.
- A sunny breakfast nook adjoins the kitchen which is also angled for visual interest and efficiency.
- Laundry area is found in the garage entryway, next to the second bath.

Plan Q-1449-1A

Bedrooms: 2	**Baths:** 2

Total living area:	1,449 sq. ft.
Garage:	387 sq. ft.

Exterior Wall Framing:	2x4

Foundation options:
Slab only.
(Foundation & framing conversion diagram available — see order form.)

Blueprint Price Code:	A

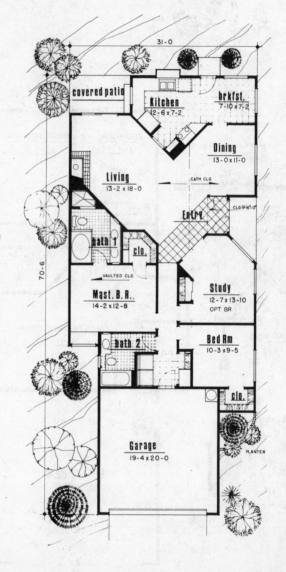

To order blueprints, call
1-800-547-5570 or see order form
and pricing information on pages 220-224.

Plan Q-1449-1A

NEW RELEASE

Easy Living in Modest-Sized Home

- Popular palladian window facing the street is echoed by the curved arch above the entryway.
- Generously sized living room includes a fireplace and features an 11'-6" ceiling.
- The roomy master bedroom suite includes a deluxe private bath with separate tub and shower, plus a large walk-in closet.
- French doors lead from master suite to outdoor patio or deck.
- A casual breakfast nook adjoins the efficient kitchen; also note the laundry area in the garage entryway.

Plan L-1507-TA

Bedrooms: 3	**Baths:** 2

Total living area:	1,507 sq. ft.
Garage:	434 sq. ft.

Exterior Wall Framing:	2x4

Ceiling Height:
    8' unless otherwise noted.

Foundation options:
    Slab only.
(Foundation & framing conversion diagram available — see order form.)

Blueprint Price Code:	B

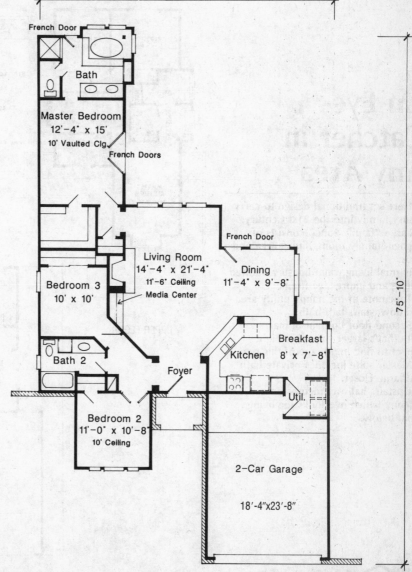

French Door

Bath

Master Bedroom
12'-4" x 15'
10' Vaulted Clg.

French Doors

Living Room
14'-4" x 21'-4"
11'-6" Ceiling
Media Center

French Door

Dining
11'-4" x 9'-8"

Bedroom 3
10' x 10'

Breakfast
8' x 7'-8"

Kitchen

Bath 2

Foyer

Util.

Bedroom 2
11'-0" x 10'-8"
10' Ceiling

2-Car Garage
18'-4"x23'-8"

44'-0"

75'-10"

HomeStyles SOURCE 1 DESIGNERS' NETWORK

To order blueprints, call
1-800-547-5570 or see order form
and pricing information on pages 220-224.

Plan L-1507-TA

187

An Eye-Catcher in Any Area

- Here's a traditional design to carry a busy family into the 21st Century.
- Large "family zone" consists of kitchen, family room, dining area and deck.
- Formal living room boasts a vaulted ceiling and impressive fireplace.
- Take note of the handy utility area and downstairs half-bath.
- Second floor contains a master suite that's larger than you might expect to find in a home of this size.
- Master suite includes private bath and large closet.
- Upstairs hallway focuses on a balcony which overlooks the living room below.

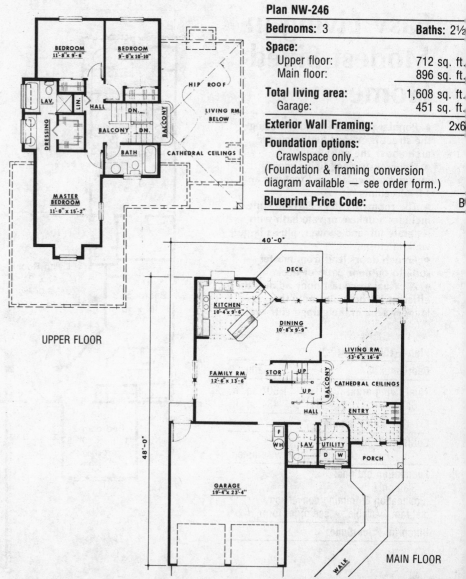

UPPER FLOOR

MAIN FLOOR

Plan NW-246

Bedrooms: 3	Baths: 2½

Space:

Upper floor:	712 sq. ft.
Main floor:	896 sq. ft.

Total living area:	1,608 sq. ft.
Garage:	451 sq. ft.

Exterior Wall Framing:	2x6

Foundation options:
Crawlspace only.
(Foundation & framing conversion diagram available — see order form.)

Blueprint Price Code:	B

HomeStyles
SOURCE 1
DESIGNERS NETWORK

188

Plan NW-246

To order blueprints, call
1-800-547-5570 or see order form
and pricing information on pages 220-224.

Traditional Charmer

- In this well-planned compact design, the traditional exterior covers a modern interior.
- The 'conversation area,' an octagon-shaped projection off the corner of the family room, has a 12-foot ceiling, and will itself be the object of much conversation.
- Large family room includes a fireplace.
- Dining room and kitchen flow together to make ample space for casual dining.
- The kitchen includes a handy work island and lots of counter space.
- A spacious master bedroom includes a big bay window, 12-foot ceiling, a deluxe bath and abundant closet space.

Plan L-1614

Bedrooms: 3	Baths: 2

Total living area: 1,614 sq. ft.
   Garage: (Plans for a 505-sq. ft. detached garage are included with blueprint.)

Exterior Wall Framing: 2x4

Ceiling Heights: 8' unless otherwise noted.

Foundation options:
   Slab only.
   (Foundation & framing conversion diagram available — see order form.)

Blueprint Price Code: B

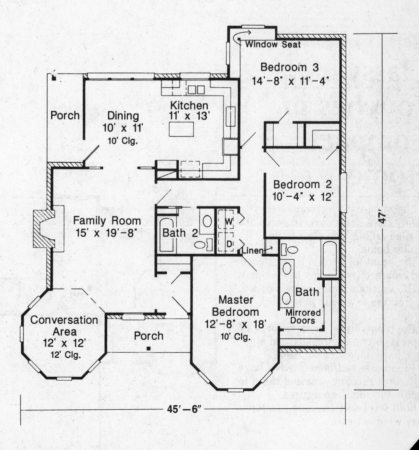

Window Seat

Bedroom 3
14'-8" x 11'-4"

Porch

Dining
10' x 11'
10' Clg.

Kitchen
11' x 13'

Bedroom 2
10'-4" x 12'

Family Room
15' x 19'-8"

Bath 2

W
D

Linen

Bath

Conversation
Area
12' x 12'
12' Clg.

Porch

Master
Bedroom
12'-8" x 18'
10' Clg.

Mirrored
Doors

47'

45'-6"

Plan L-1614

Classy Touches in Compact Home

- Charming window treatments, a quality front door, covered porch and detailed railings add class to this smaller home.
- The beautiful kitchen is brightened and enlarged by a sunny bay window.
- The spacious family room enjoys easy access to a patio in the back yard.
- The roomy living room features an impressive corner fireplace and a large bay window in the front.
- The master bedroom boasts a large bathroom, dressing area and closet in addition to the sleeping area.
- ...h secondary bedrooms feature

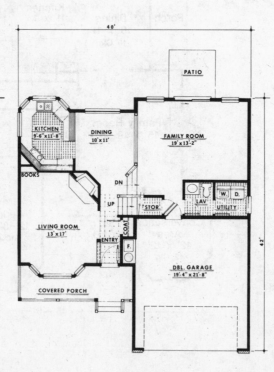

MAIN FLOOR

UPPER FLOOR

Plan NW-836

Bedrooms: 3	**Baths:** 2½

Space:

Upper floor:	684 sq. ft.
Main floor:	934 sq. ft.

Total living area:	1,618 sq. ft.
Garage:	419 sq. ft.

Exterior Wall Framing:	2x6

Foundation options:
Crawlspace only.
(Foundation & framing conversion diagram available — see order form.)

Blueprint Price Code: B

To order blueprints, call
1-800-547-5570 or see order form
and pricing information on pages 220-224.

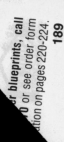
...r blueprints, call
...0 or see order form
...tion on pages 220-224.
189

Plan NW-836

Exciting Interior

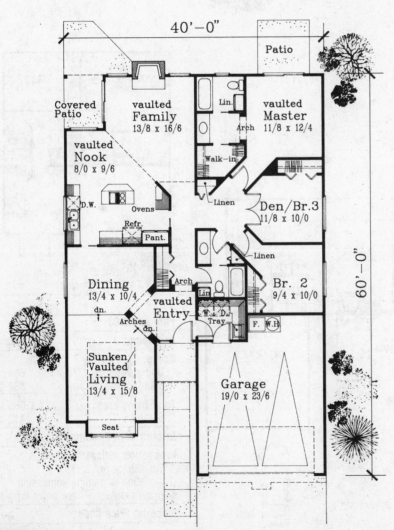

40'–0"

Patio

Covered Patio

vaulted **Family** 13/8 x 16/6

vaulted **Master** 11/8 x 12/4

Lin.

Arch

vaulted **Nook** 8/0 x 9/6

Walk-in

D.W.

Ovens

Linen

Den/Br.3 11/8 x 10/0

Refr.

Pant.

Linen

60'–0"

Dining 13/4 x 10/4

Arch

Br. 2 9/4 x 10/0

dn.

vaulted **Entry**

Lin

Arches

dn.

Tray

F. W.H.

Sunken/ Vaulted Living 13/4 x 15/8

Garage 19/0 x 23/6

Seat

- Interior angles and vaulted ceilings add excitement and visual space to this mid-sized design.
- The kitchen opens to the vaulted nook and family room, and features a handy island and convenient pantry.
- The master bedroom boasts a vaulted ceiling, private patio, walk-in closet and private bath.
- The living room is dropped down a step from the dining room, and also includes a vaulted ceiling.
- A cozy window seat in the living room provides a view to the front.
- The vaulted entry directs traffic through a hallway to the casual zones of the home, or directly to the living or dining room.
- Note the handy utility space in the garage entryway.

Plan CDG-1005

Bedrooms: 2-3	**Baths:** 2

Total living area:	1,672 sq. ft.
Garage:	446 sq. ft.

Exterior Wall Framing:	2x4

Foundation options:
Crawlspace only.
(Foundation & framing conversion diagram available — see order form.)

Blueprint Price Code:	B

HomeStyles
SOURCE 1
DESIGNERS NETWORK

Plan CDG-1005

Compact Three-Bedroom Plan

- This design makes excellent use of a small lot, requiring only a 40' x 43' 'footprint.'
- A Great-Room concept design on the first floor presents a large open space for the family room and dining area.
- A formal living room includes fireplace and vaulted ceiling.
- Note the handy laundry room and half-bath in the passageway from garage to kitchen.
- The master suite upstairs includes a private bath and large closet.

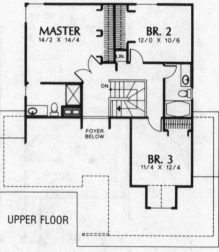

UPPER FLOOR

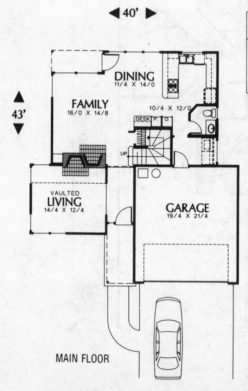

MAIN FLOOR

Plan AM-2103

Bedrooms: 3	Baths: 2½

Space:	
Upper floor:	804 sq. ft.
Main floor:	882 sq. ft.

Total living area:	1,686 sq. ft.
Garage:	412 sq. ft.

Exterior Wall Framing:	2x4

Foundation options:
Crawlspace only.
(Foundation & framing conversion diagram available — see order form.)

Blueprint Price Code:	B

Plan AM-2103

NEW RELEASE

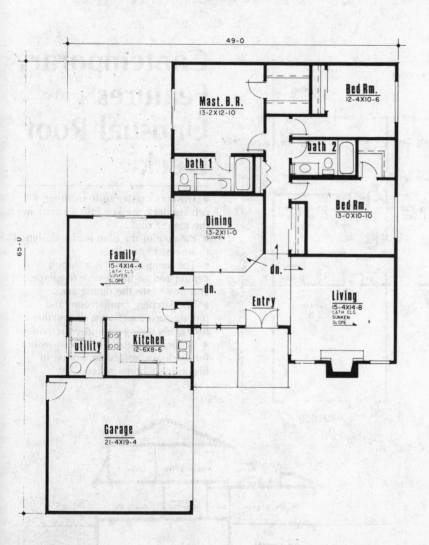

49-0

65-0

Mast. B.R.
13-2X12-10

Bed Rm.
12-4X10-6

bath 1

bath 2

Dining
13-2X11-0
SUNKEN

Bed Rm.
13-0X10-10

Family
15-4X14-4
CATH CLG
SUNKEN
SLOPE

dn.

dn.

dn.

Entry

Living
15-4X14-8
CATH CLG
SUNKEN
SLOPE

utility

Kitchen
12-6X8-6

Garage
21-4X19-4

One-Story with Contemporary Styling

- Both family room and living room are sunken down one step from the entry and feature vaulted ceilings to heighten the feeling of spaciousness.
- The roomy kitchen includes an abundance of counter space, plus a pantry/closet.
- A utility area is located in the garage entry passageway.
- The master suite includes a large walk-in closet and private bath.
- Secondary bedrooms also include large closets and share a second bath.
- A large patio is easily accessible by French doors from both the family room and the master bedroom.

Plan Q-1736-1A

Bedrooms: 3	Baths: 2
Total living area:	1,736 sq. ft.
Garage:	412 sq. ft.
Exterior Wall Framing:	2x4

Foundation options:
Slab only.
(Foundation & framing conversion diagram available — see order form.)

Blueprint Price Code:	B

HomeStyles
SOURCE 1
DESIGNERS' NETWORK

Plan Q-1736-1A

To order blueprints, call
1-800-547-5570 or see order form
and pricing information on pages 220-224.

Upper Floor

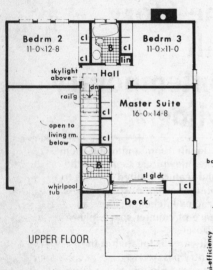

Bedrm 2
11-0×12-8

Bedrm 3
11-0×11-0

skylight above

Hall

rail'g

dn

open to living rm. below

Master Suite
16-0×14-8

whirlpool tub

sl gl dr

Deck

UPPER FLOOR

Plan K-649-P

Bedrooms: 3-4	Baths: 3

Space:

Upper floor:	724 sq. ft.
Main floor:	1,013 sq. ft.

Total living area:	**1,737 sq. ft.**
Basement:	1,013 sq. ft.
Garage:	400 sq. ft.

Exterior Wall Framing: 2x4
(with 2x6 option included)

Foundation options:
Standard basement.
Slab.
(Foundation & framing conversion
diagram available — see order form.)

Blueprint Price Code: B

HomeStyles
SOURCE 1
DESIGNERS' NETWORK

194

34-0

Terrace

hi-efficiency fireplace

sl gl dr

Dining Rm

28-8×13-0

bay

Living Rm
(sloped ceil'g)

hi-efficiency fireplace

Kit
13-0×9-0

dw

shelf

ref

dinette

Family Rm
16-0×11-0

Terr.

dn

rail'g

laundry

up

Library or
Guest Rm.
10-0×11-0

Hall

cl

up

B

stor.

cl

covered entry

up

Double Garage
20-0×20-0

52-8

sl gl dr

MAIN FLOOR

Contemporary Features Unusual Roof Deck

● Upstairs master suite includes a private deck, sunken into a cavity in the garage roof.

● Balance of the plan is also designed to be open and airy.

● The living room has a sloped ceiling and an impressive fireplace, and flows into the dining area.

● The kitchen, family room and dinette area function well together for family dining and other activities.

● A library or guest bedroom with a full bath also offers the option of becoming a home office.

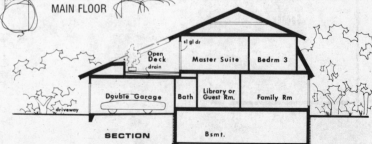

Open Deck
drain

sl gl dr

Master Suite

Bedrm 3

Double Garage

Bath

Library or
Guest Rm.

Family Rm

driveway

Bsmt.

SECTION

To order blueprints, call
1-800-547-5570 or see order form
and pricing information on pages 220-224

Plan K-649-P

MASTER BR.
14/0X14/0

DN.

BEDRM-2
11/0X11/0

BEDRM-3
11/0X9/6

UPPER FLOOR

An Impressive Facade for a Narrow Lot Plan

- Classic architectural lines set this relatively modest home apart from the ordinary.
- Low-maintenance stucco exterior will keep its good looks for decades.
- The entry leads past a convenient powder room to the angled stairway or into the living room.
- The sunny, U-shaped kitchen provides abundant counter space.
- The roomy living room includes a fireplace.
- Upstairs, the master bedroom suite includes a large walk-in closet plus a private bath with separate tub and shower.
- Two secondary bedrooms have large front windows, big closets and share a second bath.

Plan SD-9003

Bedrooms: 3	Baths: 2½

Space:

Upper floor:	821 sq. ft.
Main floor:	930 sq. ft.
Total living area:	**1,751 sq. ft.**
Basement:	930 sq. ft.
Garage:	441 sq. ft.

Exterior Wall Framing:	2x6

Foundation options:
Standard basement.
Crawlspace.
(Foundation & framing conversion diagram available — see order form.)

Blueprint Price Code:	B

FAM. RM.
13/0X17/6

LIVING
17/6 X 15/0

DINING

KITCHEN
10/0X15/6

UP

DN.

GARAGE
21/0X21/0

50' 0

32' 0

MAIN FLOOR

To order blueprints, call
1-800-547-5570 or see order form
and pricing information on pages 220-224.

Plan SD-9003

Split-Level for Narrow, Sloping Lot

- Front-to-back split level is designed to make good use of a lot sloping down from the street.
- Imposing facade makes home look bigger than it really is.
- Dining room faces front and is well-lighted by three large windows.
- Nice-sized living room includes corner fireplace.
- An upper level den overlooks the living room below.
- Lower level includes large family room, bedroom and full bath.
- Living room features sloped ceiling.

38'-0"

| BEDROOM 14'9" x 11'6" | BEDROOM 12' x 11'7" |

DEN 10'5" x 8'0"

BATH

UP

DWN

44'-0"

LIVING 13'0" x 16'6"

KITCHEN

GARAGE 14'0" x 22'0"

ENTRY

DINING 9'6" x 11'6"

UPPER FLOOR

Plan CPS-1102-S

Bedrooms: 3	**Baths:** 2

Space:	
Main floor:	1,124 sq. ft.
Lower level:	628 sq. ft.
Total living area:	1,752 sq. ft.
Garage:	308 sq. ft.

Exterior Wall Framing:	2x6

Foundation options:
Daylight basement.
(Foundation & framing conversion diagram available — see order form.)

Blueprint Price Code:	B

BEDROOM 11'6" x 9'0"

FAMILY 16'0" x 17'6"

UP

BATH

D W F WH

UNEXCAVATED

MAIN FLOOR

HomeStyles SOURCE 1 DESIGNERS NETWORK

196

Plan CPS-1102-S

Contemporary for Today's Small Lot

- Crisp contemporary styling makes this a design that will fit just about anywhere.
- Use of vaulted ceilings in the dining, living and family rooms increases the feeling of spaciousness found in this home.
- Living room and dining area flow together to create ample space for entertaining.
- Open-ended, U-shaped kitchen blends together with the nook for informal dining and food preparation.
- The family room features a fireplace and easy access to a patio in the rear.
- The master suite includes a private bath and large closet area.
- Note the washer and dryer tucked into the garage entry area.

Plans P-7651-2A & -2D

Bedrooms: 3	Baths: 2

Space:

Main floor (non-basement version):	1,700 sq. ft.
Main floor (basement version):	1,765 sq. ft.
Basement:	1,780 sq. ft.
Garage:	547 sq. ft.

Exterior Wall Framing:	2x4

Foundation options:
Daylight basement, P-7651-2D.
Crawlspace, P-7651-2A.
(Foundation & framing conversion diagram available — see order form.)

Blueprint Price Code:	B

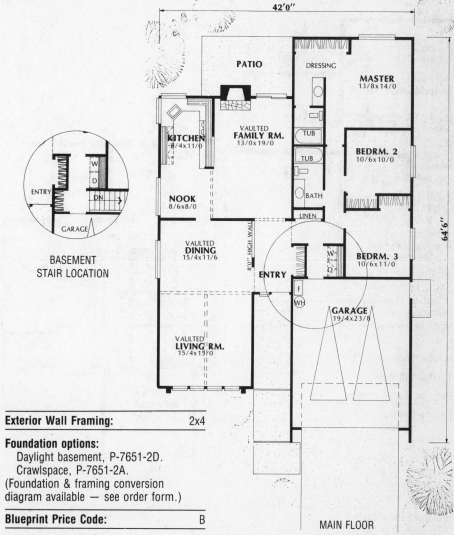

BASEMENT STAIR LOCATION

MAIN FLOOR

HomeStyles SOURCE 1 DESIGNERS' NETWORK

Plans P-7651-2A & -2D

To order blueprints, call **1-800-547-5570** or see order form and pricing information on pages 220-224

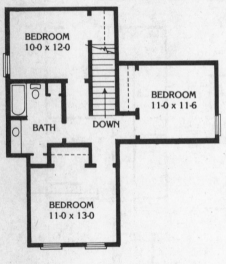

Plan V-1797

Bedrooms: 4	Baths: 2½

Space:

Upper floor:	675 sq. ft.
Main floor:	1,122 sq. ft.

Total living area: 1,797 sq. ft.

Exterior Wall Framing: 2x6

Ceiling Heights:

Upper floor:	8'
Main floor:	9'

Foundation options:
Crawlspace only.
(Foundation & framing conversion
diagram available — see order form.)

Blueprint Price Code: B

An Aura of Quiet Peace

● This charming design exudes an
aura of the peace and quiet of
simpler times.

● Note the inviting side porch off the
kitchen and laundry area which tempt
the owners to a bit of rest between
chores.

● An inviting front porch leads to an
expansive Great Room and to the
dining room beyond.

● The master suite, downstairs, faces
the front of the home, and includes
an impressive bath with oval corner
tub and separate shower.

● Upstairs, three secondary bedrooms
share another full bath.

● The fourth bedroom, on the right,
could be finished later or converted
to other uses.

To order blueprints, call
1-800-547-5570 or see order form
and pricing information on pages 220-224.

Plan V-1797

At Home in Any Setting

- This cozy and comfortable-looking plan is actually larger than it appears from the front, with 1,844 sq. ft. on one level.
- A protected entry leads into a roomy foyer which flows into the vaulted ceilinged living room.
- The family room is also vaulted, and includes an impressive fireplace.
- The spacious kitchen/nook area adjoining the family room includes a distinctive angled island counter.
- A convenient laundry area is located in the garage entryway.
- The front-facing master suite boasts a large private bath with separate tub and shower, plus a roomy walk-in closet.
- Two secondary bedrooms also have large closets and share a second full bath.

Plan AM-1124

Bedrooms: 3	Baths: 2

Total living area:	1,844 sq. ft.
Garage:	374 sq. ft.

Exterior Wall Framing:	2x4

Foundation options:
  Crawlspace only.
(Foundation & framing conversion diagram available — see order form.)

Blueprint Price Code:	B

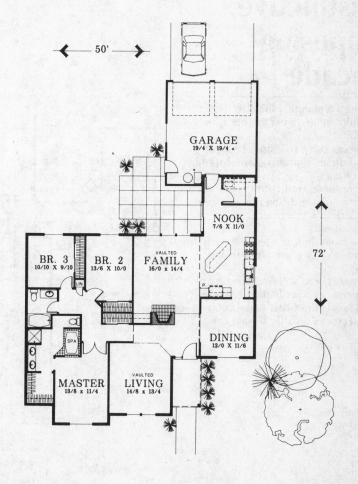

GARAGE
19/4 X 19/4 +

NOOK
7/6 X 11/0

BR. 3
10/10 X 9/10

BR. 2
13/6 X 10/0

VAULTED
FAMILY
16/0 x 14/4

MASTER
13/8 x 11/4

VAULTED
LIVING
14/8 x 13/4

DINING
12/0 X 11/6

SPA

50'

72'

HomeStyles
SOURCE 1
DESIGNERS' NETWORK

To order blueprints, call
1-800-547-5570 or see order form
and pricing information on pages 220-224.

Plan AM-1124

Distinctive, Imposing Facade

- Here's a plan that looks as though it would require a big lot, but is only 40' wide.
- The imposing two-story-high entry leads into an impressive two-story-high Great Room.
- From there, traffic flows naturally to the adjoining dining room or into the spacious kitchen/nook combination.
- The main floor master suite includes a vaulted ceiling, private bath and large closet.
- Upstairs, you will find three more bedrooms, another bath, a balcony overlooking the Great Room below and access to an attic storage area.

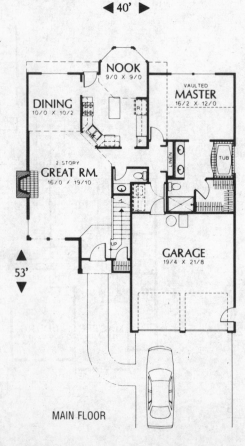

MAIN FLOOR

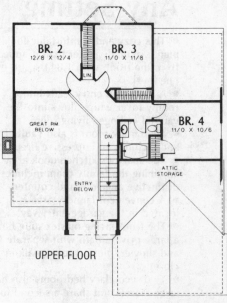

UPPER FLOOR

Plan AM-2135-A

Bedrooms: 4	Baths: 2½

Space:

Upper floor:	636 sq. ft.
Main floor:	1,230 sq. ft.

Total living area:	1,866 sq. ft.
Garage:	419 sq. ft.

Exterior Wall Framing:	2x4

Foundation options:
Crawlspace only.
(Foundation & framing conversion diagram available — see order form.)

Blueprint Price Code:	B

To order blueprints, call
1-800-547-5570 or see order form and pricing information on pages 220-224.

HomeStyles
Source1
DESIGNERS' NETWORK

Plan AM-2135-A

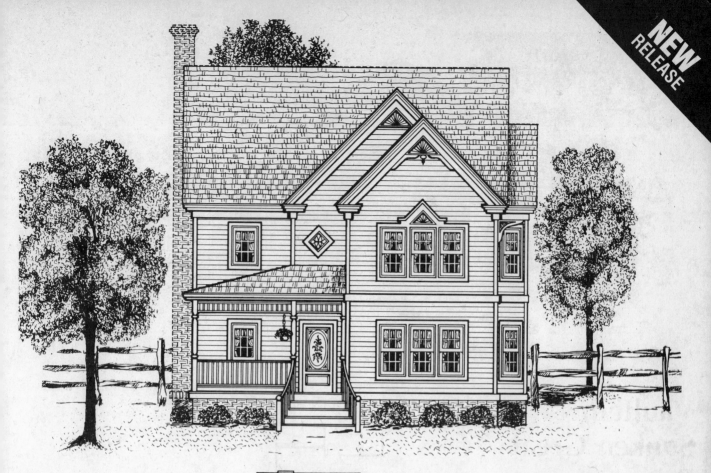

BATH

BEDROOM
10-6 x 13-0

BEDROOM
11-0 x 13-6

BATH

DOWN

MASTER BEDROOM
14-6 x 15-6

UPPER FLOOR

Nostalgic Ambience

- Ideal for a narrow lot, this design recalls days of rocking on the front porch on a warm summer's eve.
- Inside the foyer leads to a formal dining room or to the expansive Great Room.
- The generously sized kitchen can be opened directly into the Great Room or built as shown.
- Note the large work island, abundance of counter space and adjoining laundry area, not to mention the sunny bay window off the kitchen.
- Upstairs, the master suite contains a private bath with a bay window spa tub.

31'

KITCHEN

GREAT ROOM
15-0 x 19-0

36'

LAUN

UP

DINING ROOM
11-6 x 14-6

MAIN FLOOR

Plan V-1886

Bedrooms: 3	Baths: 2½
Space:	
Upper floor:	895 sq. ft.
Main floor:	991 sq. ft.
Total living area:	1,886 sq. ft.
Exterior Wall Framing:	2x6

Ceiling Heights:
Upper floor:	8'
Main floor:	9'

Foundation options:
Crawlspace only.
(Foundation & framing conversion diagram available — see order form.)

Blueprint Price Code: B

To order blueprints, call
1-800-547-5570 or see order form
and pricing information on pages 220-224.

HomeStyles
SOURCE 1
DESIGNERS' NETWORK

Plan V-1886

NEW RELEASE

Vaulted, Sunken Great Room

- Here's a modest-sized home that includes many features usually found only in larger designs.
- The large, sunken Great Room boasts a cozy fireplace and a vaulted ceiling.
- The dining room flows into the kitchen on the right while overlooking the Great Room on the left, to lend an air of spaciousness to all three areas.
- The deluxe kitchen includes a large island plus abundant counter space and a pantry.
- Also, note the convenient laundry area and half-bath on the main floor.
- The vaulted den off the foyer could become an attractive home office.
- Upstairs, the master suite includes a large walk-in closet and private bath with spa tub and separate shower.

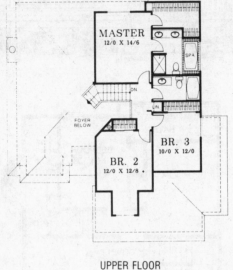

UPPER FLOOR

Plan AM-2120-BL	
Bedrooms: 3	Baths: 2½
Space:	
Upper floor:	819 sq. ft.
Main floor:	1,076 sq. ft.
Total living area:	1,895 sq. ft.
Garage:	606 sq. ft.
Exterior Wall Framing:	2x4
Foundation options: Crawlspace. (Foundation & framing conversion diagram available — see order form.)	
Blueprint Price Code:	B

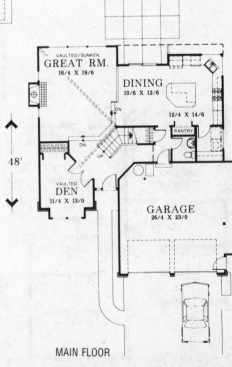

MAIN FLOOR

Plan AM-2120-BL

To order blueprints, call
1-800-547-5570 or see order form
and pricing information on pages 220-224.

Impressive Elevation on Narrow Lot Design

- With its impressive facade, this design looks much larger than its 46' width would indicate, and the interior design is equally impressive.
- Downstairs design is well-zoned into family, formal and utility areas.
- The large space devoted to family room, nook and island kitchen provides plenty of space for casual family living and entertaining.
- The vaulted living room, with its big front windows and fireplace, flows into the formal dining room to provide space for entertaining.
- The foyer, stairway, hall closet, laundry area and powder room make up the traffic-directing and utility portion of the downstairs.
- Upstairs, a delightful master suite boasts a deluxe bath and abundant closet space.

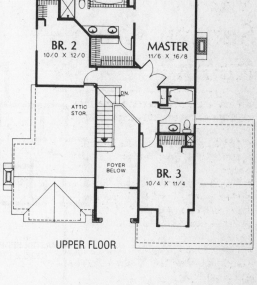

UPPER FLOOR

BR. 2
10/0 X 12/0

MASTER
11/6 X 16/8

ATTIC STOR.

DN.

FOYER BELOW

BR. 3
10/4 X 11/4

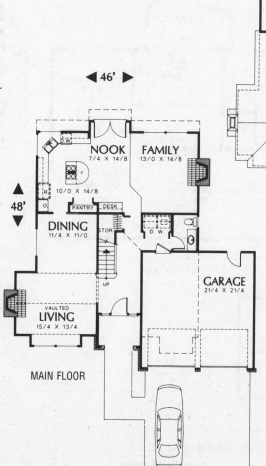

◀ 46' ▶

▲
48'
▼

NOOK
7/4 X 14/8

FAMILY
13/0 X 14/8

10/0 X 14/8

PANTRY   DESK

DINING
11/4 X 11/0

STOR.

D W

UP

GARAGE
21/4 X 21/4

VAULTED LIVING
15/4 X 13/4

MAIN FLOOR

Plan AM-2130-B

Bedrooms: 3	Baths: 2½
Space:	
Upper floor:	838 sq. ft.
Main floor:	1,062 sq. ft.
Total living area:	1,900 sq. ft.
Garage:	455 sq. ft.
Exterior Wall Framing:	2x4

Foundation options:
Crawlspace only.
(Foundation & framing conversion diagram available — see order form.)

Blueprint Price Code:	B

HomeStyles SOURCE 1 DESIGNERS' NETWORK

To order blueprints, call
1-800-547-5570 or see order form and pricing information on pages 220-224.

Plan AM-2130-B

203

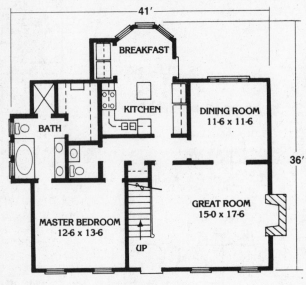

41'

BREAKFAST

KITCHEN

DINING ROOM
11-6 x 11-6

BATH

36'

GREAT ROOM
15-0 x 17-6

MASTER BEDROOM
12-6 x 13-6

UP

MAIN FLOOR

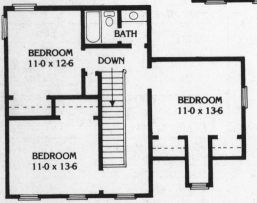

BATH

BEDROOM
11-0 x 12-6

DOWN

BEDROOM
11-0 x 13-6

BEDROOM
11-0 x 13-6

UPPER FLOOR

HomeStyles
SOURCE 1
DESIGNERS' NETWORK

Distinction and Serenity

● The elegant facade of this design promises a home of distinction and serenity.

● A generously sized Great Room, complete with fireplace, leads into a formal dining room.

● The kitchen is also large and flows into a sunny, bay-windowed breakfast nook.

● A magnificent downstairs master suite includes a superb bath with separate tub and shower, two vanities and a large closet.

● The main floor also includes a convenient laundry area (off the breakfast nook) and a powder room off the center hall.

● Upstairs, you will find three more bedrooms and another full bath. (The fourth bedroom, with the dormer, could be finished at a later date, or used for a study or play room.)

Plan V-1918

Bedrooms: 4	Baths: 2½
Space:	
Upper floor:	790 sq. ft.
Main floor:	1,128 sq. ft.
Total living area:	1,918 sq. ft.
Exterior Wall Framing:	2x6

Ceiling Heights:
Upper floor:	8'
Main floor:	9'

Foundation options:
Crawlspace only.
(Foundation & framing conversion diagram available — see order form.)

Blueprint Price Code: B

To order blueprints, call
1-800-547-5570 or see order form and pricing information on pages 220-224.

Plan V-1918

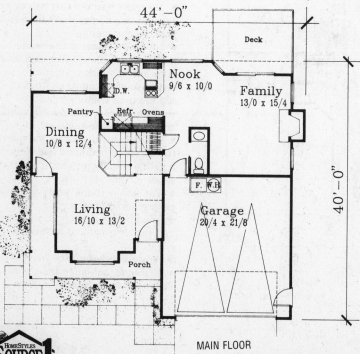

UPPER FLOOR

Br.2
10/8 x 12/0

Walk-in Wardrobe

Lin.

Master
14/8 x 11/6

dn

Open

Spa

Entry Below

W. D.

Br.4
12/4 x 11/8

Br.3
10/8 x 11/8

44'-0"

Deck

Nook
9/6 x 10/0

D.W.

Family
13/0 x 15/4

Pantry

Refr. Ovens

Dining
10/8 x 12/4

F. W.H.

40'-0"

Living
16/10 x 13/2

Garage
20/4 x 21/8

Porch

MAIN FLOOR

Country-Style Porch Welcomes Guests

● An old-fashioned porch suggests an easy, gracious, relaxing style of living.
● The main floor, although compact in size, includes a roomy living/dining area for entertaining, and a spacious family room/nook combination for family living.
● Also note the convenient downstairs powder room.
● The two-story high entry is brightened by an upper gable window.
● Upstairs, all four bedrooms include walk-in closets.
● The roomy master suite also includes a private bath with double vanities and separate tub and shower.
● The laundry area is located upstairs for the utmost in convenience.

Plan CDG-2002

Bedrooms: 4	**Baths:** 2½

Space:	
Upper floor:	1,077 sq. ft.
Main floor:	888 sq. ft.

Total living area:	1,965 sq. ft.
Garage:	440 sq. ft.

Exterior Wall Framing:	2x4

Foundation options:
  Crawlspace only.
(Foundation & framing conversion diagram available — see order form.)

Blueprint Price Code:	B

To order blueprints, call
1-800-547-5570 or see order form
and pricing information on pages 220-224.

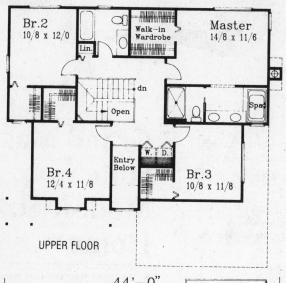

HomeStyles
SOURCE1
DESIGNERS NETWORK

Plan CDG-2002

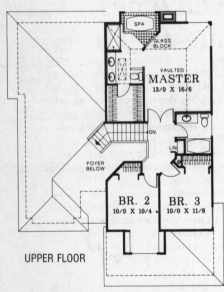

UPPER FLOOR

Plan AM-2121-C

Bedrooms: 3	Baths: 2½
Space:	
Upper floor:	823 sq. ft.
Main floor:	1,152 sq. ft.
Total living area:	1,975 sq. ft.
Garage:	514 sq. ft.
Exterior Wall Framing:	2x4

Foundation options:
Crawlspace only.
(Foundation & framing conversion
diagram available — see order form.)

Blueprint Price Code: B

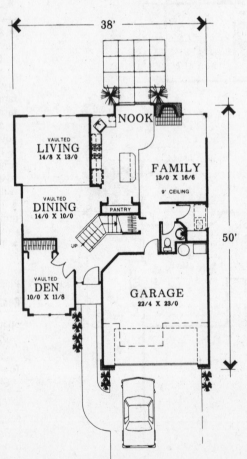

MAIN FLOOR

Grand Master Suite in Modest-Sized Home

● This home proves that narrow- or zero-lot-line homes don't have to be plain or cramped.

● Luxurious upper master suite includes a vaulted ceiling and double door entry.

● The splendid master bath boasts a spa tub area with glass block wall, a separate shower and double vanities, and a large walk-in closet.

● Downstairs, the living and dining rooms are also vaulted and flow together visually to create a grand space for entertaining.

● The family room sports a 9-foot ceiling and a fireplace.

● The kitchen is open to the nook and family room and includes large island.

● A vaulted den off the foyer is available for a home office, study, library or music room.

To order blueprints, call
1-800-547-5570 or see order form
and pricing information on pages 220-224.

Plan AM-2121-C

Crisp Contemporary Styling

- Contemporary split-level is designed for lots that slope down from the front.
- Daylight basement in rear adds extra living space.
- Angled wall and railing offer unique character to living room.
- Dining area overlooks living room through railings on either side of the fireplace.

- Living room also looks into family room below.
- Spacious kitchen/dining area provides plenty of space for casual dining.
- Master suite includes private bath and large walk-in closet.
- Lower level includes ample laundry and utility areas, plus a third bedroom and another full bath.

Plan CPS-1132-S

Bedrooms: 3	Baths: 3

Space:

Main floor:	1,185 sq. ft.
Lower level:	858 sq. ft.

Total living area:	2,043 sq. ft.
Garage:	494 sq. ft.

Exterior Wall Framing:	2x6

Foundation options:
Daylight basement only.
(Foundation & framing conversion diagram available — see order form.)

Blueprint Price Code:	C

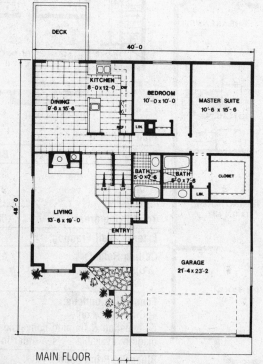

MAIN FLOOR

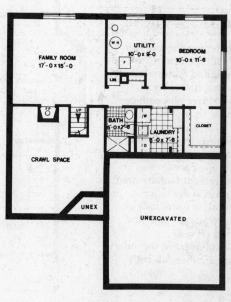

BASEMENT

Plan CPS-1132-S

To order blueprints, call
1-800-547-5570 or see order form and pricing information on pages 220-224.

207

NEW RELEASE

Delightful Victorian from 1873

- Adapted from a design originally done in 1873, this Victorian home is beautifully detailed on the exterior.
- Inside, the plan opens up to create a house ideally suited to entertaining.
- The living room, dining room, Great Room and foyer all combine and flow together to provide an abundance of well-planned space.
- For family dining, the kitchen and breakfast room are combined to create a bright, open area.
- Note the convenient laundry area and half-bath downstairs.
- The deluxe master suite upstairs includes a luxury private bath and large three-sided closet.
- Two larger-than-average secondary bedrooms share another full bath.

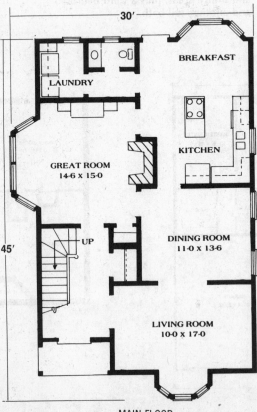

MAIN FLOOR

- 30'
- 45'
- LAUNDRY
- BREAKFAST
- GREAT ROOM 14-6 x 15-0
- KITCHEN
- UP
- DINING ROOM 11-0 x 13-6
- LIVING ROOM 10-0 x 17-0

BEDROOM 11-6 x 13-6
BEDROOM 11-6 x 13-6
BATH
BATH
DOWN
MASTER BEDROOM 11-6 x 17-0

UPPER FLOOR

Plan V-2084-C

Bedrooms: 3	Baths: 2½
Space:	
Upper floor:	979 sq. ft.
Main floor:	1,105 sq. ft.
Total living area:	2,084 sq. ft.
Exterior Wall Framing:	2x6
Ceiling Heights:	
Upper floor:	8'
Main floor:	10'

Foundation options:
Crawlspace only.
(Foundation & framing conversion diagram available — see order form.)

Blueprint Price Code: C

To order blueprints, call **1-800-547-5570** or see order form and pricing information on pages 220-224.

Plan V-2084-C

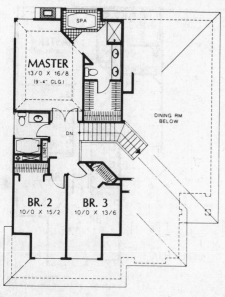

UPPER FLOOR

Plan AM-2285

Bedrooms: 3	Baths: 2½

Space:

Upper floor:	854 sq. ft.
Main floor:	1,257 sq. ft.
Total living area:	2,111 sq. ft.
Garage:	427 sq. ft.

Exterior Wall Framing:	2x4

Foundation options:
Crawlspace only.
(Foundation & framing conversion
diagram available — see order form.)

Blueprint Price Code: C

HomeStyles
SOURCE1
DESIGNERS NETWORK

◄ 38' ►

NOOK
7/4 X 8/0

FAMILY
13/0 X 16/8
(9'-0" CLG.)

SHELVES

VAULTED
LIVING
14/8 X 13/0

PLANT SHELF

VAULTED
DINING
14/8 X 11/0 +/-

PLANT SHELF

UP

GARAGE
20/4 X 21/0

DEN
10/8 X 11/8
(CLG. @ 10'-8")

▲
50'
▼

MAIN FLOOR

Elegantly Simple Design

● Clean lines and stucco exterior create a design that is elegant in its basic simplicity.

● On the main floor, the family room, nook and kitchen are designed as a unit to make best use of the space available.

● The living and dining rooms and the foyer are separated only by plant shelves, giving the area a super-spacious look.

● A handy half-bath and laundry area are located near the garage entry.

● The upstairs master suite is comprised of a luxurious bath with separate tub and shower, plus two vanities.

● Both secondary bedrooms face the front and include bright front windows.

MASTER
13/0 X 16/8
(9'-4" CLG.)

SPA

DINING RM
BELOW

DN.

LINEN

BR. 2
10/0 X 15/2

BR. 3
10/0 X 13/6

To order blueprints, call
1-800-547-5570 or see order form
and pricing information on pages 220-224.

Plan AM-2285

209

Dignity and Grace

- A 40' width need not present an insurmountable obstacle to creativity, and this design is proof of that fact.
- The impressive facade includes design elements often found only on larger homes.
- Downstairs, the living and dining rooms are designed to be used separately or together, depending on the occasion and the number of people involved.
- The casual family living area across the rear is spacious, and encompasses a roomy kitchen, sunny nook and family room with fireplace.
- Upstairs, the sumptuous master suite displays a coffered ceiling and includes a deluxe bath and large walk-in closet.
- Three secondary bedrooms share a second upstairs bath.
- Note the convenient half-bath and laundry area downstairs near the entry from the garage.

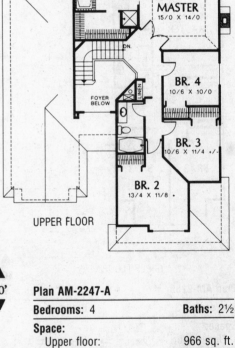

UPPER FLOOR

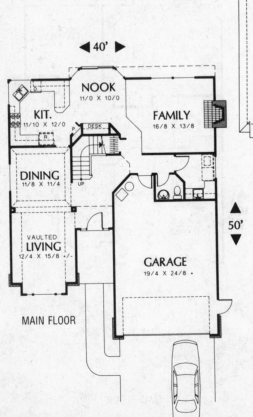

MAIN FLOOR

Plan AM-2247-A

Bedrooms: 4	Baths: 2½

Space:	
Upper floor:	966 sq. ft.
Main floor:	1,150 sq. ft.
Total living area:	**2,116 sq. ft.**
Garage:	476 sq. ft.

Exterior Wall Framing:	2x4

Foundation options:
Crawlspace only.
(Foundation & framing conversion diagram available — see order form.)

Blueprint Price Code:	C

To order blueprints, call
1-800-547-5570 or see order form and pricing information on pages 220-224.

Plan AM-2247-A

Tasteful Simplicity

● A basically very simple design on the exterior, this home presents a welcoming look to the world.
● Inside, the spacious foyer channels traffic to the living, dining or family rooms, or upstairs to the two secondary bedrooms.
● The master suite is downstairs and includes a deluxe double-vanity bath, plus separate tub and shower.
● The kitchen, nook and family room are designed as a unit for casual family activities.
● The dining room and living room with vaulted ceiling function together when needed for formal entertaining.

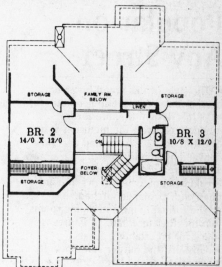

UPPER FLOOR

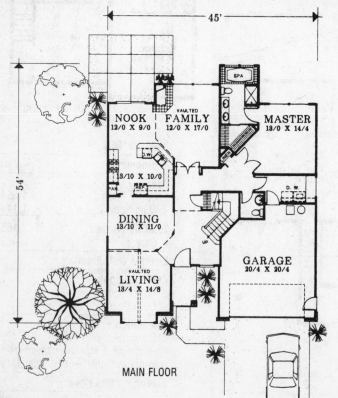

MAIN FLOOR

Plan AM-2222

Bedrooms: 3	Baths: 2½

Space:

Upper floor:	565 sq. ft.
Main floor:	1,574 sq. ft.

Total living area:	2,139 sq. ft.
Garage:	413 sq. ft.

Exterior Wall Framing:	2x4

Foundation options:
Crawlspace only.
(Foundation & framing conversion diagram available — see order form.)

Blueprint Price Code:	C

To order blueprints, call
1-800-547-5570 or see order form
and pricing information on pages 220-224.

Plan AM-2222

Popular on Any Street

- The style of this grand home has been popular for several generations.
- In this design, the interior is modernized, with the inclusion of a Great Room, 2½ baths and a convenient laundry area.
- The Great Room adjoins a bright breakfast nook which flows into an open-end, U-shaped kitchen.
- The formal living and dining rooms join together to create an impressive space for entertaining guests.
- Upstairs, the master suite includes a private bath and large closet; three secondary bedrooms complete the upstairs.

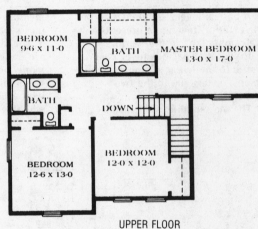

UPPER FLOOR

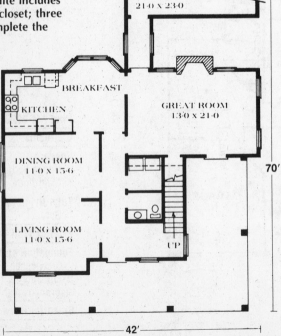

MAIN FLOOR

Plan V-2165-C

Bedrooms: 4	Baths: 2½
Space:	
Upper floor:	1,054 sq. ft.
Main floor:	1,111 sq. ft.
Total living area:	2,165 sq. ft.
Garage:	483 sq. ft.
Exterior Wall Framing:	2x6
Ceiling Heights:	
Upper floor:	8'
Main floor:	10'

Foundation options:
  Crawlspace only.
(Foundation & framing conversion diagram available — see order form.)

Blueprint Price Code: C

To order blueprints, call
1-800-547-5570 or see order form
and pricing information on pages 220-224

Plan V-2165-C

Stylish Traditional Design

- Large kitchen/nook/family room combination creates generous space for a busy, growing family.
- Living room, dining room and foyer combine to create impressive space for friends, neighbors and other visitors.
- Upstairs master suite includes a luxury bath with separate tub and shower, plus a large closet.
- Bedroom 2 exhibits a vaulted ceiling and a sunny window seat.

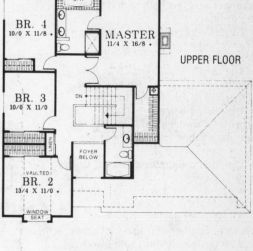

UPPER FLOOR

BR. 4
10/0 X 11/8

MASTER
11/4 X 16/8

SPA

BR. 3
10/0 X 11/0

DN

LINEN

FOYER BELOW

VAULTED
BR. 2
13/4 X 11/0

WINDOW SEAT

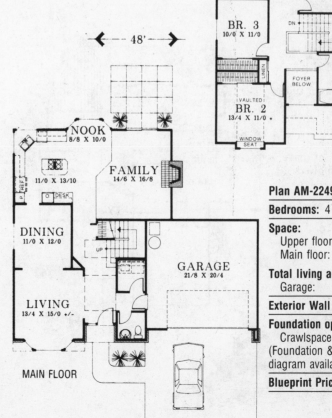

← 48' →

44'

NOOK
8/8 X 10/0

FAMILY
14/6 X 16/8

11/0 X 13/10

DESK

DINING
11/0 X 12/0

UP

GARAGE
21/8 X 20/4

LIVING
13/4 X 15/0 +/-

MAIN FLOOR

Plan AM-2249

Bedrooms: 4	**Baths:** 2½

Space:
Upper floor:	1,138 sq. ft.
Main floor:	1,043 sq. ft.
Total living area:	**2,181 sq. ft.**
Garage:	440 sq. ft.

Exterior Wall Framing:	2x4

Foundation options:
Crawlspace only.
(Foundation & framing conversion diagram available — see order form.)

Blueprint Price Code:	C

HomeStyles SOURCE
DESIGNERS NETWORK

Plan AM-2249

To order blueprints, call
1-800-547-5570 or see order form and pricing information on pages 220-224.

Soaring Contemporary

- Contemporary flair of soaring rooflines sets this home apart from the ordinary.
- Large living room includes sunken "conversation pit" in front of the fireplace.
- The family and dining areas flow together to create a large space for gatherings of family and friends.
- Upstairs, a balcony hallway provides a vantage point for looking into the vaulted ceiling area of the living room below.
- Upstairs, a sumptuous master suite includes a deluxe bath and a separate private room for a wardrobe, sewing room, library or exercise area.
- An optional daylight basement provides another 800 sq. ft. of space, and an upstairs bonus room offers numerous possibilities.

UPPER FLOOR

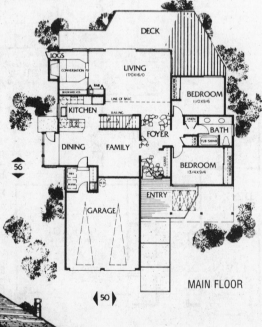

MAIN FLOOR

◄ 50 ►

Plan SD-2165

Bedrooms: 3	Baths: 2

Space:	
Upper floor:	789 sq. ft.
Main floor:	1,376 sq. ft.

Total living area:	2,165 sq. ft.
Bonus area:	212 sq. ft.
Basement:	800 sq. ft.
Garage:	438 sq. ft.

Exterior Wall Framing:	2x4

Foundation options:
Daylight basement.
Crawlspace.
(Foundation & framing conversion diagram available — see order form.)

Blueprint Price Code:	C

**To order blueprints, call
1-800-547-5570** or see order form
and pricing information on pages 220-224

214

Plan SD-2165

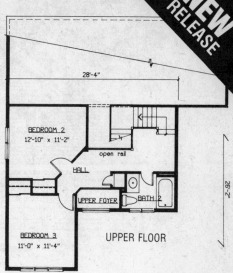

UPPER FLOOR

BEDROOM 2
12'-10" x 11'-2"

open rail

BEDROOM 3
11'-0" x 11'-4"

HALL

UPPER FOYER

BATH 2

28'-4"

26'-2"

Your Choice of Exteriors

- This roomy two-story plan comes with two different exterior treatments for the same interior design.
- Great Room and dining area together create a huge space for entertaining and family living across the rear of the home.
- Roomy kitchen includes abundant counter and cabinet space, and a convenient pantry.
- An elegant downstairs master bedroom suite includes a sumptuous private bath and large walk-in closet.
- A convenient den off the foyer would make a nice home office.
- The upstairs offers two more bedrooms, another bath and a balcony hallway overlooking the foyer below.

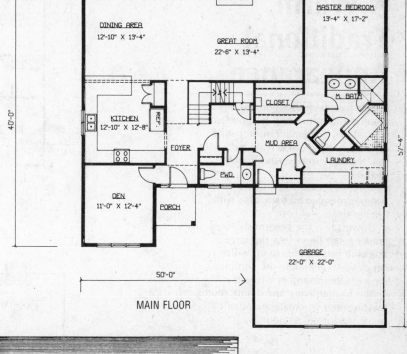

MAIN FLOOR

DINING AREA
12'-10" x 13'-4"

GREAT ROOM
22'-6" x 13'-4"

MASTER BEDROOM
13'-4" x 17'-2"

KITCHEN
12'-10" x 12'-8"

REF.

CLOSET

M. BATH

FOYER

MUD AREA

LAUNDRY

PWD.

DEN
11'-0" x 12'-4"

PORCH

GARAGE
22'-0" x 22'-0"

40'-0"

50'-0"

57'-4"

Plan GL-2250-P

Bedrooms: 3	Baths: 2½

Space:	
Upper floor:	540 sq. ft.
Main floor:	1,710 sq. ft.

Total living area:	**2,250 sq. ft.**
Basement:	1,710 sq. ft.
Garage:	484 sq. ft.

Exterior Wall Framing:	2x6

Foundation options:
Standard basement only.
(Foundation & framing conversion diagram available — see order form.)

Blueprint Price Code:	C

HomeStyles
SOURCE 1
DESIGNERS' NETWORK

Plan GL-2250-P

To order blueprints, call
1-800-547-5570 or see order form
and pricing information on pages 220-224.

A Warm, Traditional Appearance

- This four-bedroom home offers a grand solution to small lot problems.
- Upstairs, a splendid master suite includes a gorgeous private bath with spa, separate shower and double vanities.
- Three secondary bedrooms share a compartmentalized bath, also with double sinks.
- Downstairs, the generously sized family room flows into the large nook/kitchen combination, which is designed to eliminate the confined feeling often found in kitchens.
- The formal living and dining rooms join together to create abundant space for formal gatherings.

Plan AM-2202-L

Bedrooms: 4	Baths: 2½

Space:

Upper floor:	1,213 sq. ft.
Main floor:	1,150 sq. ft.
Total living area:	**2,363 sq. ft.**
Garage:	455 sq. ft.

Exterior Wall Framing:	2x4

Foundation options:
Crawlspace only.
(Foundation & framing conversion diagram available — see order form.)

Blueprint Price Code:	C

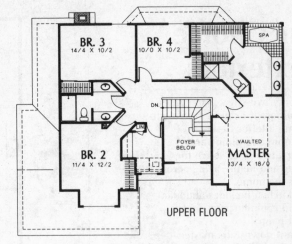

UPPER FLOOR

◀ 50' ▶

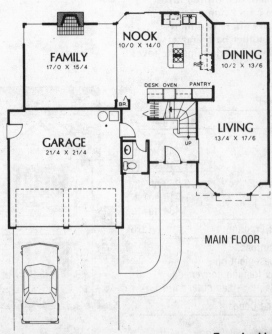

MAIN FLOOR

▲ 40' ▼

HomeStyles SOURCE 1 DESIGNERS' NETWORK

216

To order blueprints, call
1-800-547-5570 or see order form
and pricing information on pages 220-224.

Plan AM-2202-L

Charming Economy

- This plan is economical to construct, but still charming in its visual appeal and restful interior.
- The interior presents abundant space for family or informal entertaining.
- A roomy Great Room adjoining the breakfast nook includes a handsome fireplace.
- A formal dining room is available for dressier occasions.
- The downstairs guest bedroom would make a great home office if not needed for sleeping.
- Note the full bath downstairs, in addition to two baths upstairs.
- The large master suite includes a sumptuous private bath with separate tub and shower.
- Bedrooms 2 and 3 are roomy and share access to a compartmentalized bath.

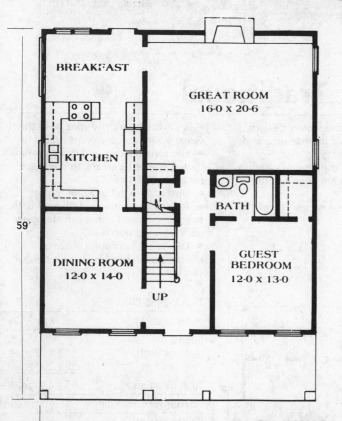

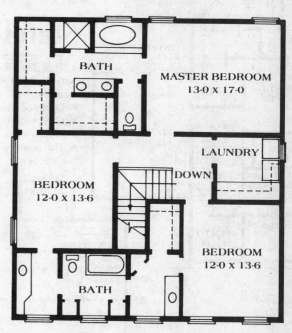

Plan V-2398-C

Plan V-2398-C	
Bedrooms: 3-4	**Baths:** 3

Space:

Upper floor:	1,174 sq. ft.
Main floor:	1,224 sq. ft.
Total living area:	**2,398 sq. ft.**
Exterior Wall Framing:	2x6

Ceiling Heights:

Upper floor:	9'
Main floor:	9'

Foundation options:
Crawlspace only.
(Foundation & framing conversion diagram available — see order form.)

Blueprint Price Code:	C

To order blueprints, call
1-800-547-5570 or see order form
and pricing information on pages 220-224.

Stately Traditional

- This dignified and stately design puts forth an air of permanence and stability.
- Updated interior includes a fine kitchen with cooktop counter and breakfast area.
- The laundry area is convenient to the kitchen.

- A covered porch adjoins both the Great Room and breakfast area.
- The formal living and dining rooms flow together to create ample space for dinner parties.
- Upstairs, an extravagant master suite includes a unique L-shaped bath, two large closets and a private upper deck covered porch.
- Two other bedrooms share a compartmentalized bath with double vanities.

Plan V-2450-CH

Bedrooms: 3		**Baths:** 2½

Space:
Upper floor:	1,150 sq. ft.
Main floor:	1,300 sq. ft.

Total living area:	2,450 sq. ft.

Exterior Wall Framing:	2x6

Ceiling Heights:
Upper floor:	9'
Main floor:	10'

Foundation options:
Crawlspace only.
(Foundation & framing conversion diagram available — see order form.)

Blueprint Price Code:	C

Plan V-2450-CH

**To order blueprints, call
1-800-547-5570** or see order form
and pricing information on pages 220-224.

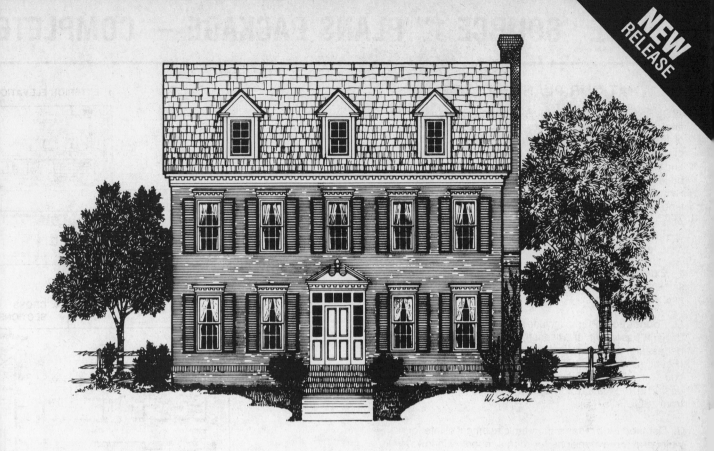

W. Sidruns

Classic Design Offers Big Space on Small Lot

● Symmetrical colonial design presents a classic facade to visitors and passersby.

● Interior also follows tradition, but includes plenty of modern amenities, such as a thoroughly modern kitchen, three full baths and a powder room.

● Note the convenient wet bar located between the Great Room and living room.

● An old-fashioned touch that is making a welcome come-back is the large walk-in pantry in the kitchen.

● Upstairs, an elegant master suite includes a bath our ancestors could never even dream about.

● Three other bedrooms and two more baths complete the upstairs.

● A third floor can be finished off for more bedrooms, a study, exercise room or many other uses.

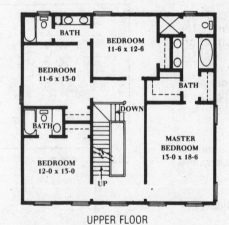

BATH

BEDROOM
11-6 x 12-6

BEDROOM
11-6 x 13-0

BATH

BATH

BEDROOM
12-0 x 13-0

DOWN

UP

MASTER BEDROOM
13-0 x 18-6

UPPER FLOOR

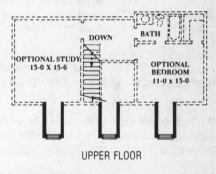

DOWN

BATH

OPTIONAL STUDY
13-0 X 15-6

OPTIONAL BEDROOM
11-0 x 13-0

UPPER FLOOR

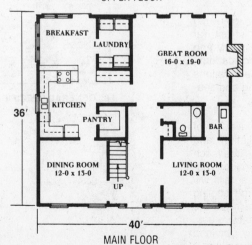

BREAKFAST

LAUNDRY

GREAT ROOM
16-0 x 19-0

KITCHEN

PANTRY

BAR

DINING ROOM
12-0 x 13-0

LIVING ROOM
12-0 x 13-0

UP

36'

40'

MAIN FLOOR

Plan V-2649	
Bedrooms: 4-5	**Baths:** 3½
Space:	
Upper floor:	1,281 sq. ft.
Main floor:	1,368 sq. ft.
Total living area:	2,649 sq. ft.
Bonus area:	605 sq. ft.
Exterior Wall Framing:	2x6
Ceiling Heights:	
Upper floor:	9'
Main floor:	10'

Foundation options:
Crawlspace.
(Foundation & framing conversion diagram available — see order form.)

Blueprint Price Code: D

HomeStyles
Source 1
DESIGNERS NETWORK

Plan V-2649

To order blueprints, call
1-800-547-5570 or see order form
and pricing information on pages 220-224.

WHAT OUR PLANS INCLUDE

"SOURCE 1" construction blueprints are detailed, clear and concise. All blueprints are designed by members of the A.I.A. (American Institute of Architects) and/or the A.I.B.D. (American Institute of Building Designers), and each plan is designed to meet nationally recognized building codes (either the Uniform Building Code, Standard Building Code or Basic Building Code) at the time they were drawn.

Although blueprints will vary depending on the size and complexity of the home and on the individual designer's style, each set will include the following elements:

1. **Exterior Elevations** show the front, rear, and the sides of the house including exterior materials, details, and measurements.

2. **Foundation Plans** include drawings for a full or daylight basement, crawlspace, or slab foundation. All necessary notations and dimensions are included. (Foundation options will vary for each plan. If the home you want does not have the type of foundation you desire, a foundation conversion diagram is available from "SOURCE 1".)

3. **Detailed Floor Plans** show the placement of interior walls and the dimensions for rooms, doors, windows, stairways, etc. of each level of the house.

4. **Cross Sections** show details of the house as though it were cut in slices from the roof to the foundation. The cross sections detail the home's construction, insulation, flooring and roofing details.

5. **Interior Elevations** show the specific details of cabinets (kitchen, bathroom, and utility room) fireplaces, built-in units, and other special interior features.

6. **Roof Plans** provide the layout of rafters, dormers, gables, and other roof elements including clerestory windows and skylights.

7. **Schematic Electrical Layouts** show the suggested location for switches, fixtures, and outlets.

8. **General Specifications** provide general instructions and information regarding structural specifications, excavating and grading, masonry and concrete work, carpentry and wood specifications, thermal and moisture protection, and specifications about drywall, tile, flooring, glazing, caulking and sealants.

NOTE: Due to regional variations, local availability of materials, local codes, methods of installation, and individual preferences, it is impossible to include much detail on heating, plumbing, and electrical work on your plans. The duct work, venting, and other details will vary depending on the type of heating and cooling system (forced air, hot water, electric, solar) and the type of energy (gas, oil, electricity, solar) that you use. These details and specifications are easily obtained from your builder, contractor, and/or local suppliers.

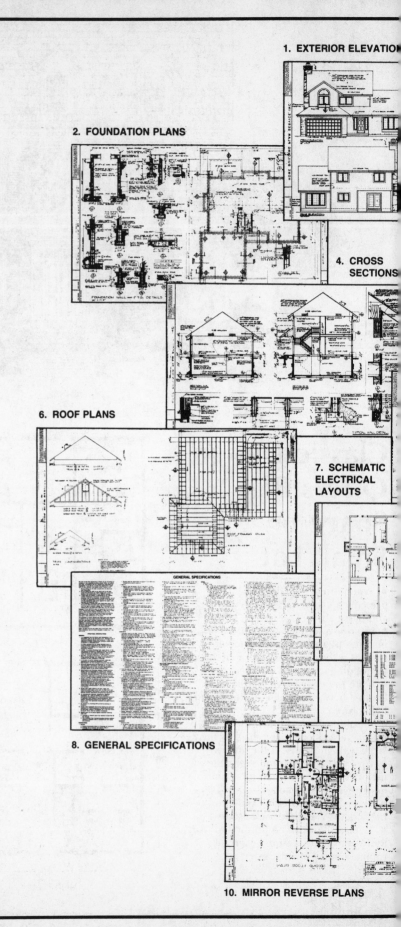

1. EXTERIOR ELEVATION

2. FOUNDATION PLANS

4. CROSS SECTIONS

6. ROOF PLANS

7. SCHEMATIC ELECTRICAL LAYOUTS

8. GENERAL SPECIFICATIONS

10. MIRROR REVERSE PLANS

CONSTRUCTION BLUEPRINTS TO BUILD YOUR HOME

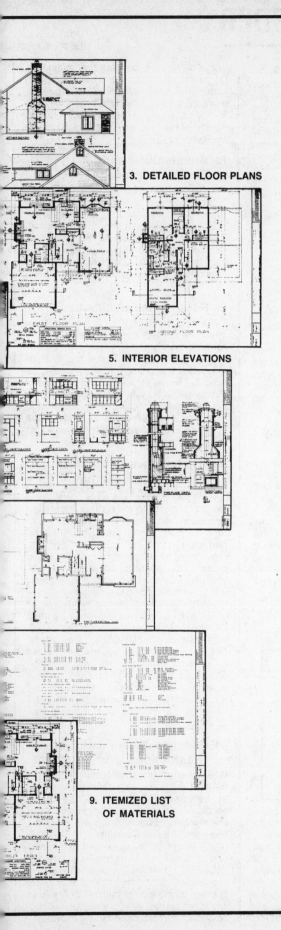

3. DETAILED FLOOR PLANS

5. INTERIOR ELEVATIONS

9. ITEMIZED LIST OF MATERIALS

11. HELPFUL "HOW-TO" DIAGRAMS

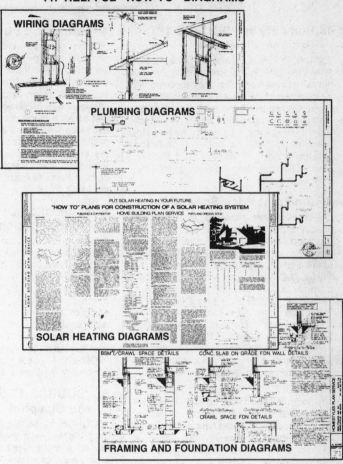

WIRING DIAGRAMS

PLUMBING DIAGRAMS

SOLAR HEATING DIAGRAMS

FRAMING AND FOUNDATION DIAGRAMS

Important Extras and Helpful Building Aids
(Sold Separately)

Every set of plans that you order will contain all the details that your builder will need. However, "Source 1" provides additional guides and information as follows:

9. **Itemized List of Materials** details the quantity, type, and size of materials needed to build your home. (This list is extremely helpful in acquiring an accurate construction estimate. It is not intended for use to order materials.)

10. **Mirror Reverse Plans** are useful if you want to build your home in the reverse of the plan that is shown. Reverse plans are available for an additional charge. However, since the lettering and dimensions will read backwards, we recommend that you order at least one regular-reading set of blueprints.

11. **Helpful "How-To" Diagrams — Plumbing, Wiring, Solar Heating, and Framing and Foundation Conversion Diagrams**

Each of these diagrams details the basic tools and techniques needed to plumb, wire, and install a solar heating system, convert plans with 2 x 4 exterior walls to 2 x 6 (or vice versa), or adapt a plan for a basement, crawlspace, or slab foundation.

WHAT YOU NEED TO KNOW
BEFORE YOU ORDER

1. HomeStyles "SOURCE 1" Designers' Network

"SOURCE 1" is a consortium of over 25 of America's leading residential designers. All the plans presented in this book are designed by members of the A.I.A. (American Institute of Architects) and/or the A.I.B.D. (American Institute of Building Designers), and each plan is designed to meet nationally recognized building codes (either the Uniform Building Code, Standard Building Code or Basic Building Code) at the time that they were drawn.

2. Blueprint Price Schedule

Our sales volume allows us to offer quality blueprints at a fraction of the cost it takes to develop them. Custom designs cost thousands of dollars, usually 5 to 15 percent of the cost of construction. Design costs for a $100,000 home, for example, can range from $5,000 to $15,000. A HomeStyles "SOURCE 1" plan costs only $165 to $395 depending on the size of the home and the number of sets of blueprints that you order. By ordering a "SOURCE 1" plan, you save enough money to add a deck, swimming pool, beautiful kitchen, luxurious master bedroom, elegant bathroom, or other extras.

The "SOURCE 1" pricing schedule is based on "total finished living space." When we calculate "living space" we do not include garages, porches, decks, unfinished space or unfinished basements. The schedule below outlines the value and savings you get from ordering "SOURCE 1" plans and multiple sets:

NUMBER OF SETS	PRICE CODE GROUP				
	A under 1,900 sq. ft.	B 1,900-1,999 sq. ft.	C 2,000-2,499 sq. ft.	D 2,500-2,999 sq. ft.	E over 3,000 sq. ft.
7 sets	$240	$290	$325	$360	$395
4 sets	$210	$250	$280	$315	$350
1 set	$165	$200	$230	$260	$295

*Prices guaranteed to December 31, 1990.
We expect a $25 increase on all plans in 1991.

3. Revisions, Modifications, and Customizing

The tremendous variety of designs available through "SOURCE 1" allows you to choose the home that best suits your lifestyle, budget and building site. Your home can be easily customized through your choice of siding, roof, trim, decorating, color, and other non-structural alterations and materials.

Most "SOURCE 1" plans are easily modified by qualified professionals. Minor changes and material substitutions can be made by any professional builder without the need for expensive blueprint revisions. However, if you are considering making major changes to your design, we strongly recommend that you seek the services of an architect or professional designer to assist you.

Also, every state, county, and municipality has its own codes, zoning requirements, ordinances, and building regulations. Modifications may be necessary to comply with your specific requirements — snow loads, energy codes, seismic zones, etc.

4. Estimating Building Costs

Building costs vary widely depending on style and size, the type of finishing materials you select, and the local rates for labor and building materials. With an average cost per square foot of construction, you can multiply this figure by the total living area of your home and derive a rough estimate. More accurate estimates will require a professional review of the working blueprints and the types of materials you choose. To get a rough estimate, call a local contractor, your state or local Builders Association, the NAHB, or the AIBD.

5. Foundation Options and Exterior Construction

Depending on your specific geography and climate, your home will be built with either a slab, crawlspace, or basement type foundation and the exterior walls will either be 2 x 4 or 2 x 6. Most professional contractors and builders can easily adapt a home to meet the foundation and exterior wall requirements that you desire. If the specific home that you select does not meet your foundation or exterior wall requirements, "SOURCE 1" has a foundation and framing conversion diagram available.

6. "SOURCE 1" Service Policy and Blueprint Delivery

"SOURCE 1" service representatives are available to answer questions and assist you in placing your blueprint order. All telephone orders are entered directly into our computer. Mail orders are entered upon receipt. We try to process and ship every order within 48 hours. For regular mailing (US First Class Mail or UPS Second Day Air) you should receive your blueprints within 4 to 5 working days. For express mail (UPS Next Day Air or Federal Express) please expect 1 to 2 days for delivery.

7. How Many Blueprints Should I Order?

BLUEPRINT CHECKLIST
____ OWNER'S SET(S)
____ BUILDER (usually requires at least three sets: one for legal document, one for inspections, and a minimum of one set for subcontractors.)
____ BUILDING PERMIT DEPARTMENT (at least one set; check with your local governing body for number of sets required.)
____ LENDING INSTITUTION (usually one set for conventional mortgage; three sets for FHA or VA loans.)
____ TOTAL NUMBER OF SETS NEEDED

A single set of blueprints is sufficient to study and review a home in greater detail. However, if you are planning to get cost estimates or are planning to build, you will need a minimum of 4 sets and more likely 7 sets — sometimes more. Once you begin the process of building your home, everyone seems to need a set. As the owner, you will want to retain a set (1), your lending institution (2), the local building authorities (3), your builder/contractor (4), and of course, subcontractors — foundation, framing, plumbing, heating, electrical, insulation, etc. (5-10) To help you determine the exact number of sets you will need, please refer to the Blueprint Checklist.

8. Architectural and Engineering Seals

With increased concern over energy costs and safety, many cities and states are now requiring that an architect or engineer review and "seal" a blueprint prior to construction. There may be an additional charge for this service. Please contact your local lumber yard, municipal building department, Builders Association, or the local chapter of the AIBD or AIA.

9. Returns and Exchanges

Each set of "SOURCE 1" blueprints is specially printed and shipped to you in response to your specific order; consequently, we cannot honor requests for refunds. If the prints you order cannot be used, we will be pleased to exchange them. Please return all sets to us within 30 days. For the new set of plans that you select in exchange, there will simply be a flat charge of $50 (plus $5 for each additional set up to the original number of sets ordered).

10. Compliance With Local Codes and Building Regulations

Because of the tremendous variety of geography and climate throughout the U.S. and Canada, every state, county, and municipality will have its own building regulations, codes, zoning requirements and ordinances. Depending on where you live, your plan may need to be modified to comply with your local building requirements — snow loads, energy codes, seismic zones, etc. All of "SOURCE 1" plans are designed to meet the specifications of seismic zones I or II. HomeStyles "SOURCE 1" Designers' Network authorizes the use of our blueprints expressly conditioned upon your obligation and agreement to strictly comply with all local building codes, ordinances, regulations, and requirements — including permits and inspections at the time of and during construction.

11. License Agreement, Copy Restrictions, and Copyright

When you purchase your blueprints from "SOURCE 1", we, as Licensor, grant you, as Licensee, the right to use these documents to construct a single unit. All of the plans in this publication are protected under the Federal Copyright Act, Title XVII of the United States Code and Chapter 37 of the Code of Federal Regulations. "SOURCE 1" retains title and ownership of the original documents. The blueprints licensed to you cannot be used or resold to any other person. Also, these plans cannot be copied or reproduced by any means.

How to Order Your Blueprints

Ordering blueprints is fast and easy. You can order by mail, by fax (use our International Fax number 1-612-927-5149) or call our toll free number **1-800-547-5570.** When ordering by phone, please have your credit card ready. Thank you for your order. Good luck building your dream home.

------- BLUEPRINT ORDER FORM --------

Mail to: **For Faster Service**
HomeStyles "Source 1"   **Call Toll-Free**
Suite 115, 6800 France Avenue South   **1-800-547-5570**
Minneapolis, MN 55435
Please send me the following:

Plan Number _____ **Price Code** _____

Foundation _____
(Please review your plan carefully for foundation options — basement, crawlspace, or slab. Many plans offer all three options, others offer only one.)

Number of Sets	A	B	C	D	E	Amount
☐ 7 SETS	$240	$290	$325	$360	$395	$ _____
☐ 4 SETS	$210	$250	$280	$315	$350	$ _____
☐ 1 SET	$165	$200	$230	$260	$295	$ _____

*Prices guaranteed to December 31, 1990. We expect a $25 increase on all plans in 1991.

☐ **Additional Sets** of this plan, $25 now; $ _____
$35 later, each. (Number of sets _____)

☐ **Itemized List of Materials,** $30, each $ _____
additional set $10.
(Sold only with blueprint purchase. Lists are only available for plans with prefix letters AH, AM, B, C, CPS, E, H, I, J, K, N, NW*, P, R, S, SD, U, W)
*Please ask when ordering, not available on all plans

☐ **Description of Materials:** Two sets $25 $ _____
(For use in obtaining FHA or VA financing)
(Only available for Plans with prefix letters C, E, H, J, K, N, P, U)

☐ **Mirror Reverse Plans,** $25 one-time charge. $ _____
(Number of sets to be reversed _____.)
*The writing on Mirror Reverse plans will be backwards. Order at least one regular set.

☐ **Typical How-To Diagrams** $ _____
☐ Plumbing ☐ Wiring ☐ Solar Heating
☐ Framing & Foundation Conversion
One set @ $12.50, any two @ $23.00, any three @ $30.00, all four only $35.

☐ **Sales Tax** (MN Residents, please add 6%) $ _____

Please Add Postage Charges (Check One)
☐ First-Class Priority or UPS Blue Label $ _____
(U.S. only), $10.50
Allow 4-5 working days for delivery. *Must have street address for UPS delivery.
☐ First-Class Priority (Canada only) $10.50 $ _____
Allow 2-3 weeks for delivery.
☐ Overnight Express Delivery (U.S. only) $25.00 $ _____
Allow 1-2 working days for delivery. *Must have street address.
☐ Express Delivery (Canada only) $40.00 $ _____
Allow 4-5 working days for delivery. *Must have street address.
☐ Overseas Airmail Delivery $40.00 $ _____
Allow approx. 7 working days.

Payment   **TOTAL ORDER** $ _____
☐ Check/money order enclosed (in U.S. funds)
☐ VISA ☐ MasterCard ☐ AmEx ☐ Discover   Exp. Date _____

Card Number _____

Signature _____

Name _____

Street _____

City _____ State ____ Zip _____

Daytime Telephone (____) _____
☐ Builder-Contractor ☐ Home Owner ☐ Renter   PG4

------- BLUEPRINT ORDER FORM --------

Mail to: **For Faster Service**
HomeStyles "Source 1"   **Call Toll-Free**
Suite 115, 6800 France Avenue South   **1-800-547-5570**
Minneapolis, MN 55435
Please send me the following:

Plan Number _____ **Price Code** _____

Foundation _____
(Please review your plan carefully for foundation options — basement, crawlspace, or slab. Many plans offer all three options, others offer only one.)

Number of Sets	A	B	C	D	E	Amount
☐ 7 SETS	$240	$290	$325	$360	$395	$ _____
☐ 4 SETS	$210	$250	$280	$315	$350	$ _____
☐ 1 SET	$165	$200	$230	$260	$295	$ _____

*Prices guaranteed to December 31, 1990. We expect a $25 increase on all plans in 1991.

☐ **Additional Sets** of this plan, $25 now; $ _____
$35 later, each. (Number of sets _____)

☐ **Itemized List of Materials,** $30, each $ _____
additional set $10.
(Sold only with blueprint purchase. Lists are only available for plans with prefix letters AH, AM, B, C, CPS, E, H, I, J, K, N, NW*, P, R, S, SD, U, W)
*Please ask when ordering, not available on all plans

☐ **Description of Materials:** Two sets $25 $ _____
(For use in obtaining FHA or VA financing)
(Only available for Plans with prefix letters C, E, H, J, K, N, P, U)

☐ **Mirror Reverse Plans,** $25 one-time charge. $ _____
(Number of sets to be reversed _____.)
*The writing on Mirror Reverse plans will be backwards. Order at least one regular set.

☐ **Typical How-To Diagrams** $ _____
☐ Plumbing ☐ Wiring ☐ Solar Heating
☐ Framing & Foundation Conversion
One set @ $12.50, any two @ $23.00, any three @ $30.00, all four only $35.

☐ **Sales Tax** (MN Residents, please add 6%) $ _____

Please Add Postage Charges (Check One)
☐ First-Class Priority or UPS Blue Label $ _____
(U.S. only), $10.50
Allow 4-5 working days for delivery. *Must have street address for UPS delivery.
☐ First-Class Priority (Canada only) $10.50 $ _____
Allow 2-3 weeks for delivery.
☐ Overnight Express Delivery (U.S. only) $25.00 $ _____
Allow 1-2 working days for delivery. *Must have street address.
☐ Express Delivery (Canada only) $40.00 $ _____
Allow 4-5 working days for delivery. *Must have street address.
☐ Overseas Airmail Delivery $40.00 $ _____
Allow approx. 7 working days.

Payment   **TOTAL ORDER** $ _____
☐ Check/money order enclosed (in U.S. funds)
☐ VISA ☐ MasterCard ☐ AmEx ☐ Discover   Exp. Date _____

Card Number _____

Signature _____

Name _____

Street _____

City _____ State ____ Zip _____

Daytime Telephone (____) _____
☐ Builder-Contractor ☐ Home Owner ☐ Renter   PG4

A Masterpiece of Proportion and Scale

- The splendid facade of this well-designed home will lend elegance and distinction to any street.
- The interior boasts an expansive Great Room, formal living and dining rooms and a roomy kitchen/breakfast area combination.
- Four bedrooms upstairs include a roomy master suite with private bath and large closet.
- The three secondary bedrooms are larger than typically found in homes of this size, and share two additional bathrooms.
- Note the convenient laundry area downstairs, as well as the half-bath powder room in the hallway.

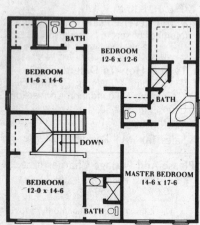

UPPER FLOOR

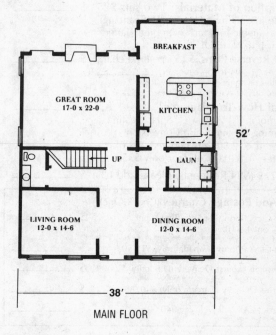

MAIN FLOOR

Plan V-2911-C

Bedrooms: 4	Baths: 3½

Space:

Upper floor:	1,374 sq. ft.
Main floor:	1,537 sq. ft.
Total living area:	2,911 sq. ft.

Exterior Wall Framing:	2x6

Ceiling Heights:

Upper floor:	9'
Main floor:	10'

Foundation options:
Crawlspace only.
(Foundation & framing conversion diagram available — see order form.)

Blueprint Price Code:	D

Plan V-2911-C

To order blueprints, call
1-800-547-5570 or see order form
and pricing information on pages 220-224.